IMAGES
of America

ROANE COUNTY

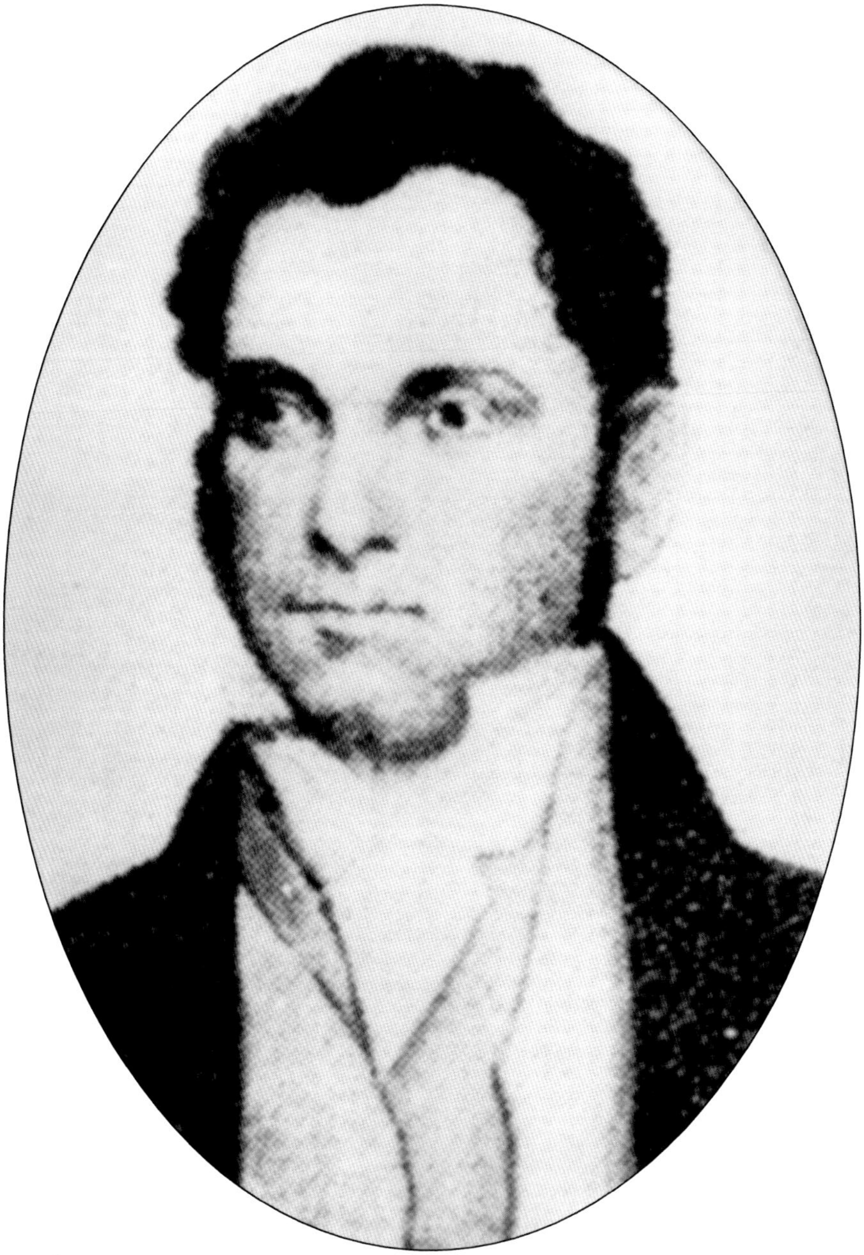

On the 11th day of March 1856, a bill was passed in Richmond, Virginia, for the formation of a new county. This county would be named Roane in honor of Spencer Roane, a local circuit court judge. (R. Nester Collection courtesy of Mark Sergent.)

ON THE COVER: Steam-powered oil field drilling rigs were very common between 1910 and 1920. A boiler was hauled to the site by ox-drawn wagons and set up to power a steam engine. This engine provided power to a walking beam that lifted and dropped the drilling stem and bit. A bailer was run down the hole to remove the drill cuttings. Upon completion of the drilling, the well was shot with nitroglycerine to fracture the oil- and gas-bearing sand formation to increase production. (Courtesy of Mark Sergent.)

IMAGES
of America

ROANE COUNTY

Jack Nida and
Roane County Historical Society

ARCADIA
PUBLISHING

ISBN 978-0-7385-5275-0

Published by Arcadia Publishing
Charleston, South Carolina

Printed in the United States of America

Library of Congress Catalog Card Number: 2007924370

For all general information contact Arcadia Publishing at:
Telephone 843-853-2070
Fax 843-853-0044
E-mail sales@arcadiapublishing.com
For customer service and orders:
Toll-Free 1-888-313-2665

Visit us on the Internet at www.arcadiapublishing.com

This book is dedicated to all the pioneer families who forged a livelihood from this part of West Virginia by clearing a wilderness and building their homes in this mountainous state.

Contents

ACKNOWLEDGMENTS

This is a pictorial story that had to be told. It reveals the life and times of a small section of our country through some images that date back over 100 years. Included are brief descriptions of people and a way of life, including landmarks that they left for future generations. It portrays a life of hard work, dedication, perseverance, and a lifestyle that is far removed from what we know today. Many of us refer to this as the good old days, and the youth often want to know more about that time in history.

Many of the photographs herein were gathered from the library of the Roane County Historical Society and its members, while residents of West Virginia and adjoining states contributed others. To all of those who assisted in this project, you have my heartfelt gratitude and appreciation. To Carol Board and Carol Cronin, I can only say that without your perseverance, this book would not have been possible, and I am forever grateful for your assistance.

Introduction

Prior to 1749, western Virginia was not trodden by the foot of white man except for an occasional trader who may have ventured a short distance west of the Allegheny Mountains. The race to colonize this area by French and English traders resulted in what was known as the French and Indian War from 1754 to 1763. During the period of 1764 to 1774, the British government would attempt to secure an amicable relationship with the Native Americans through various modes of peace. Several treaties were established with the Native Americans, which resulted in many boundary disputes. George Washington was among the earlier operators in western Virginia in the survey and settlement authorized by Lord Dunmore, then governor of Virginia. Had it not been for the Revolutionary War, Washington would in all possibility have become the leading settler of the West.

The people in the western section of the state of Virginia felt that their political and industrial interests were not being equitably divided between the two sections of the state. A constitutional convention was finally called in 1829 in response to western demands with little results. Attention to the need of road construction was paramount in the minds of most local citizens to assist in development of the area. The first improved road into the Greenbrier Valley was built in 1782 and was called the Midland Trail. It would connect Warm Springs, Virginia, to Lewisburg and would later be extended to the headwaters of the Kanawha River at Gauley Bridge. By 1800, the turnpike would reach the Ohio River where Huntington now stands. The road was further improved by 1824 and was the chief route of east-west travel in the South. It was now known as the Kanawha Turnpike. In 1838, the last section of the Northwestern Turnpike between Clarksburg and Parkersburg was opened for traffic. The next 20 years would find the construction of several connecting roads, including the Gilmer, Ripley, and Ohio Turnpike, which had the greatest impact on the settlement of Roane County. These dirt roads offered wagons access to the wilderness area of western Virginia for families moving westward.

Areas described as island communities developed at the present sites of Spencer, Walton, Reedy, Newton, Harper, and Reedyville. The church played an important part in the social and moral control of the people in each little community, and its members agreed to abide by the Rules of Decorum, a list of prohibitions against a variety of acts. Foremost among these were immoral acts and adultery, but the rules also included dancing, swearing, drunkenness, fighting, gambling, lying, horse racing, and a host of things not to do on the Sabbath. William Bishop in his book, *History of Roane County West Virginia, 1774–1927*, remarked that the early settlers of the county were "fully conscious of the value of the Christian faith as a stabilizer among them and its preachment, a best measure of self-control." Church meetings were held in the homes of the most prominent citizens prior to the building of a church house.

Original settlers at Spencer were the family of Samuel Tanner and Jonathan Wolfe in 1812. Few other families would follow before the early 1830s. Population of the county would continue to be slow until the late 1840s. By 1850, the original land grants had been dissolved, and land ownership was passing into local hands. It was about this time that plans for a new county were being discussed. Reasons were dissatisfaction with the tax system and a belief that local government would enhance development of the area. Looneyville, Arnoldsburg, and New California (later to become Spencer) were considered as county seats, with the majority favoring New California. This resulted in two new counties being formed with Arnoldsburg becoming the county seat of Calhoun County on March 5, 1856, and New California becoming the county seat of Roane County on March 11, 1856. Roane County would later be divided into six magisterial districts that were named Spencer, Geary, Reedy, Smithfield, Harper, and Walton.

Principal centers of trade within the new county of Roane were New California, Walton, Newton, Reedy, Osborne's Mill, and Reedyville. Early settlers in the Spencer District were the Boggs, Vandale, DePue, Tanner, Miller, and Carpenter families. The first post office to be established in the county was named Walton on July 1, 1856, at the mouth of McKown's Creek.

Geary District, the southeastern section of the new county, had two major business centers that were known then as Geary's Mills and Newton, which was originally called the Three Forks of Sandy. Geary's Mills, originally called Ashley's Settlement, was named for Matthew Geary, who had built a sawmill on his property. The area also had a tub mill, and the community grew around these businesses. A general store was built in the early 1850s, and a post office was established there July 3, 1855. The name of the settlement was then changed to Osborne's Mills in honor of Archibald Osborne, who had built the first store.

Some of the first pioneers to come to the area of what is now called Geary District were John Kelly, Ware Long, and Francis Garner. These men and their families settled along Big Sandy Creek in 1809, about three miles below the mouth of Left Hand Creek. The Geary, Osborne, and John Ashley families followed the next year, and the area became known as Ashley's Settlement. William King and William Noe were the first settlers in Newton, arriving in 1833 and 1835 respectively. The Drake, Keen, Ross, and Wright families were soon to follow. The name of this community was changed from the Three Forks of Sandy to Newton when Rev. Davidson Ross established a post office in 1857 and named it in honor of his two-year-old son, Isaac Newton Ross. A gristmill and a blacksmith shop were the center of activity in the village. New communities soon sprang up along Left Hand and Big Sandy Creeks as the Tawney, Smith, Justice, Nida, Geary, and Engle families arrived.

The Stewart, Board, Carney, Roach, Seaman, and Burdette families settled in Reedy District. Hiram Chancey and family were the first settlers to come to the Middle Fork of Reedy Creek in 1819. The post office in Reedy was established in 1853 as Jackson County, Virginia, and was not changed to Roane County in the records until September 14, 1875. James W. Seaman erected a tannery in Reedy about 1859 on the Ravenswood and Spencer Turnpike. The products made of leather—harnesses, saddles, and footwear—were all required by local demand. Peter Bush had a large farm in 1866 and was the first, largest, and last distiller of alcoholic liquors in Reedy. His still house was built of logs with a large, copper boiler about 3 feet in diameter. His orchard of 100 trees or more would supply ingredients for his apple and peach brandies.

Reedyville had a gristmill, a carding mill, blacksmith shops, and two general stores when the post office was established in 1854. A general merchandise store was opened by Mathias B. Armstrong in Peniel that would also house a post office. By 1892, there were a total of 10 post offices within the county to establish a public communications network.

The Vineyard, Looney, Gandee, Lowe, Summer, Hammack, Whited, and Droddy families were early settlers in Smithfield District. Joseph Lyons and Henry Mace settled on the waters of Henrys Fork in 1814. Peter McCune is said to have settled there in the year 1817. Robert Looney and his family settled at the crossroads on the headwaters of Flat Fork of Pocatalico River in 1839. He was a veteran of the War of 1812 and served many years as a justice of the peace upon settling in Roane County. The post office of Looneyville would later be erected in his honor. Capt. John W. Spencer made his first home on the upper Henrys Fork above the mouth of Canoe Run, where he was owner of 1,000 acres or more about 1865. The William Ferrell family arrived in 1842. John B. Stone, a Virginian, made his home and farm in the gap of the dividing ridge on an old buffalo and Native American trail. He established the first post office in Smithfield District, called Roxalana.

In 1835, the John Harper family arrived in Harper District. John Bishop was among the first settlers of Upper Harper, while the John Taylor family located in Lower Harper. The Hughes, Gandee, Riley, Romine, Cox, and Conley families would soon locate in the area of Cox's Fork and Flat Fork Creeks.

The first settler to live in Walton District was Paul Shafer. William Hammack built a water gristmill at the mouth of McKown's Creek, and Presley Vineyard did the same at the mouth of Johnson Creek. Carding machinery, a sawmill, and a tannery were soon to follow. Charles Droddy arrived in the area about 1821.

A church and school would closely follow the establishment of the post office in each community with the Flat Fork Baptist Church being one of the oldest churches in the county that is still in operation. It was founded in 1850 and located near Looneyville in Smithfield District. In 1870, the author's great-grandfather, Caleb Nida, was reprimanded by members of this church for "playing the fiddle for others and having frolics at his house."

One

The Early Years

An act of the Virginia General Assembly created Roane County on March 11, 1856, from Kanawha, Gilmer, Wirt, and Jackson Counties. Major waterways were Reedy Creek, Spring Creek, and West Fork, which flowed northward into the Little Kanawha River. The Pocatalico River and Big Sandy Creek flowed southward into the Kanawha and Elk Rivers, respectively. These waterways would assist in floating logs to a mill where they would be cut into lumber or barrel staves.

A major decision would soon confront the people of Roane County. They had to declare, through a public, oral vote called by the election board, their approval or disapproval in seceding from the Union. The population of the county in 1860 was 5,309, of which only 1,010 were eligible voters. Of those, 540 voters chose to secede from the Union and join the Confederacy, while 304 voters chose to give their allegiance to the Union. This split resulted in brother-against-brother armed conflict in Roane County. The first fighting occurred during August 1861 in Spencer, and guerrilla warfare was prevalent throughout the area for the next three years. During these war-torn years, a new state constitution was adopted, and West Virginia became the 35th state in the Union on June 20, 1863.

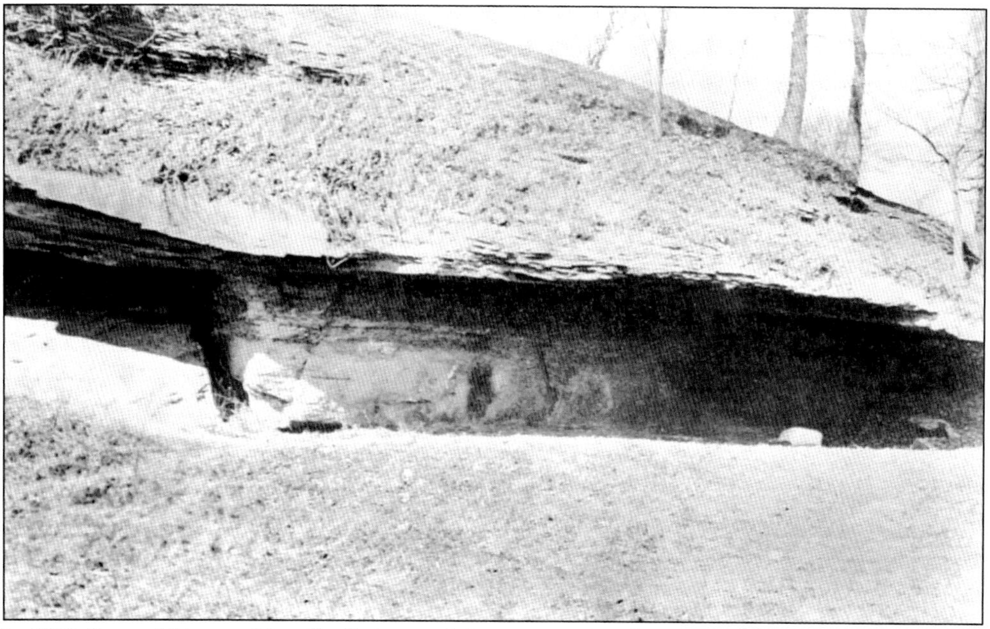

In 1812, Samuel Tanner, his wife, Sudna, and their young daughter moved from Harrison County, Virginia, with friend Jonathan Wolfe. This large outcropping of rock provided shelter for the family, who took small poles, trees, and boughs to cover the entrance. A daughter was born in this cave and was reported to be the first white child to be born in what is now Roane County. (Ralph Nester Collection courtesy of Mark Sergent.)

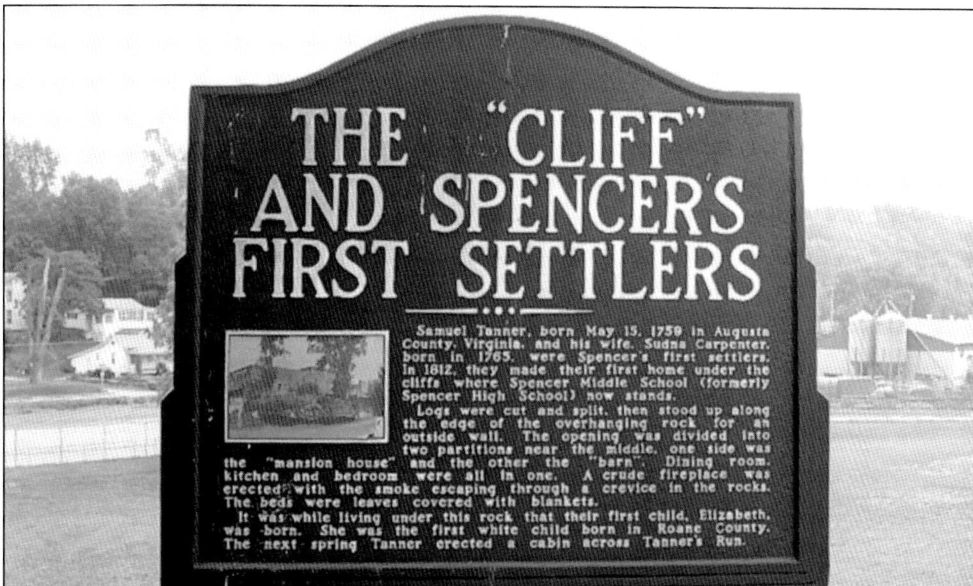

This plaque was placed at the top of the rock cave and adjacent to the old Spencer High School building to commemorate this historical location. The permanent home of Jesse Tanner, son of Samuel Tanner, was built on what was known as the Raymond Carper farm but probably better known as the Minnie B. Simmons farm. It was built about the time of the Civil War and was occupied until about 1905. (Courtesy of Jack Nida.)

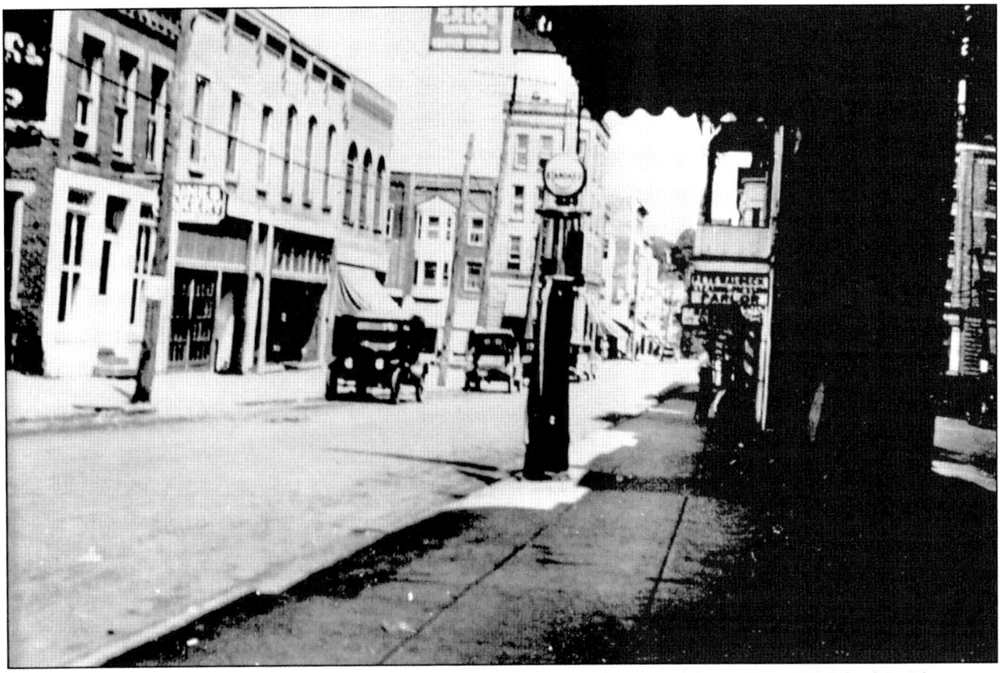

This view of Market Street shows Raines Bakery in the Robey Building. Pete Waldeck's Cleaning and Pressing was upstairs over Morrison's. In 1907, voters approved a bond issue to pave the streets in Spencer. About three miles of paving had been completed by 1926 within the city limits. (Courtesy of Donna Walbrown.)

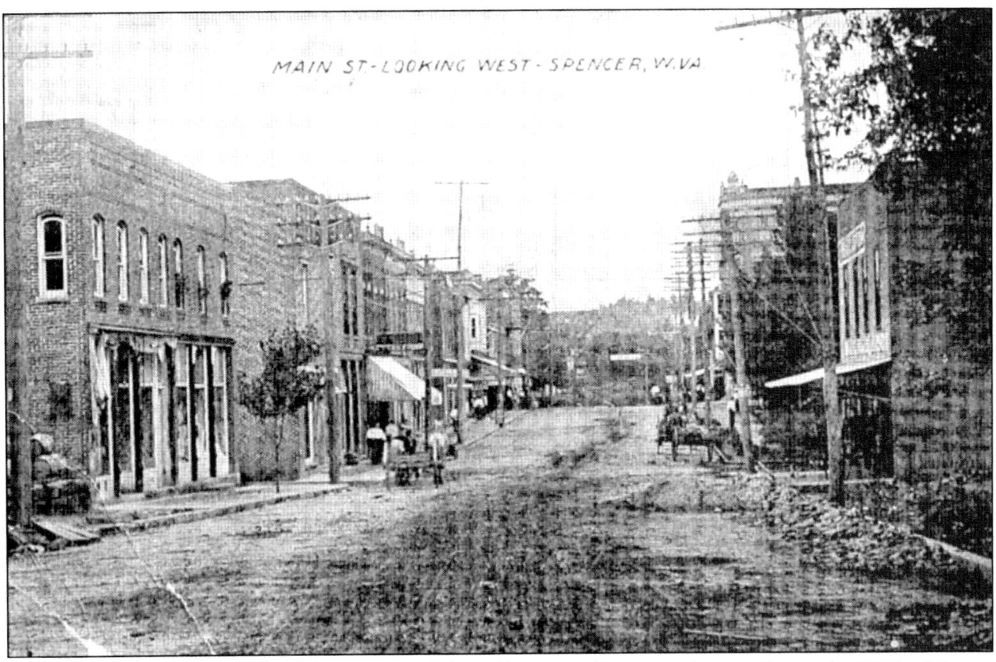

This was a typical scene looking west on Main Street in Spencer during the early 1900s. Horses and buggies were the common mode of transportation on the dirt streets, and travel during the rainy days was very difficult. (Courtesy of Donna Walbrown.)

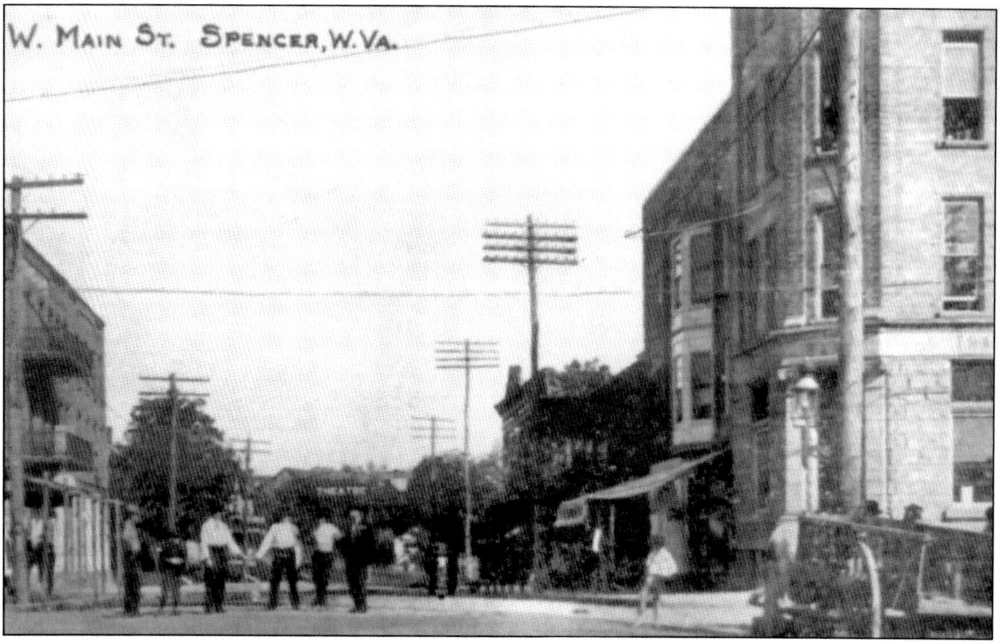

In 1910, West Main Street was paved, and travel improved for the growing community. New places of business were thriving with the arrival of workers for the oil and gas industry. (Courtesy of Donna Walbrown.)

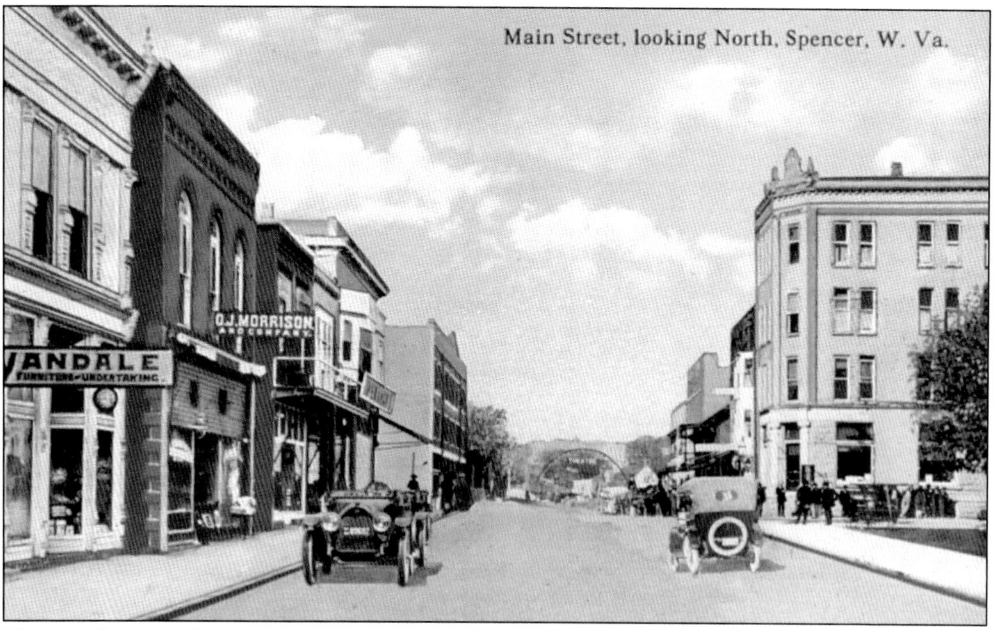

The population in Spencer grew from 143 people in 1870 to 431 in 1890. The arrival of the railroad had also increased the growth of the community and expanded the influence of the town past the county lines. This would become the major shipping point for the adjacent counties of Clay and Calhoun. (Courtesy of Donna Walbrown.)

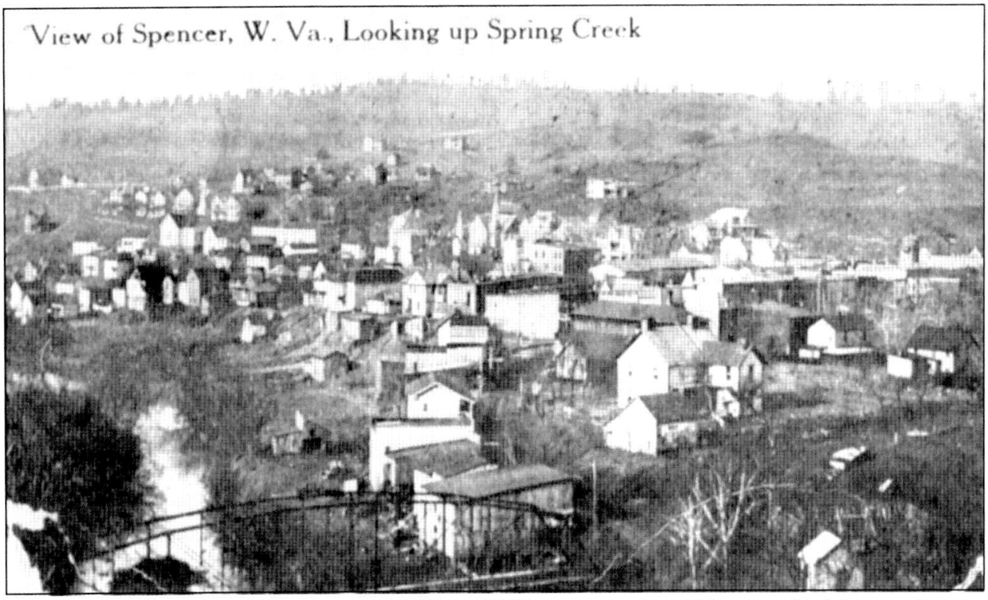

This image of Spencer, from around 1910 to 1920, gives a view of homes, looking up Spring Creek. Houses were generally constructed of lumber during this era, and the popular residential area of Alvord is shown on the right in the picture. (Ralph Nester Collection courtesy of Mark Sergent.)

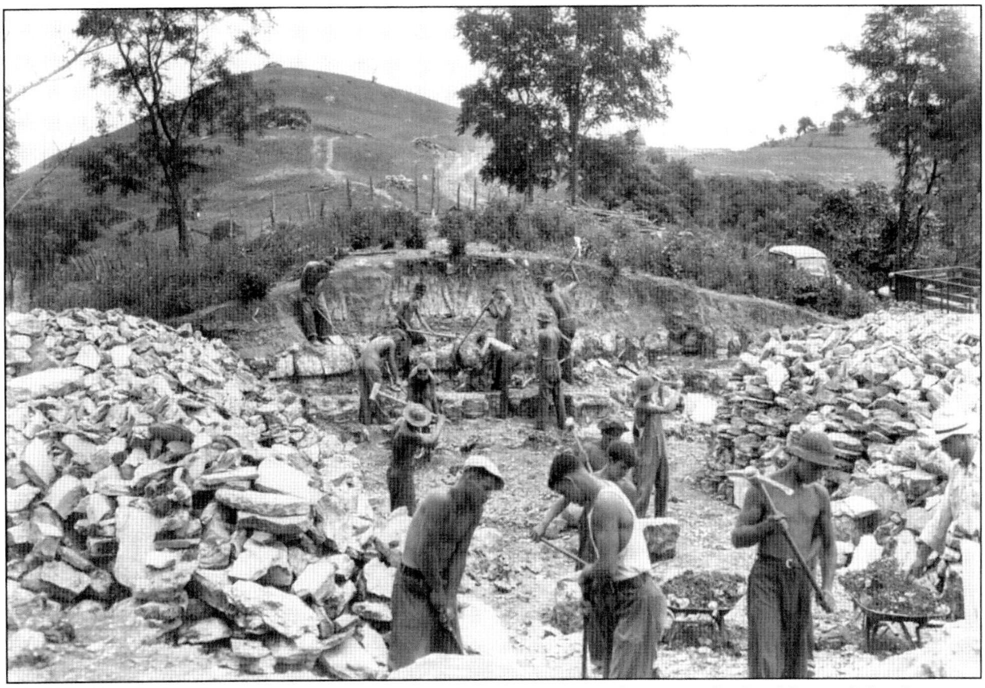

These prisoners from the Moundsville Penitentiary were working on the building of the Spencer State Hospital, originally designated as the second hospital for the insane in the state of West Virginia. The overcrowding of the first hospital in Weston prompted the need for an additional facility. The use of prison labor was quite common during the early part of the 20th century. (Courtesy of Dr. Harry H. Camp Sr. family.)

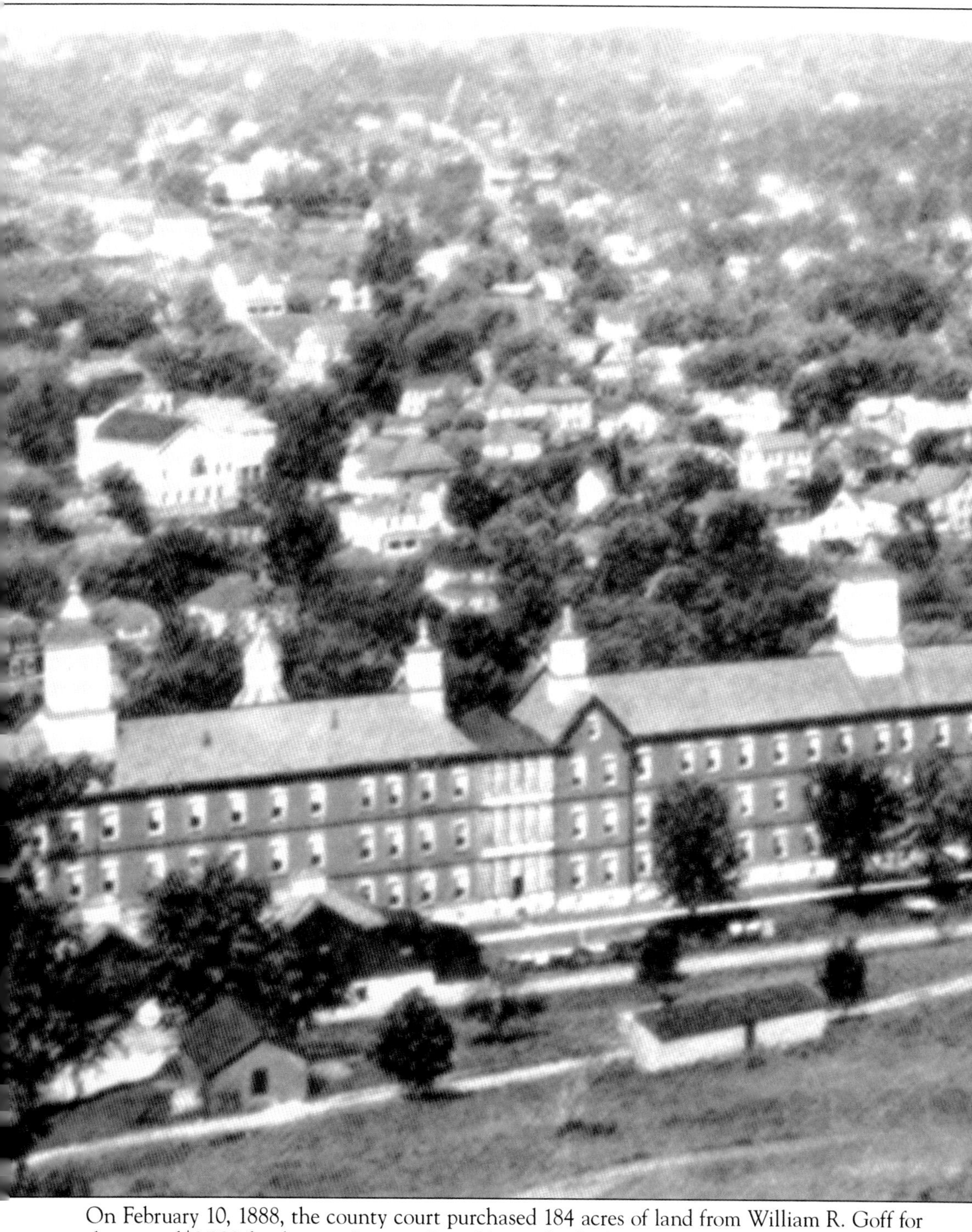

On February 10, 1888, the county court purchased 184 acres of land from William R. Goff for the sum of $9,200 for the new Spencer State Hospital. The building was a quarter-mile long and was sometimes referred to as the longest continuous brick building in America. Bricks for the hospital's Gothic structure were made on the grounds. Native Roane County stone was hand cut by Henry Waldeck and Lee Kelley and was used for facings and adornments. The slate roof

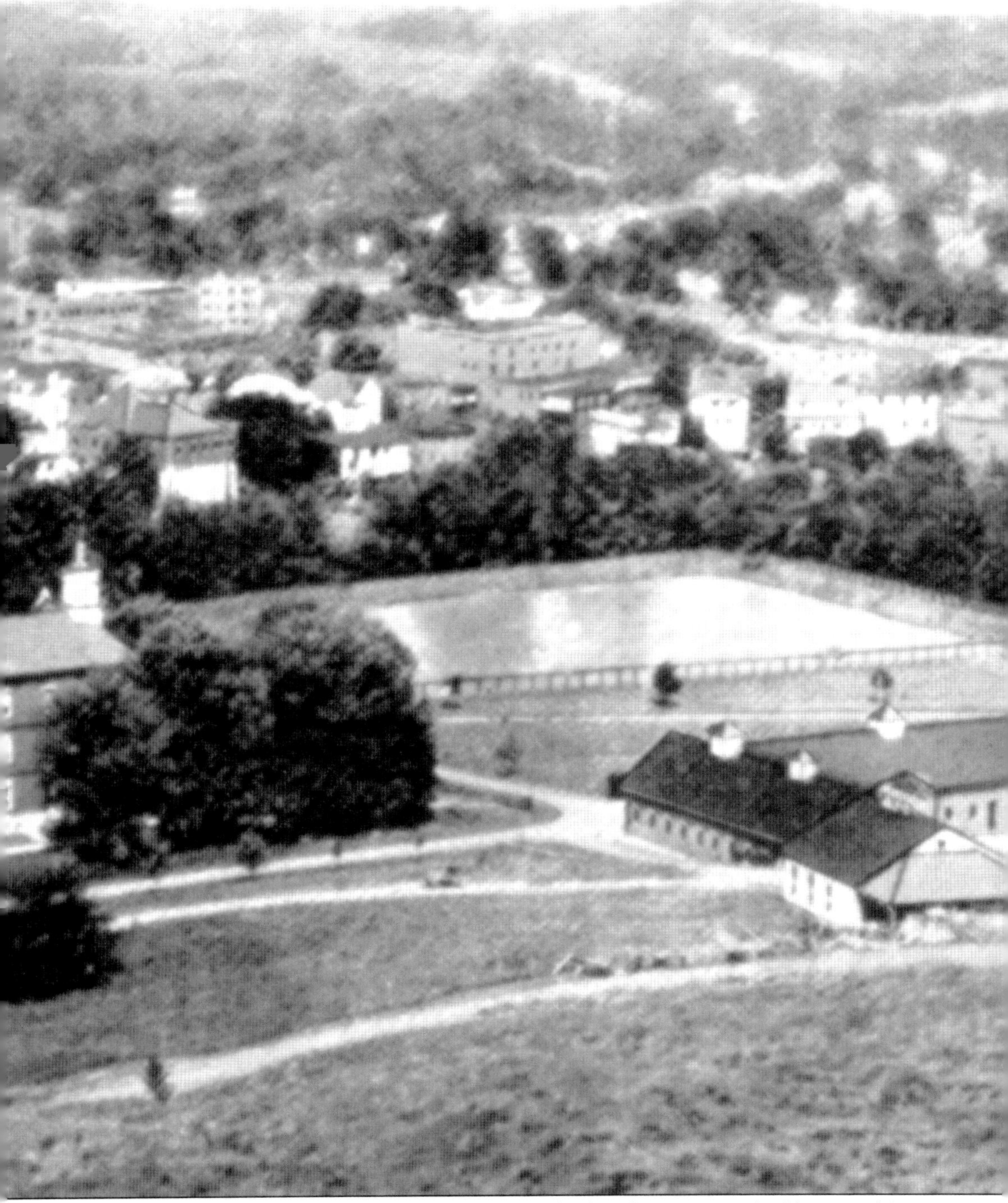

was adorned with cupolas that were typical of the period. The administration building stood four stories high and was topped with two round towers. On each side of the administration building were two three-story wards, one for men and one for women. The building was completed in 1893 at a total cost of $93,393. (Ralph Nester Collection courtesy of Mark Sergent.)

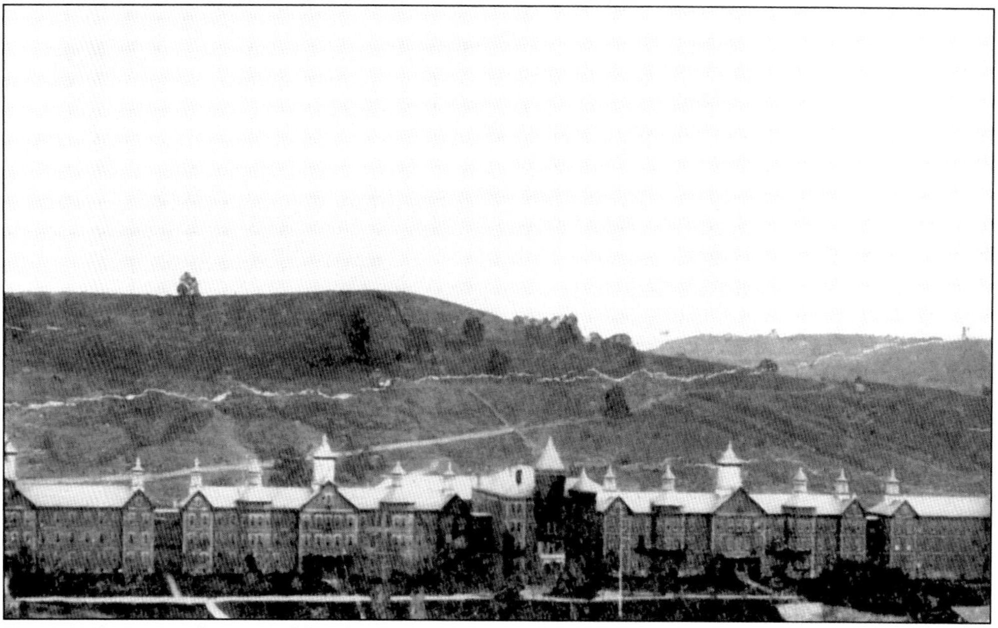

In 1893, the Second Hospital for the Insane was opened in Spencer for the state of West Virginia. Within a few years, this institution would also admit elderly patients and unwanted children. It would officially become known as the Spencer State Hospital. Specialized units were maintained for the physically ill and infirm, alcoholic treatment programs, Medicare and Medicaid patients, and rehabilitation programs. (Courtesy of Donna Walbrown.)

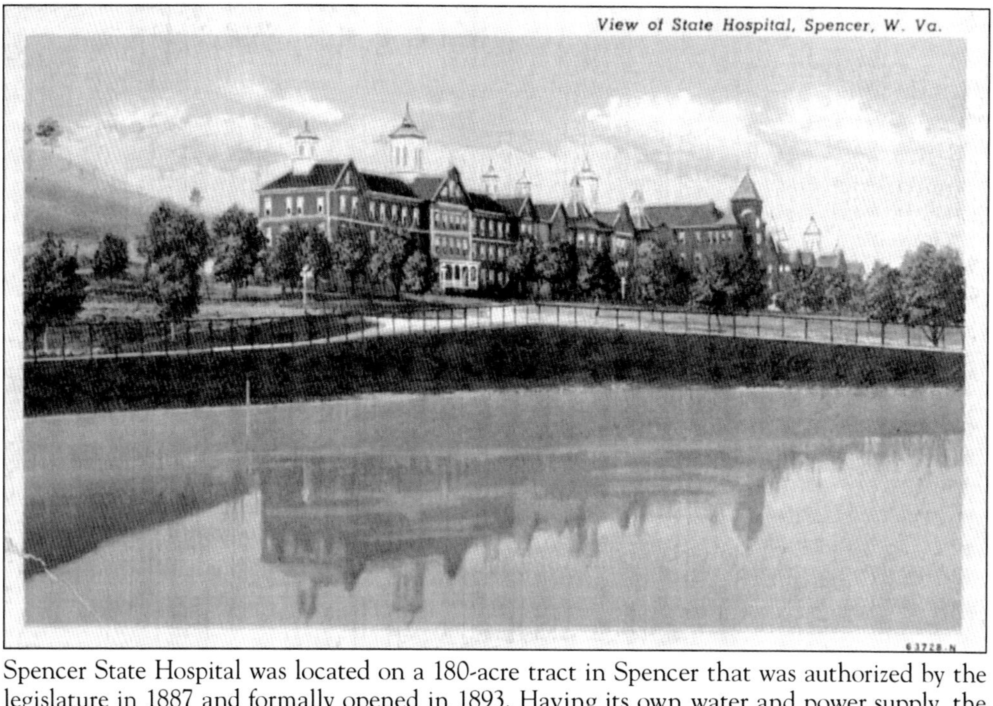

Spencer State Hospital was located on a 180-acre tract in Spencer that was authorized by the legislature in 1887 and formally opened in 1893. Having its own water and power supply, the hospital served an eight-county area. It was closed in 1989, and most of the buildings were torn down to make room for a Wal-Mart store. (Courtesy of Gene Ashley.)

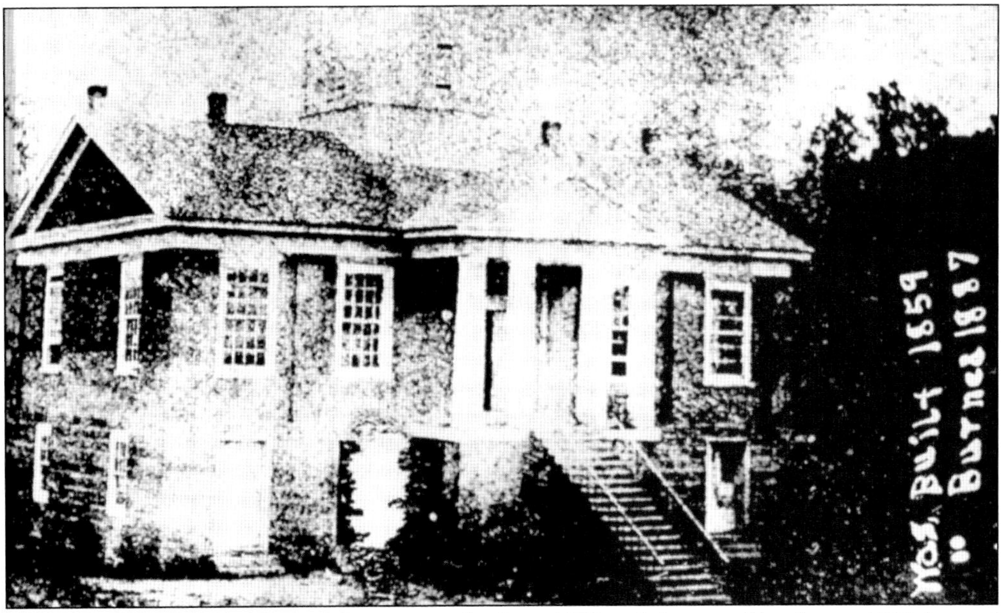

The first courthouse of Roane County was built in 1859 and destroyed by fire in 1887. Its roof was of shingles, and the cupola sides were made of paneling. The building was made of stone and brick with no basement or rooms below the surface of the ground. The interior woodwork was of lumber that was sawed at McKown's Mill. (Courtesy of Donna Walbrown.)

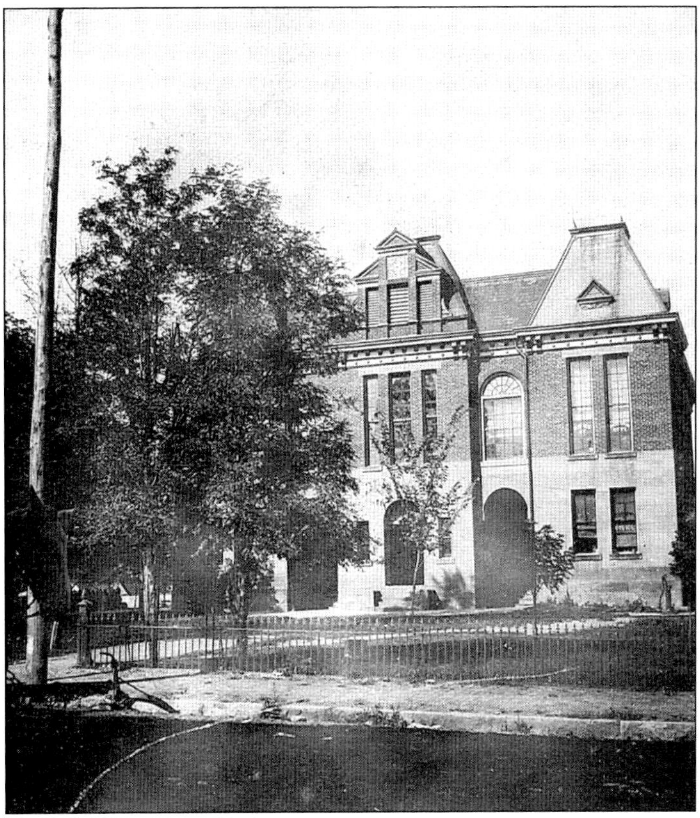

The second courthouse was completed in 1889, and the task of restoring the burned records began. It remained the official center of the county until it was razed for the 1964 construction of a modernistic, rectangular, brick-and-plate-glass edifice. (Courtesy of Donna Walbrown.)

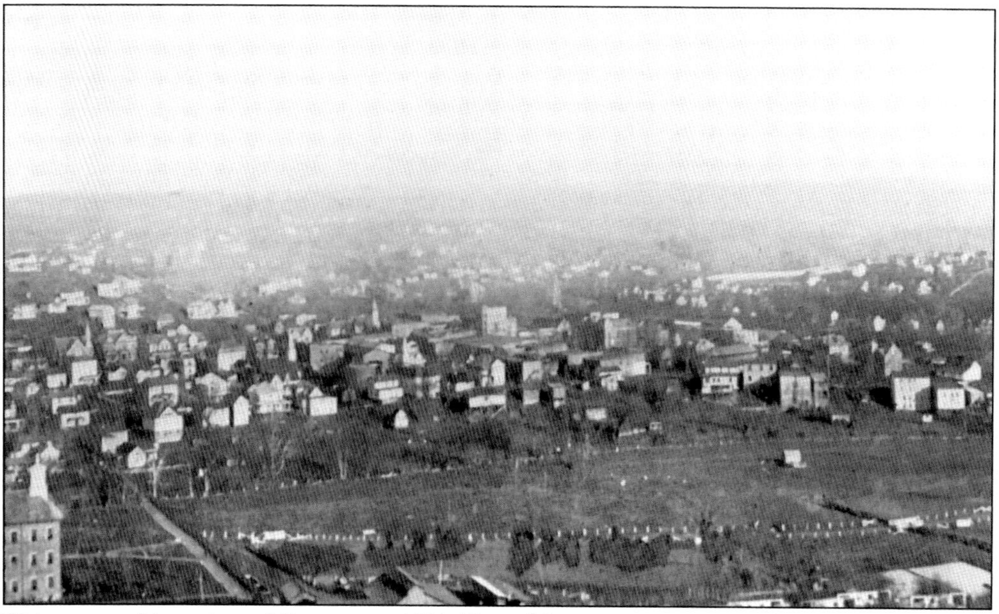

This postcard is a view of Spencer in 1914. Typical businesses operating during this time were general stores, tanneries, blacksmith shops, and boarding houses. They had followed the gristmill and offered the basic needs of the farmers that could not be met on the farm. (Courtesy of Dr. Harry H. Camp Sr. family.)

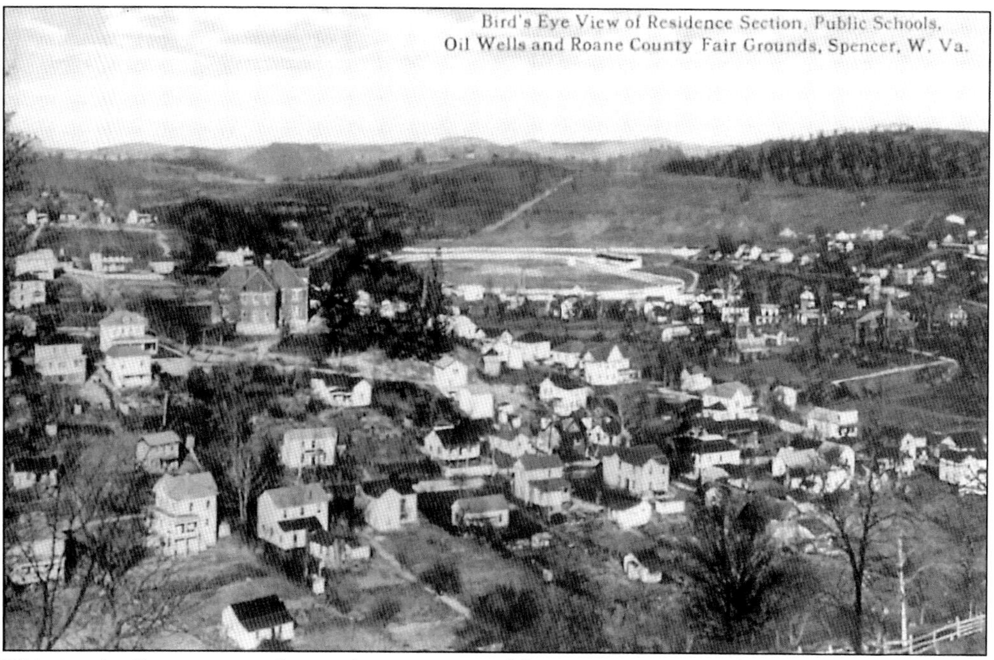

This is a bird's-eye view of a northern section of Spencer in 1912. Oil wells, schools, and the county fairgrounds can also be seen. In the lower right of this image, the Ripley and Spencer Turnpike intersects with Main Street. (Courtesy of Eve Southall.)

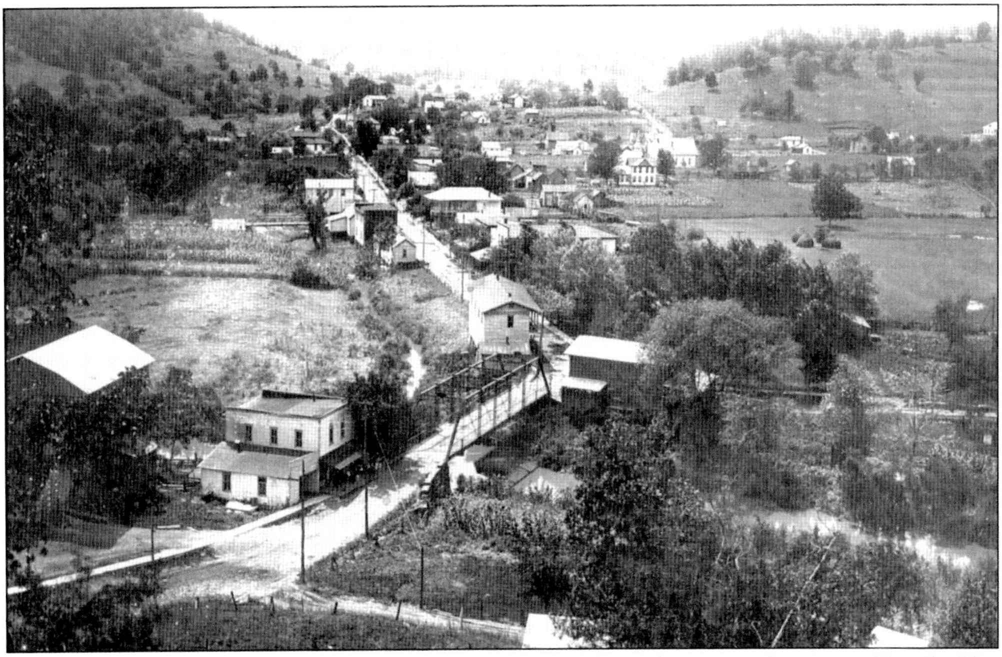

The three forks of Reedy Creek created the site of the early settlement in the town of Reedy. The first bridge built across main Reedy Creek was opened for traffic in 1870 and was washed away in the flood of 1901. It was a covered bridge that was replaced by a steel structure. Andrew Callison built a store building and later enlarged it to include a hotel. (Courtesy of Sharon Christ.)

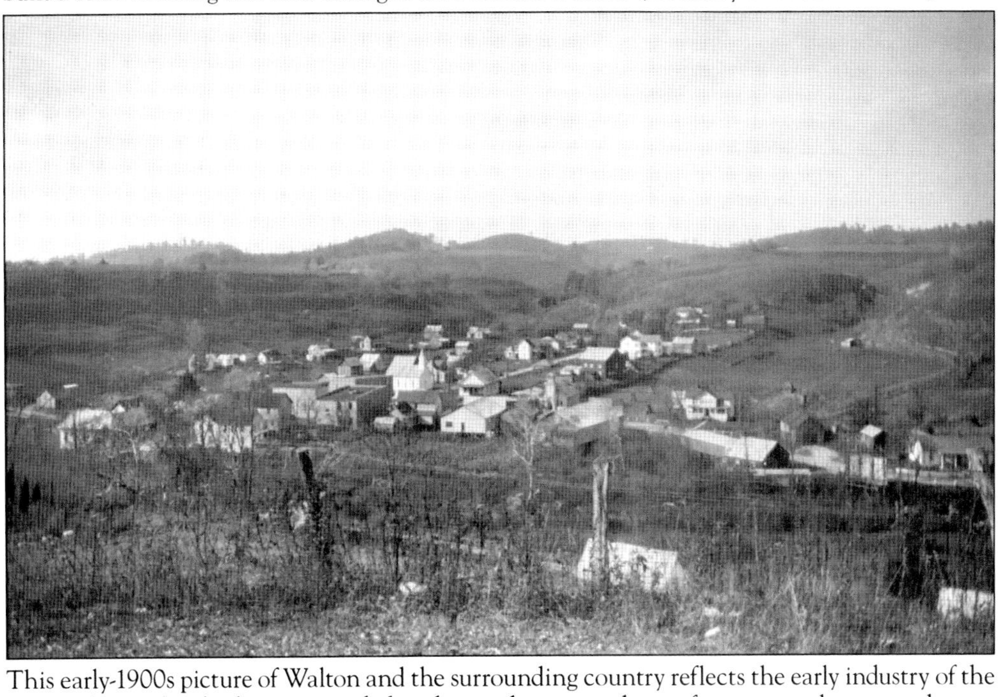

This early-1900s picture of Walton and the surrounding country reflects the early industry of the town. The settlers had constructed churches and stores and were fortunate to have two doctors living in Walton by 1905. They ground the last grist around 1902, as the mill had to succumb to the great mills of the northwest. (Courtesy of Dr. Harry H. Camp Sr. family.)

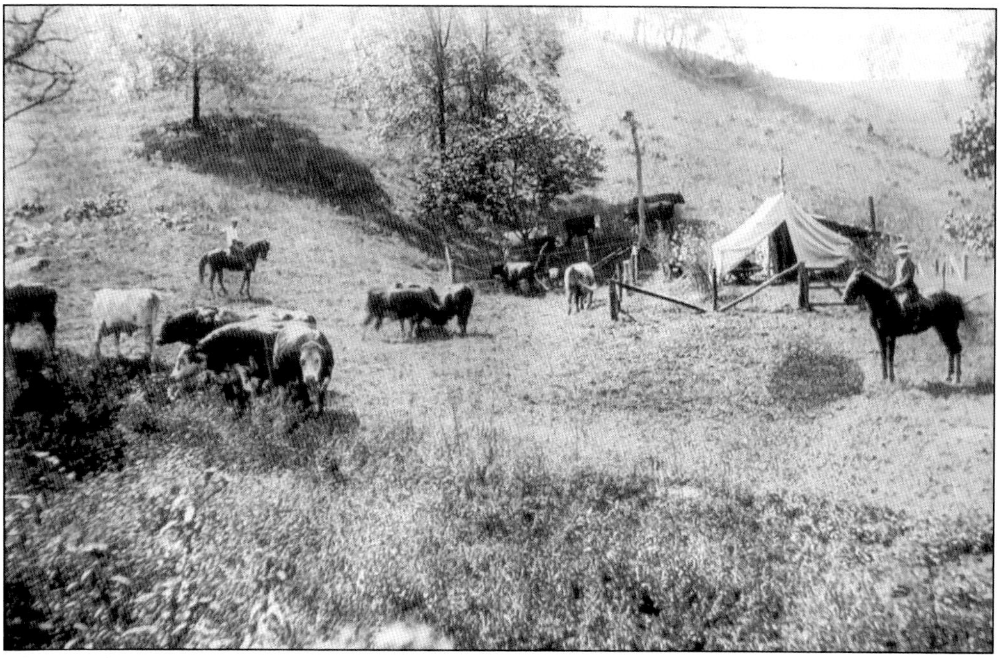

The first home of Fredrick Kirby and Nancy Augusta (Boggs) Vineyard was a tent on the headwaters of the Pocatalico River near Looneyville in 1915. By that winter, they had bought and moved into a small house on the wooded hilltop near the Looneyville store on Flat Fork. (Courtesy of Carol Cronin.)

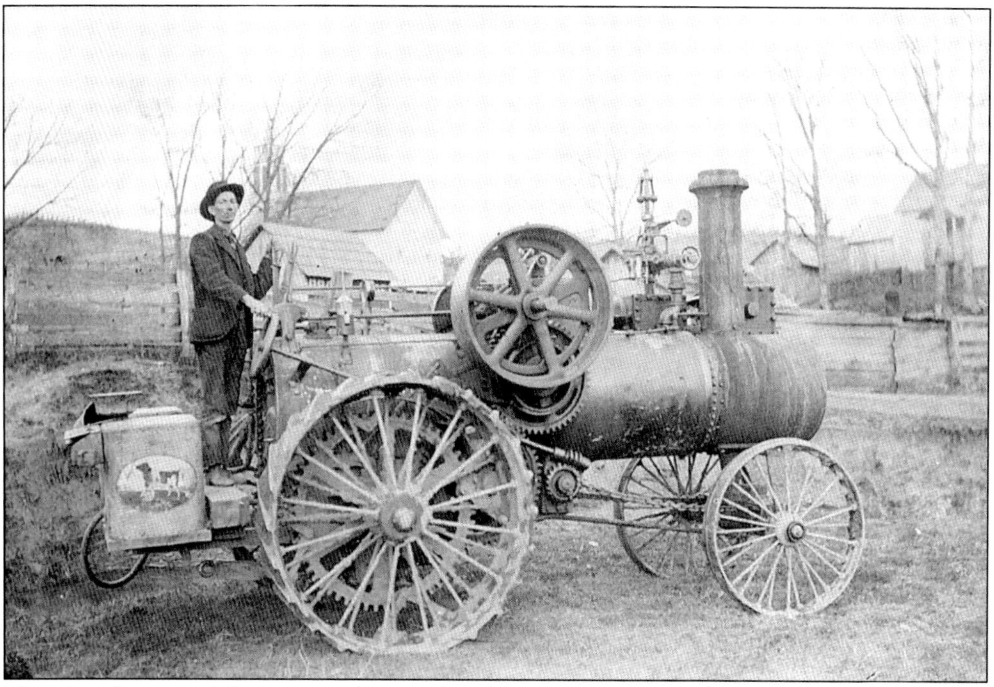

The identification of the person riding on this old steam tractor is unknown. It is from the Ralph Nester Collection of old photographs from in and around Spencer. (Ralph Nester Collection courtesy of Mark Sergent.)

This plaque stands on the courthouse lawn as a reminder of early history in the area. The present drilling of gas wells in Roane County to a depth of 12,000 feet is not uncommon. (Courtesy of Jack Nida.)

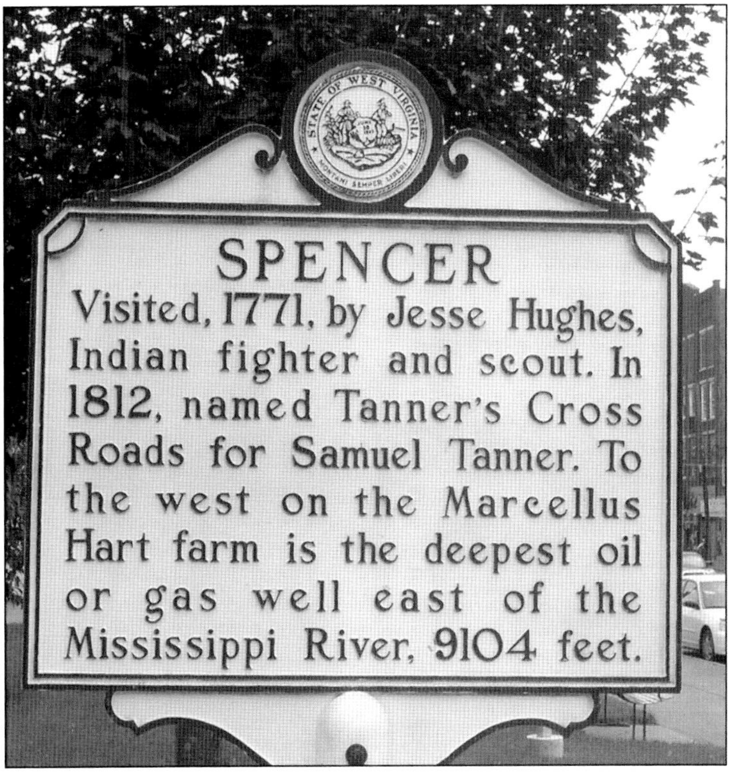

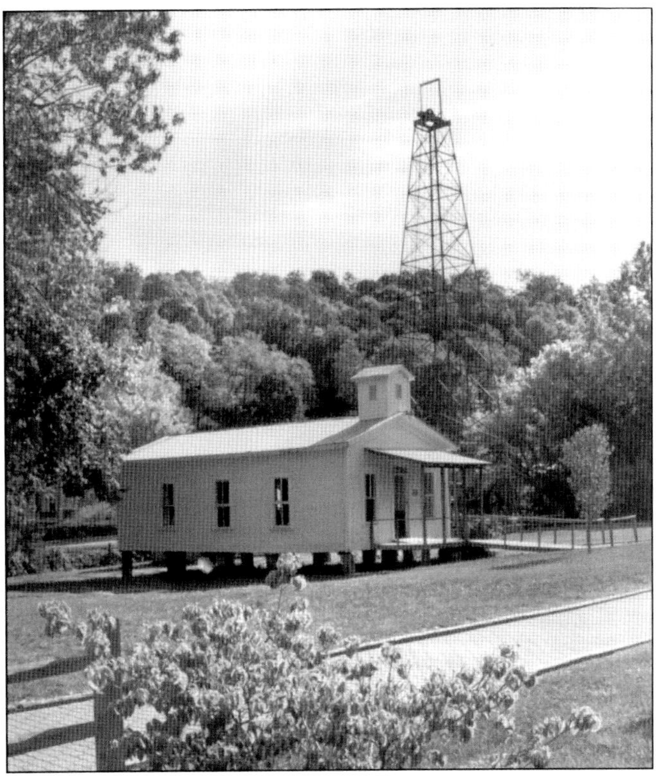

In 1989, the Spencer Heritage Park became a reality as the completed facility was opened to the public. The park contains a new community building, and the old Baltimore and Ohio (B&O) train depot was converted into a museum. A one-room school building in Looneyville was transported to its new home in 1986. The Pennzoil Company donated an 84-foot-tall oil derrick that was moved from Wallback to Spencer. (Courtesy of Donna Walbrown.)

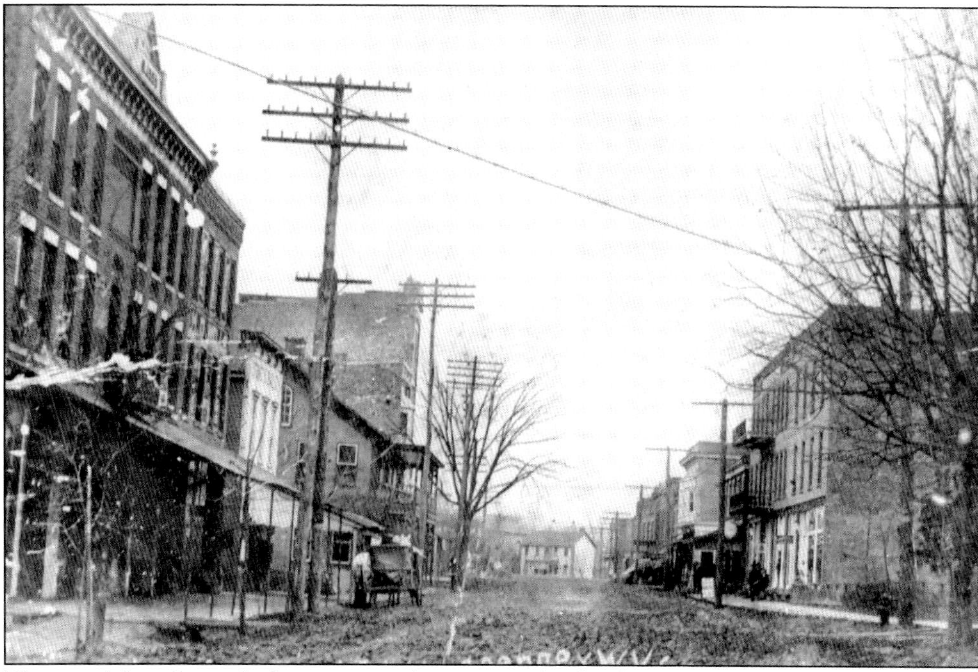

This was Main Street looking east in the year 1905. The dirt streets were heavily traveled by oxen, wagons, and carriages as supplies were moved into the oil and gas fields of the county. (Courtesy of Donna Walbrown.)

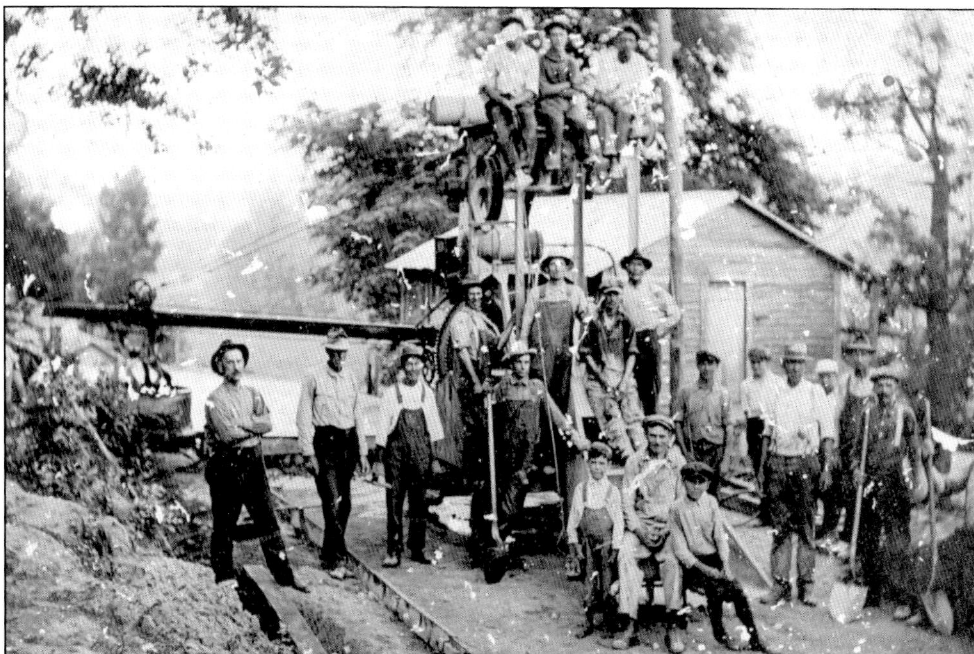

The paving of Lynn Street in Spencer took place in 1924. The person on the far left is Bill Poling, a local merchant and contractor. He built the brick building that houses part of Monarch Rubber Company, and his home was on the same property. (Ralph Nester Collection courtesy of Mark Sergent.)

Two

Timber Industry

It was necessary that new landowners clear their land for the development of crops and livestock. Removing the larger trees supplied wood that could be hewn into logs for the construction of homes and barns. By the year 1875, a market for timber and lumber would develop, and landowners could sell timber for 50¢ per tree. The value would increase to $1 per tree during the next decade. As the sawmills were built, lumber would soon replace hand-hewn logs for construction of new homes. The best oak and poplar lumber was sold in 1885 at the mill for about $10 per 1,000 feet. By the year 1900, the price had more than doubled. The salt industry was booming on the Kanawha River, and the demand was great for barrels and long boats for transporting the salt to market. The high quality of white oak lumber from this area became recognized by the shipbuilding industry. Wood was also readily available as a fuel source for the new landowners. The first commercial enterprise was hardwood timber for lumber used for building long boats and barrels for the Kanawha Salt Works. The coal industry would first begin development in the 1850s with oil and gas to follow near the beginning of the 20th century.

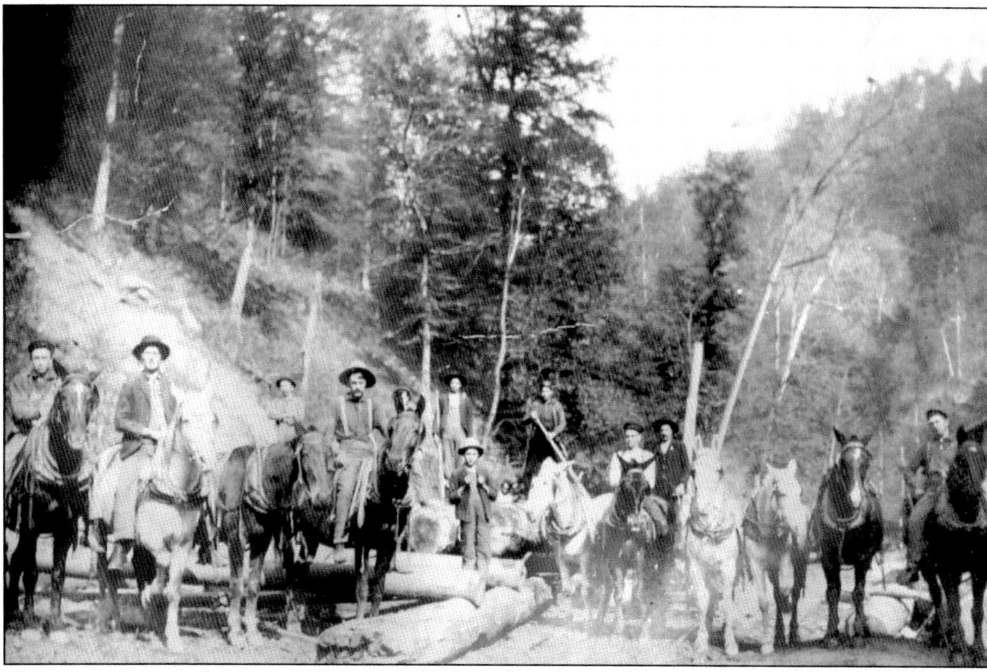

This group was working with the construction of the Dan's Run Dam in 1913–1914. These logs would be shaped for use as wall timbers for building new homes or barns for the new settlers. As the sawmill came into existence, the demand for lumber increased and slowly replaced the log buildings in the area. (Ralph Nester Collection courtesy of Mark Sergent.)

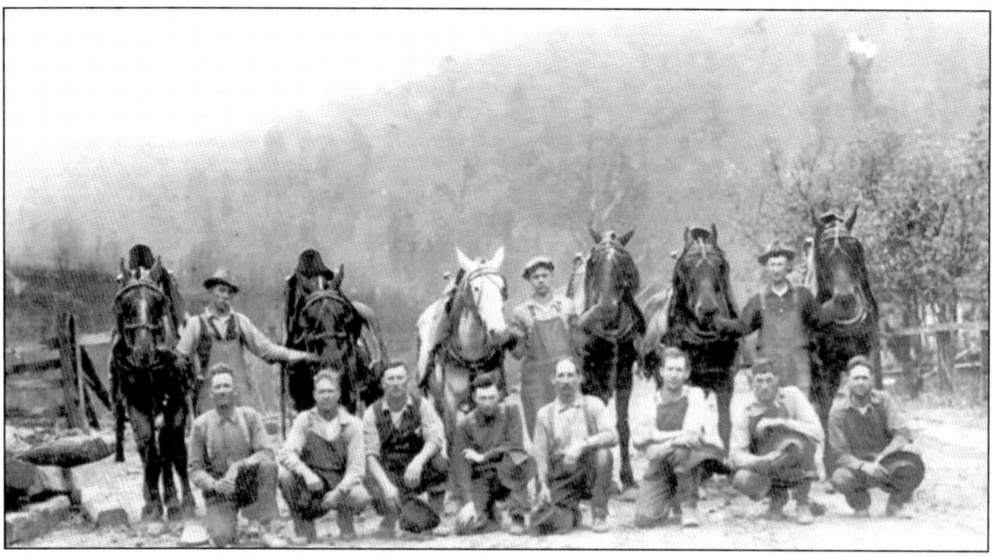

These teamsters worked in the Tariff area and provided a great service to the urban and rural areas of the county. They continued their work after the railroads came into being by using their teams and wagons to transport goods to and from the rail heads. They assisted in the building of the county roads, pipeline construction, and rigs for the new oil and gas business in addition to the timbering. (Courtesy of Goldie [Morris] Douglas.)

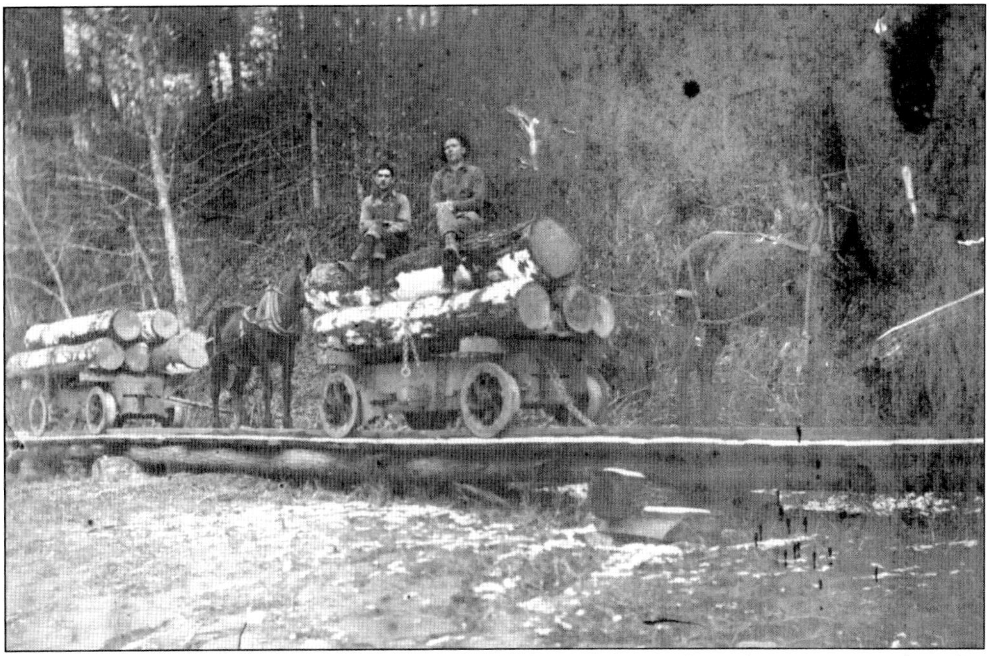

One of the means of transportation for moving the logs to a sawmill was by wagon on rail tracks. The teamster on the right was Benjamin Bullis. The log cars ran on a metal rail much like railroad tracks and were usually pulled by mules, horses, or oxen. The location of this image is believed to be in the Clover Ridge area. (Courtesy of Tresa [O'Brien] Mitchell.)

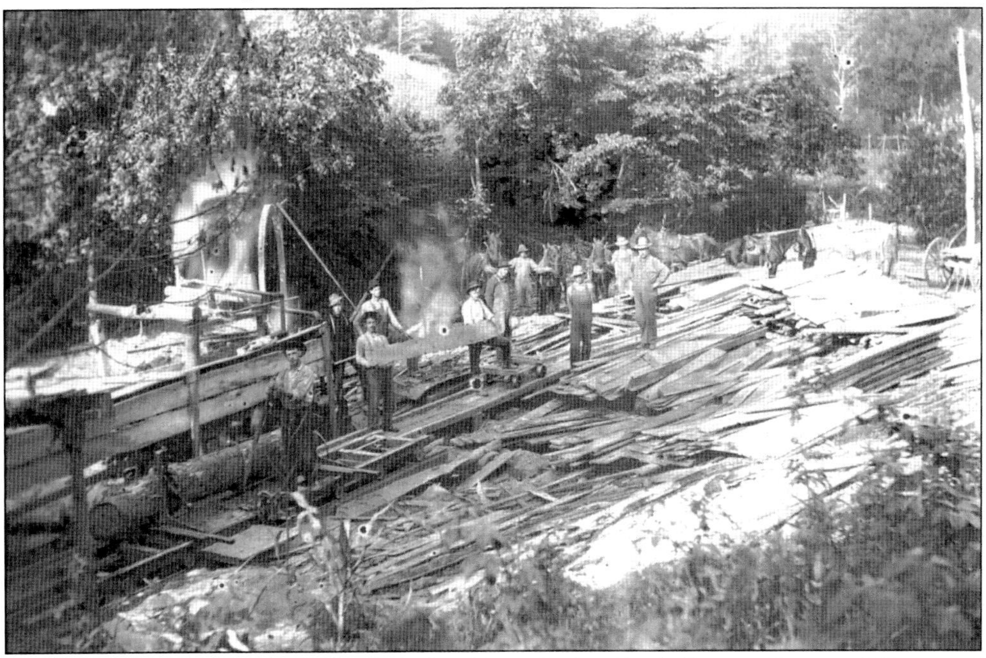

This sawmill and crew was located in the Clover Ridge, Rush Run, or Banner Hill area of Smithfield District near the beginning of the 20th century. Sawmills were established throughout Roane County as the timbering industry flourished and the demand for lumber increased with the arrival of new settlers to the area. (Courtesy of Tresa [O'Brien] Mitchell.)

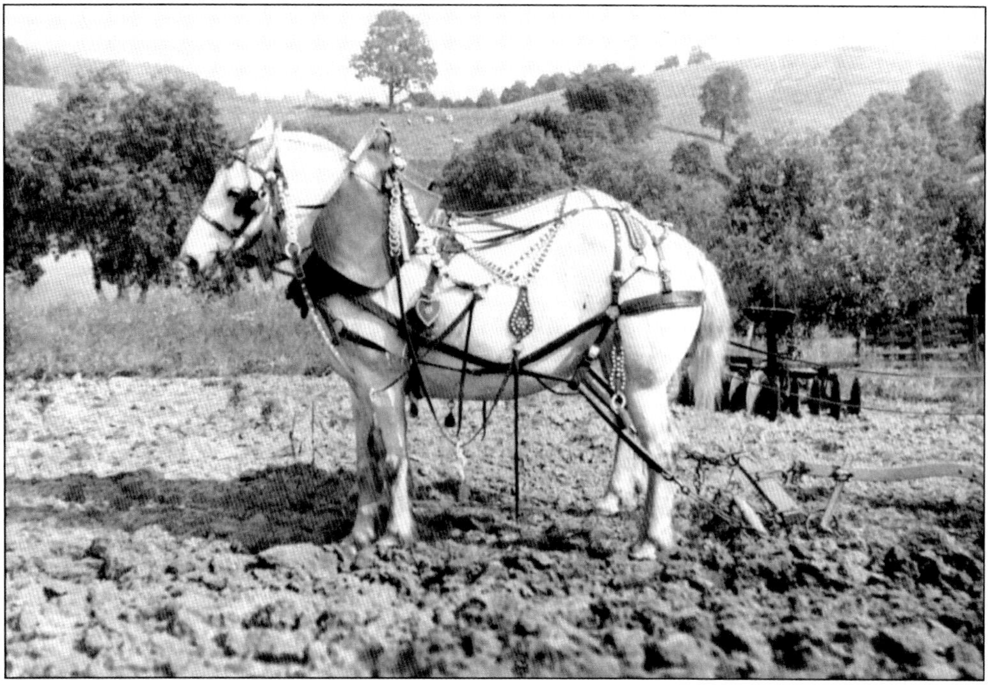

This draft horse was owned by Phil Miller around 1930. Horses like this were necessary to the farmer for plowing and working the fields and gardens and hauling things needed in everyday farm life. (Ralph Nester Collection courtesy of Mark Sergent.)

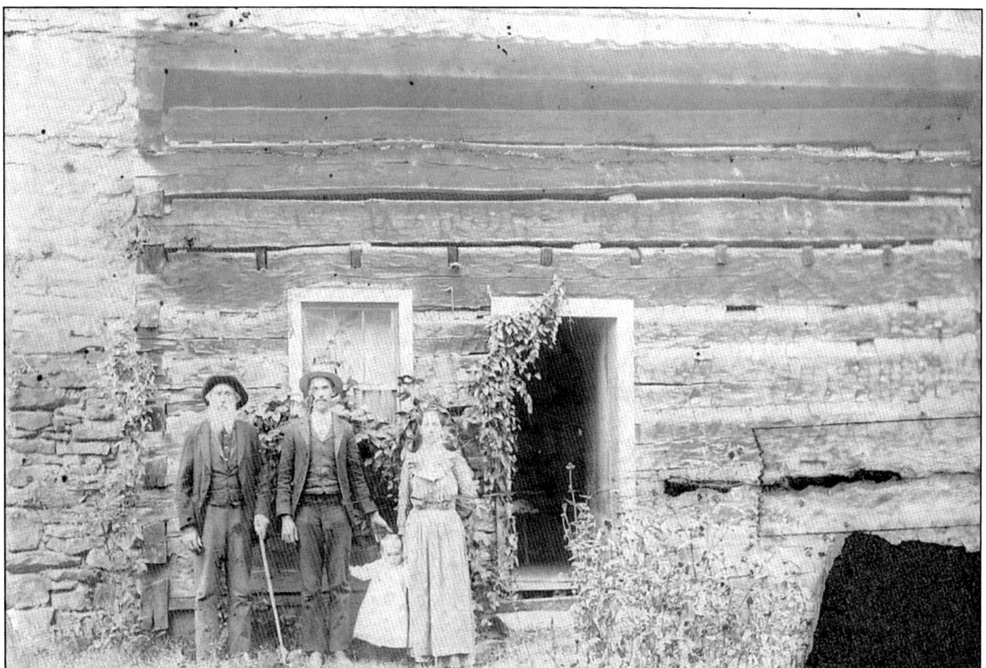

This log house in the Johnson Creek area was the home of Abraham Dye. The image is of, from left to right, Abraham, Creed, unidentified, and Minnie Dye taken before the year 1900. (Courtesy of Mark Sergent.)

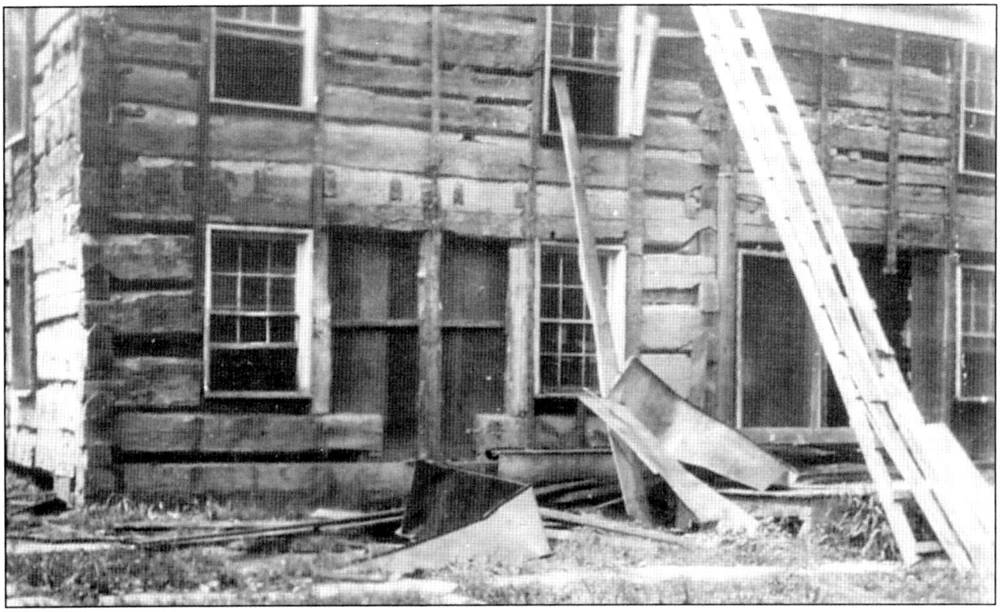

This log house was built at Looneyville by Robert Looney about 1840. Three generations of the Looney family lived here. Abraham Looney inherited the house and farm and lived there for 56 years. His son, John W. Looney, inherited the farm, and a new two-story frame house was built by 1912. The first Looneyville Post Office was located in this log house. (Courtesy of Philip Crane.)

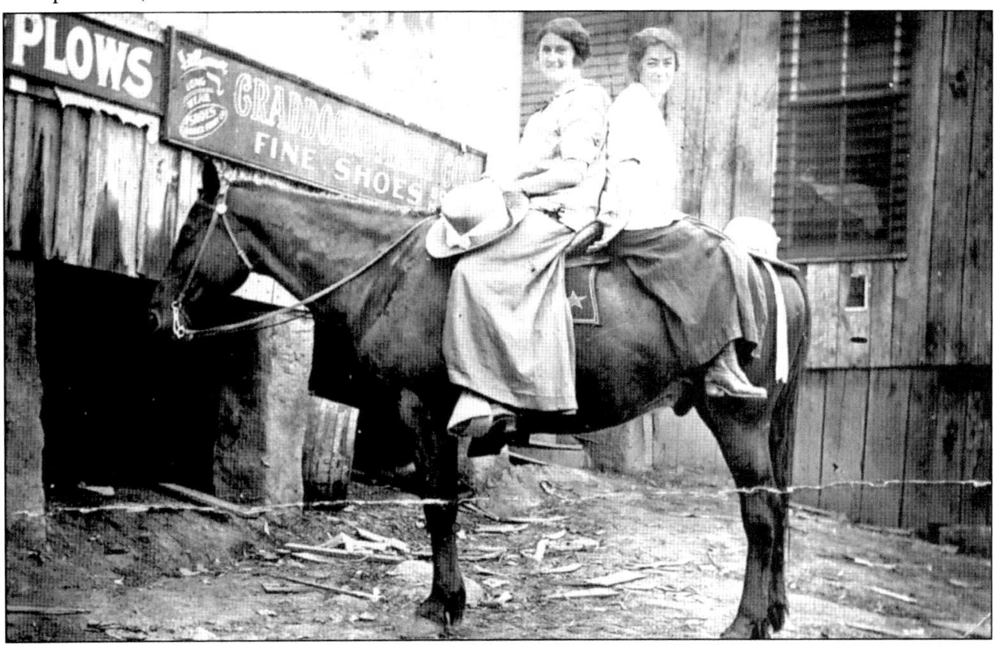

This Geary Brothers store in Amma was owned by Clyde and Harry Geary about 1918. Shorty Haddox (left) and Edith Geary model their new bonnets on horseback. There were two buildings with a covered driveway where wagons could be unloaded out of the weather. The Gearys relocated their store to Clendenin and demolished the old building with its contents of caskets, shoes, and other dry goods. (Courtesy of Philip Crane.)

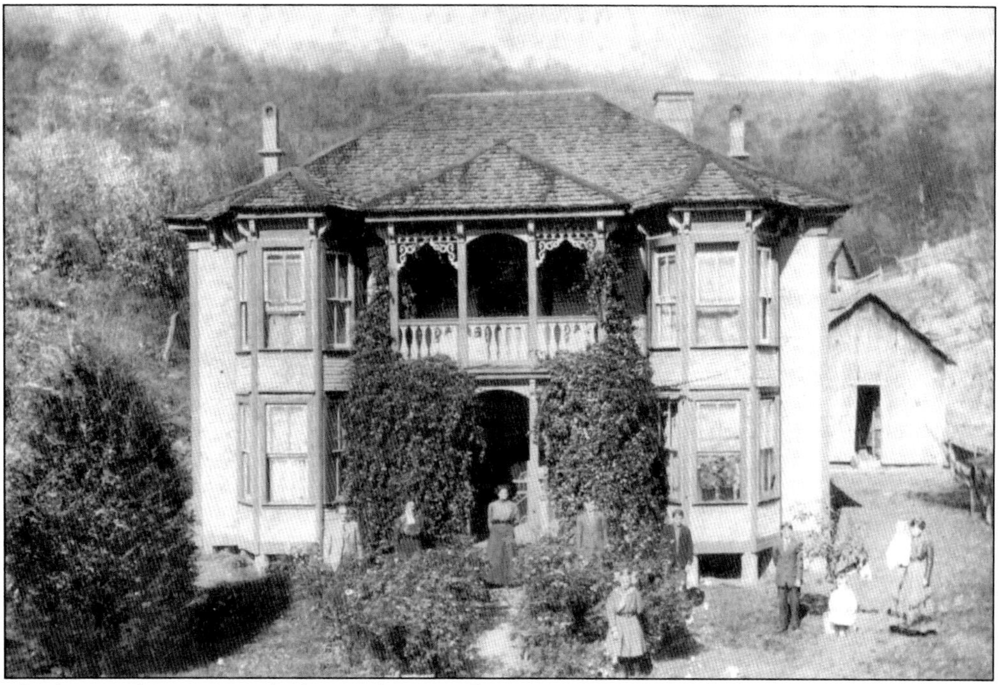

The home of Peter C. and Charity (Vineyard) Looney was built in the late 1800s or very early 1900s. This family was reported to be some of the oldest settlers in Roane County. He was a teacher and county superintendent of schools of Roane County. The house is still standing in the head of Canoe Run at upper Henrys Fork near Tariff. (Courtesy of Carol Cronin.)

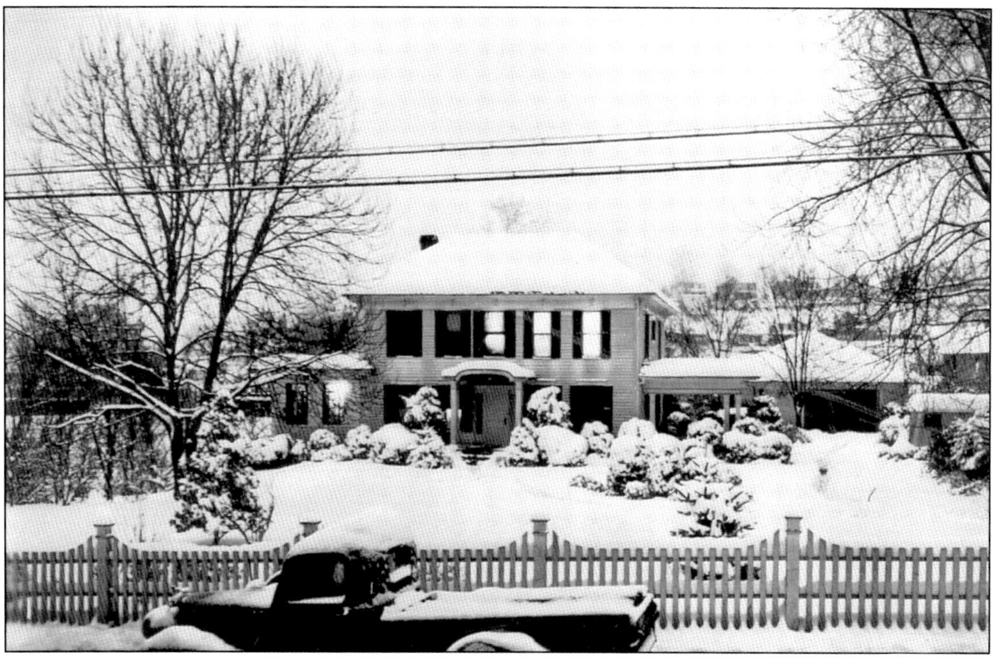

The home of Fred McIntosh on Main Street in Spencer is a good example of some fine homes being built in the town in the early 1900s. He was in the hardware business about 1906, and the McIntosh Hardware Store remains in business today. (Courtesy of Dr. Harry H. Camp Sr. family.)

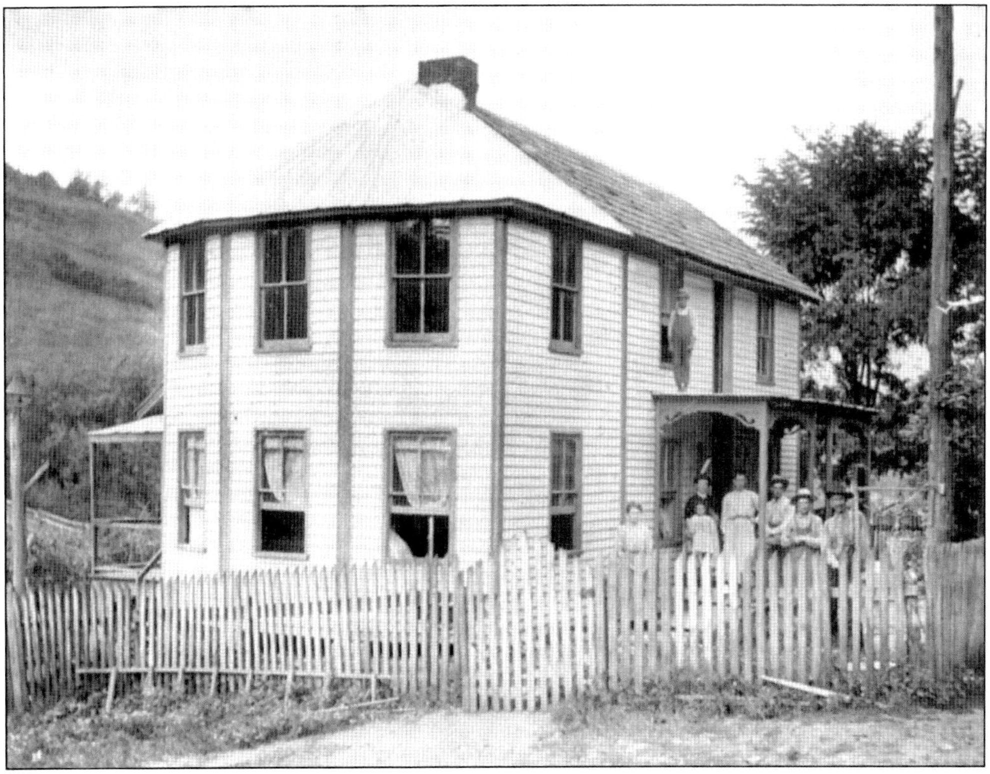

This is the Elihu Whited home located near Peniel. It was built about 1910. (Courtesy of Wilma Rhodes.)

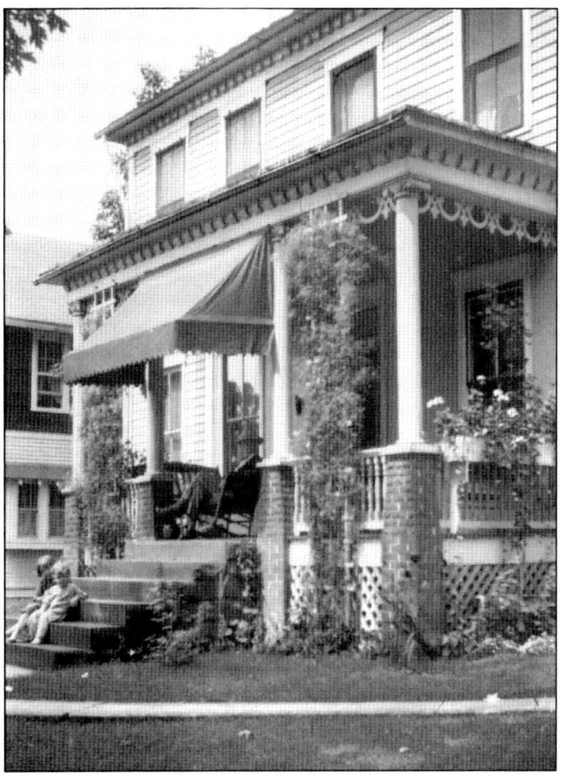

The home of James M. Cleavenger is located on Church Street in Spencer. He was a merchant and a Civil War veteran, joining the Union army when 14 years of age. He carried on various businesses and held public office. (Courtesy of Dr. Harry H. Camp Sr. family.)

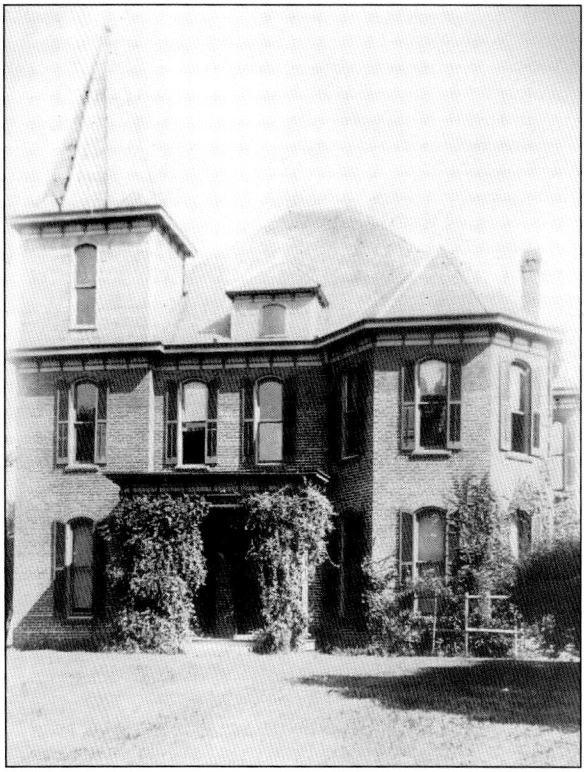

This was the home of William Woodyard, born in Wirt County, Virginia, in 1840. He moved to Spencer about the time of the Civil War and married Isabelle Chapman in 1866. He raised his family and later became a West Virginia state senator. He died in 1895, and their house would be sold and remodeled in 1911 to become the first Spencer High School. (Courtesy of Dr. Harry H. Camp Sr. family.)

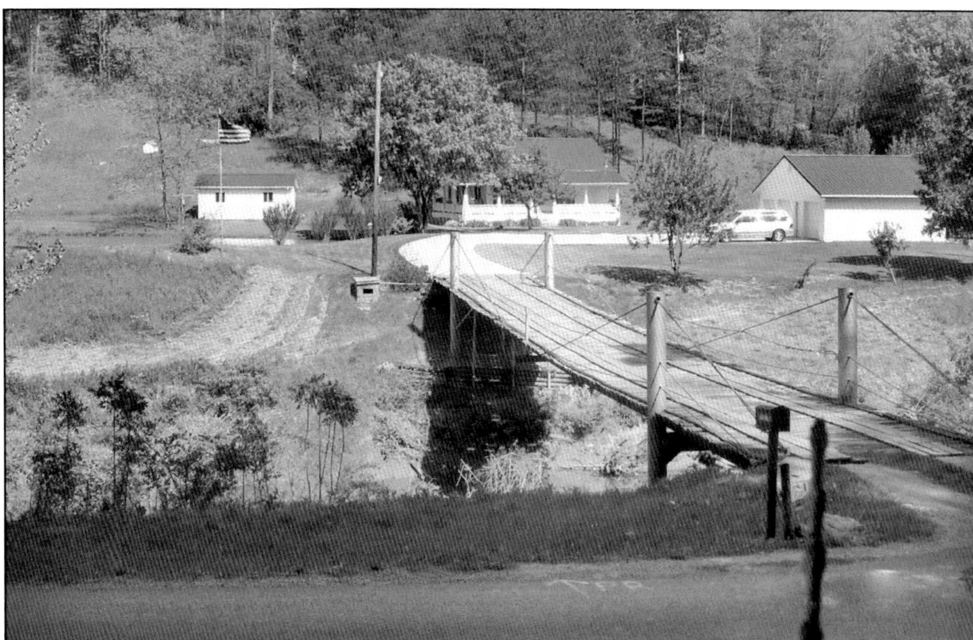

This house was built by Roy J. Nida in 1929 at Amma. He was employed by the United Fuel Gas Company for 43 years before retiring. He married Ruby G. Looney, daughter of Henry C. Looney, a merchant and schoolteacher of Newton. Roy and Ruby would live here until their deaths. Ruby taught in elementary schools of Roane County for over 40 years. (Courtesy of Jack Nida.)

Three

OIL AND GAS

William Bishop's *History of Roane County West Virginia, 1774–1927* (1927) describes the natural gas fields of Roane County as being "the greatest in the world." This may not be entirely true in 2007, but its contribution to the economy of this county places it at or near the top of the list of exported products. Fortunes were made by families who held the mineral rights to this vast industry as they received royalties from the production of wells drilled on their land.

In the early 1800s, David and Joseph Ruffner inherited a large tract of land in Kanawha County from their father. There were several natural salt springs on this property, so it was decided that they should develop these for increased production. In 1808, they drilled through rock formations to a depth of 58 feet and struck a strong vein of saltwater brine. Tubing and packers were used to convey the brine to the surface, and this method would later be used extensively in the petroleum industry.

The industrial use of natural gas preceded the domestic use by about a decade. Glass factories, iron and steel mills, and carbon black factories developed production techniques for natural gas that led to the creation of a market for this product. Other industries began the use of natural gas as a fuel source in the 1880s. This demand precipitated the expansion of oil and gas exploration during the 1890s, especially in the northern and western part of the state, including Roane County. The American Oil Development Company held leases on 65,000 acres of land in Roane, Jackson, and Clay Counties. By 1898, the town of Spencer was being supplied natural gas for domestic use at a price of 22¢ per 1,000 cubic feet. Drilling technology continued to improve, and by 1910, many wells were approaching 2,000 feet in depth. Pipelines were constructed to transport the natural gas to the metropolitan areas of the northeast, including the compressor stations along the way to furnish the necessary pressure boost over hills and mountains. The major company in the construction of high-pressure gas transport lines in Roane County was the United Fuel Gas Company (UFGC), which would later become part of the Columbia Gas System. The first well to be drilled by this company was at Clio in 1899 and produced gas for 55 years. A small bronze plaque now marks the location of UFGC Well No. 1 and the Lewis Compressor Station that is now just a memory at Clio.

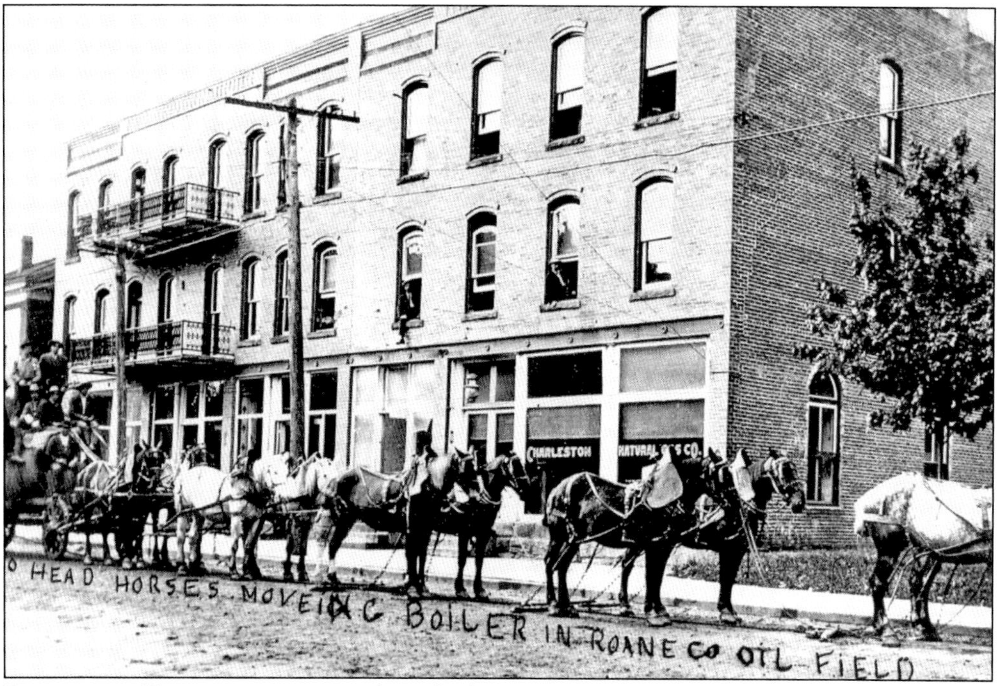

Five teams of horses are moving a large boiler on a wagon past the Charleston Natural Gas Company office on the way to the Curtis oil field about 1900. The building shown is the Grand Hotel in Spencer. (Ralph Nester Collection courtesy of Mark Sergent.)

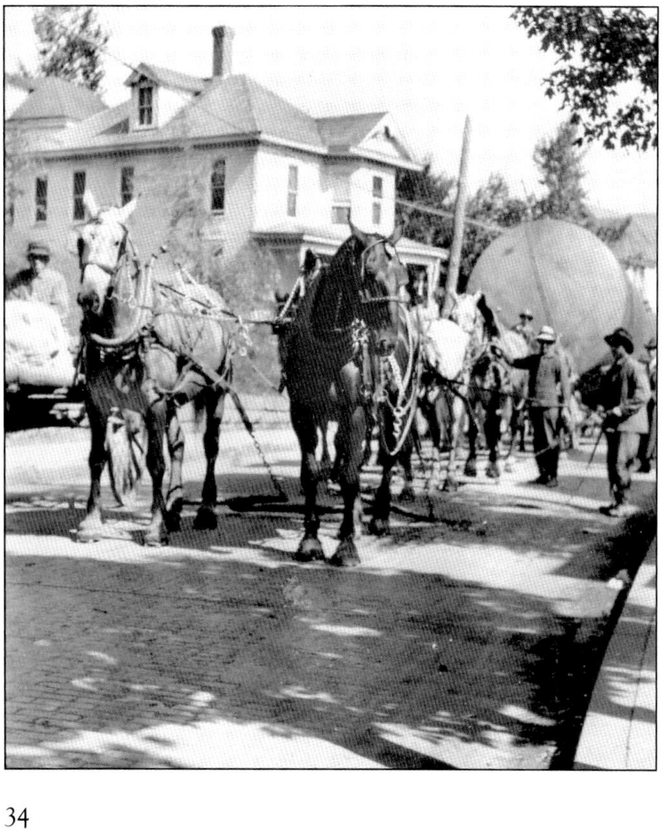

A steam boiler is being delivered to the Clover Ridge oil field. Teamsters with their horses were the precursor of the semi-trucks for hauling heavy loads. Old-timers told of mud so deep on Spencer's Main Street that horses' and oxen's bellies would mire in the streets while pulling loads through town. (Ralph Nester Collection courtesy of Mark Sergent.)

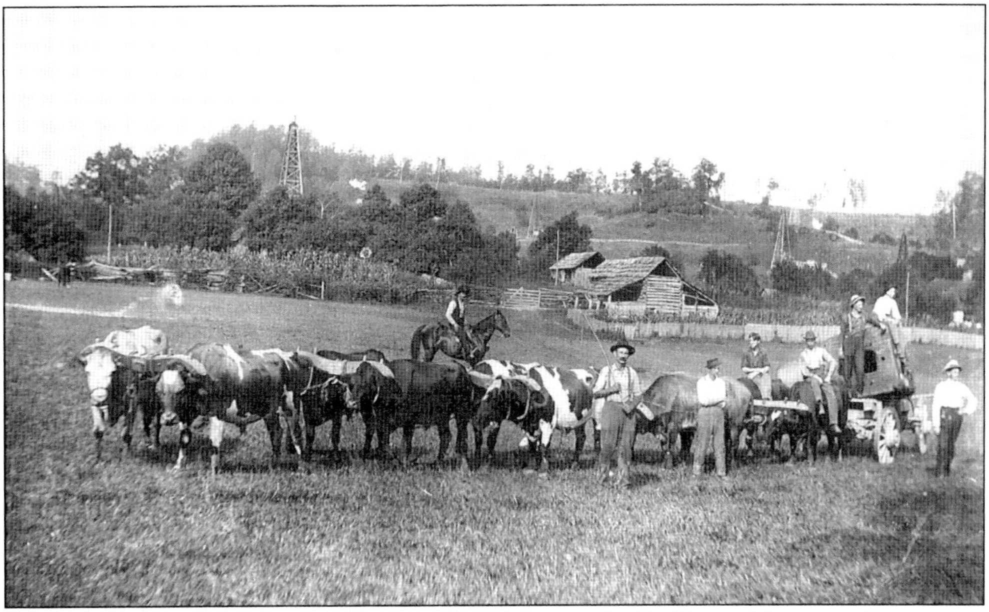

A steam boiler is being transported by five yokes of oxen on the Ott Kincaid farm near Stringtown. Boilers were utilized to produce steam that powered the steam engines. Oxen were used more often than horses to pull heavier loads. (Courtesy of Mark Sergent.)

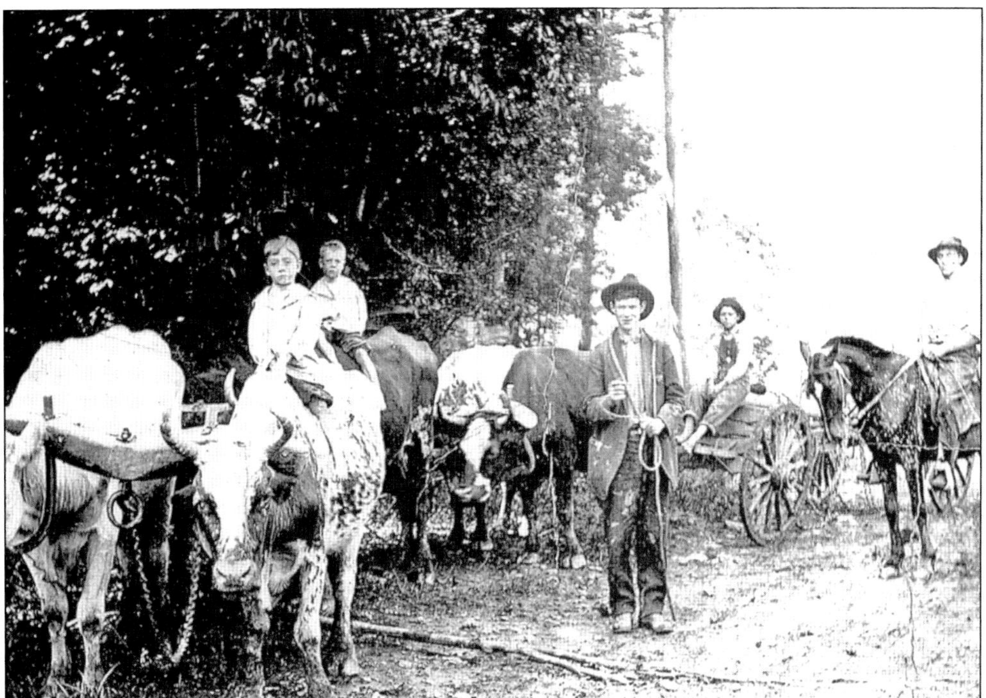

A double yoke of oxen was used to pull a wagon of supplies for the oil and gas fields. It was a fun time for the children when they hitched a ride. (Courtesy of Dan Looney.)

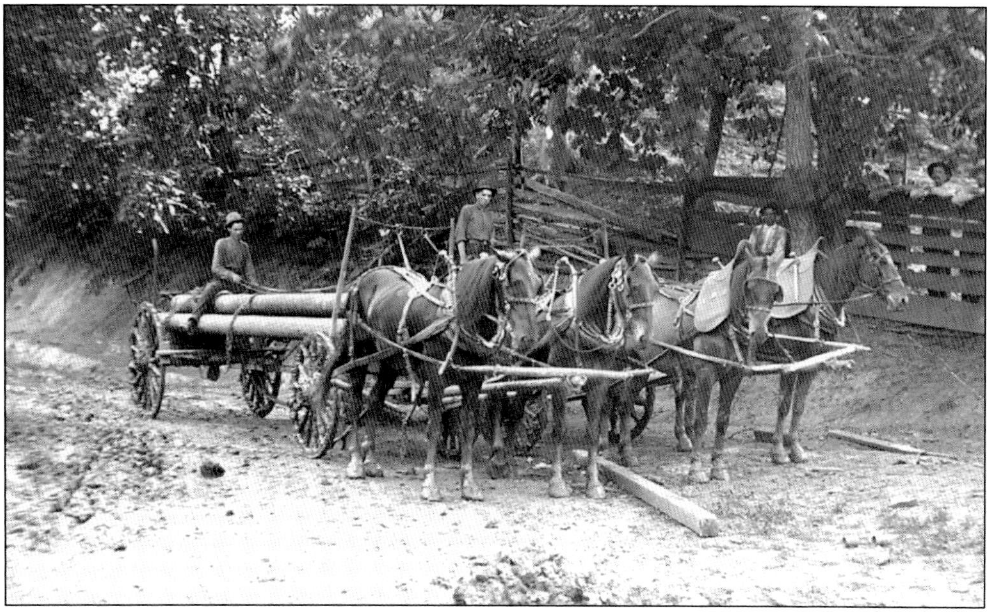

Isaiah Daniel Looney rides on a load of pipe being moved to the Tariff oil fields about 1911. Teamsters took great pride in their horses and harness equipment. The driver was not identified. (Courtesy of Madge [Looney] Crane.)

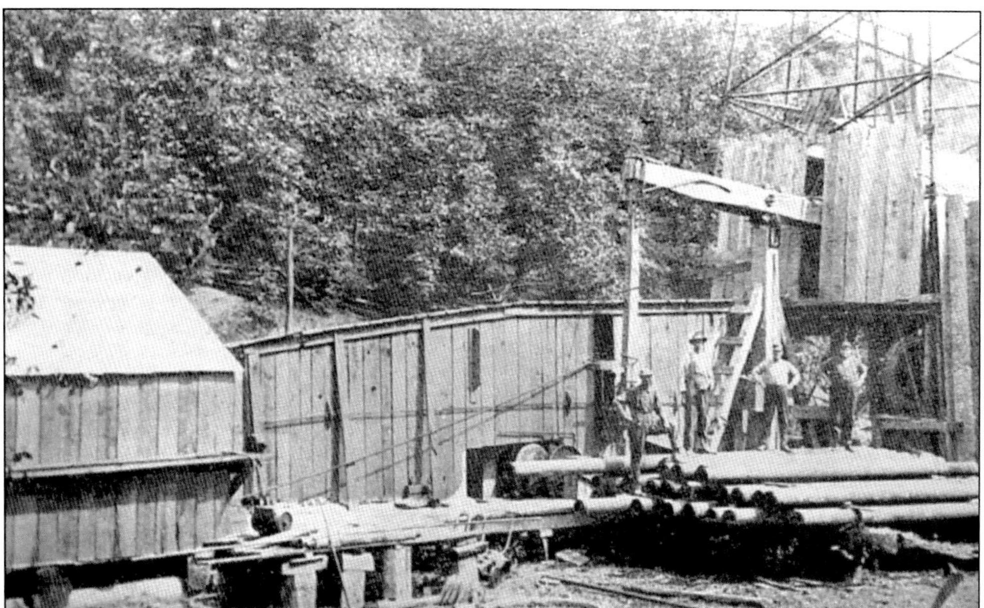

The men working on this oil well were, from left to right, John Wright, P. C. Lowman, Cliff Lamp, and a Mr. Slaughter. It is on the property of Irvin Conley. (Courtesy of Eleanor Stotts.)

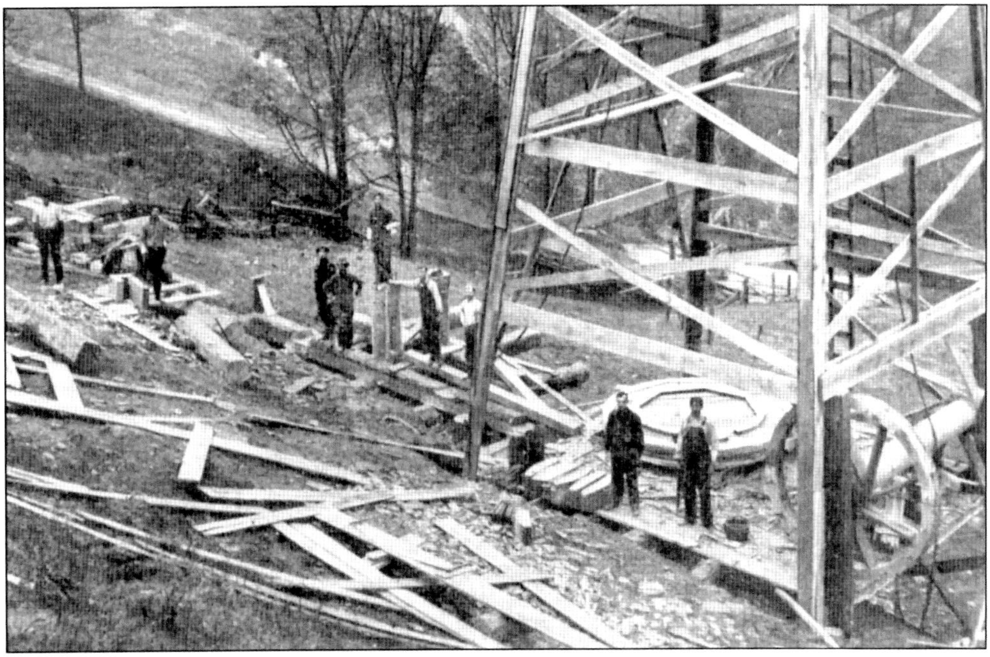

A wooden oil rig is under construction in 1914 near Spencer. (Courtesy of Donna Walbrown.)

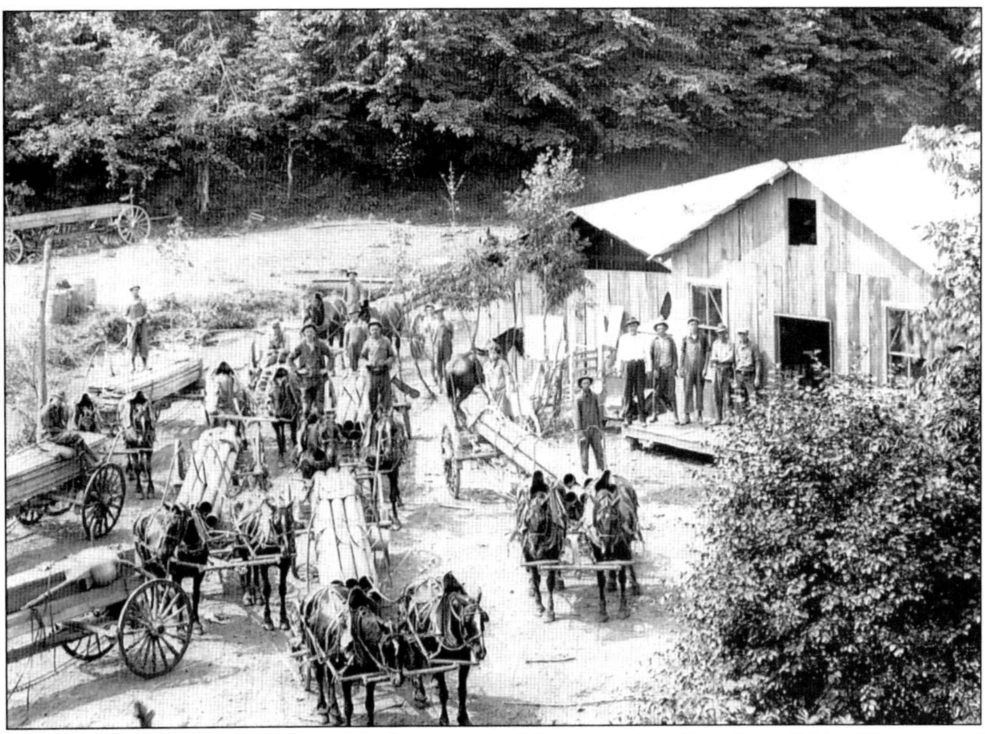

Wagonloads of supplies are being made ready for delivery to the oil and gas fields. (Courtesy of Dan Looney.)

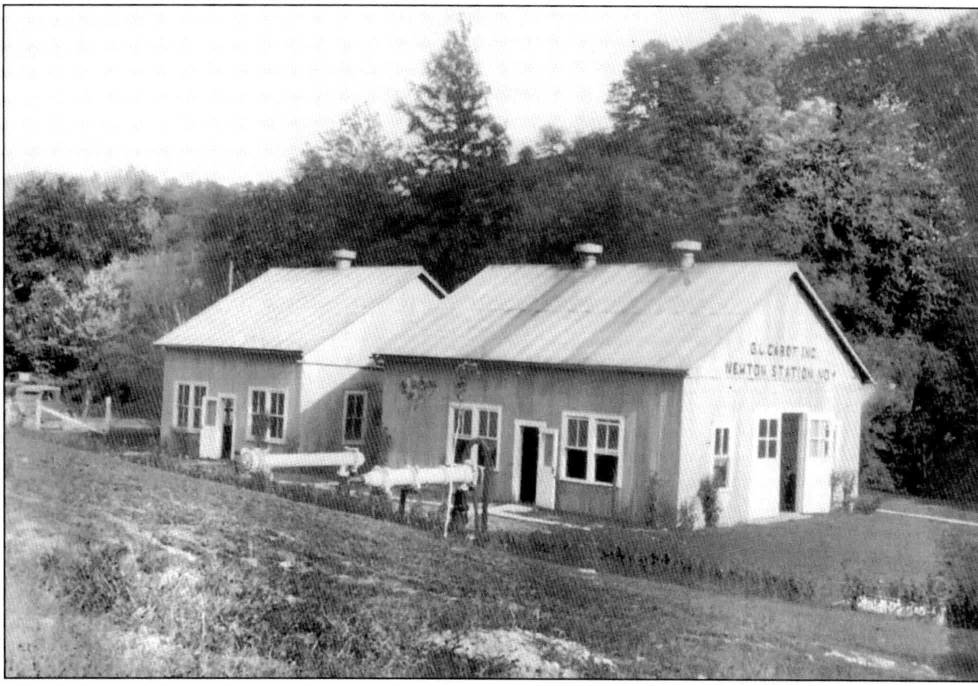

The Cabot Company compressor station in Newton provided the energy to push the gas farther north to the next station. Additional stations would be needed to move the gas to Pennsylvania on its way to the markets in the Northeast. (Courtesy of Carol Cronin.)

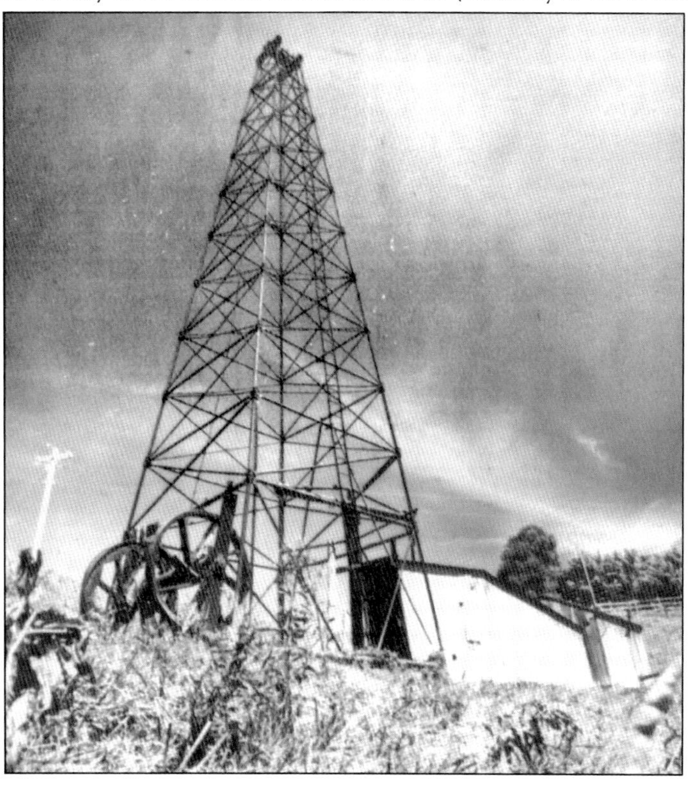

This steel oil rig is located on Clover Ridge in one of the best producing areas of the county. (Courtesy of Corlis Harris Collection.)

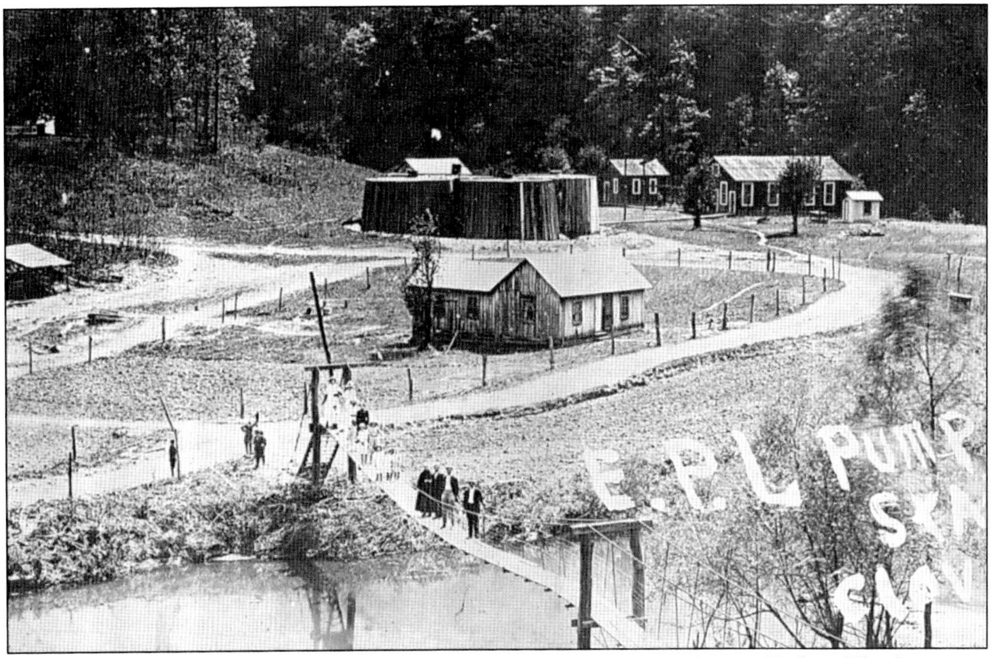

The Eureka Pipe Line Pumping Station is located at Otto near Clover Ridge. The house in the foreground was the home of Hal and Letha McMillan about 1911. (Courtesy of Evelyn [Bissell] Starcher.)

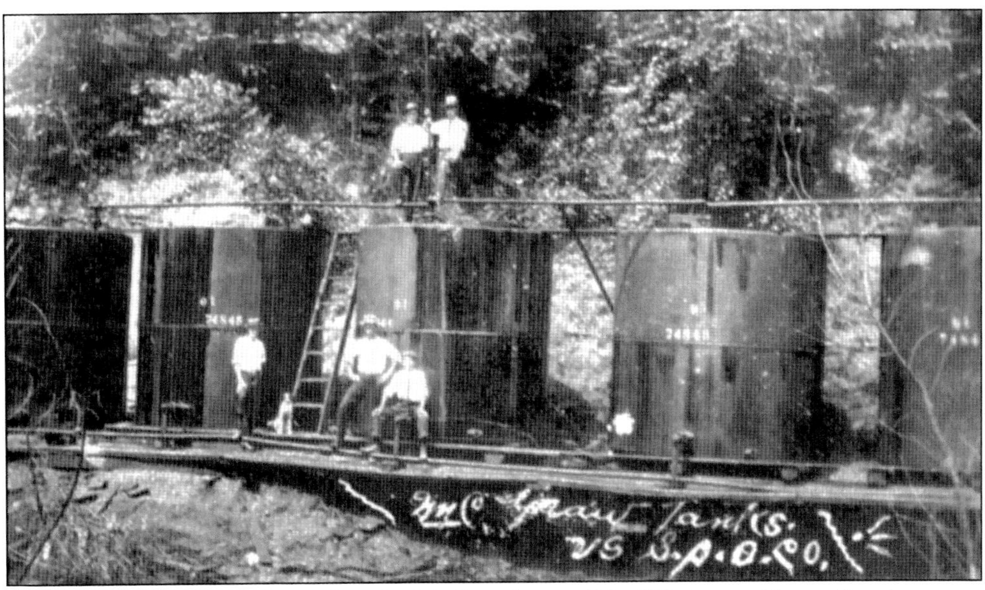

This battery of tanks was located on the McGraw farm at Edgell Fork near Clover. Royalties were paid per the amount of oil pumped from local wells into such storage tanks. (Courtesy of David Boothe and David Freshwater.)

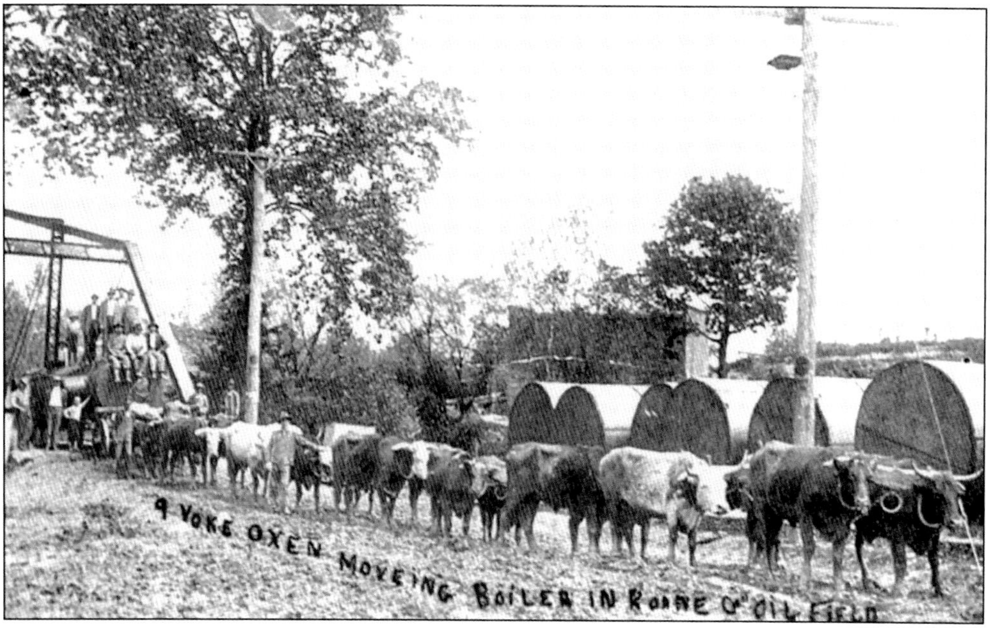

Nine yokes (18 head) of oxen are moving a heavy steam boiler from Spencer to the oil fields. (Courtesy of David Boothe and David Freshwater.)

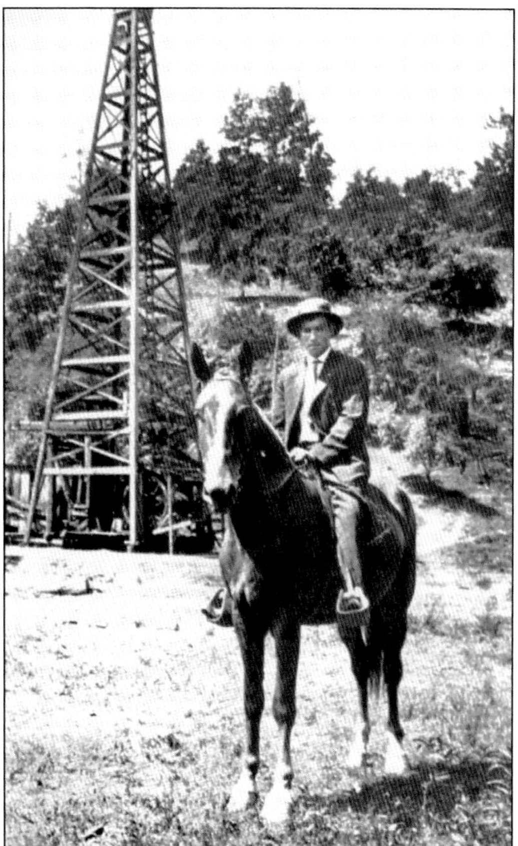

The J. O. Fisher Oil Well No. 1 was drilled in 1910 on Edgell Fork near Clover to a depth of 1,934 feet. The wooden derrick was later replaced by a steel tower. Homer A. Harris of the South Penn Oil Company is mounted on his horse in this 1915 photograph. His son Corlis W. Harris founded Harris Oil Company, and his grandson C. Willard Harris Jr. became its president in 1972. (Courtesy of David Boothe and David Freshwater.)

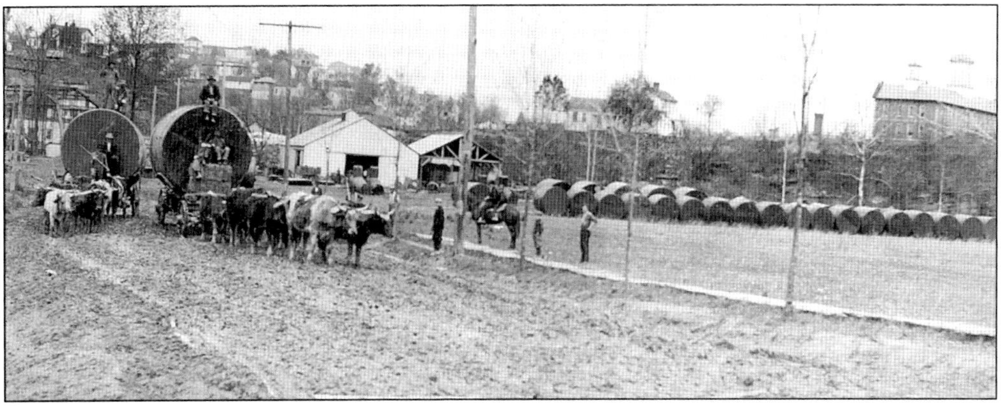

South Penn Oil Company, a major participant in the growth of the Roane County oil and gas industry, was located on Capitol Street in Spencer in 1913. This lot was utilized for storage of their drilling supplies that were being moved into the oil fields. The property, with the Spencer State Hospital in the background, is now owned by East Resources. (Courtesy of Marlin Morris.)

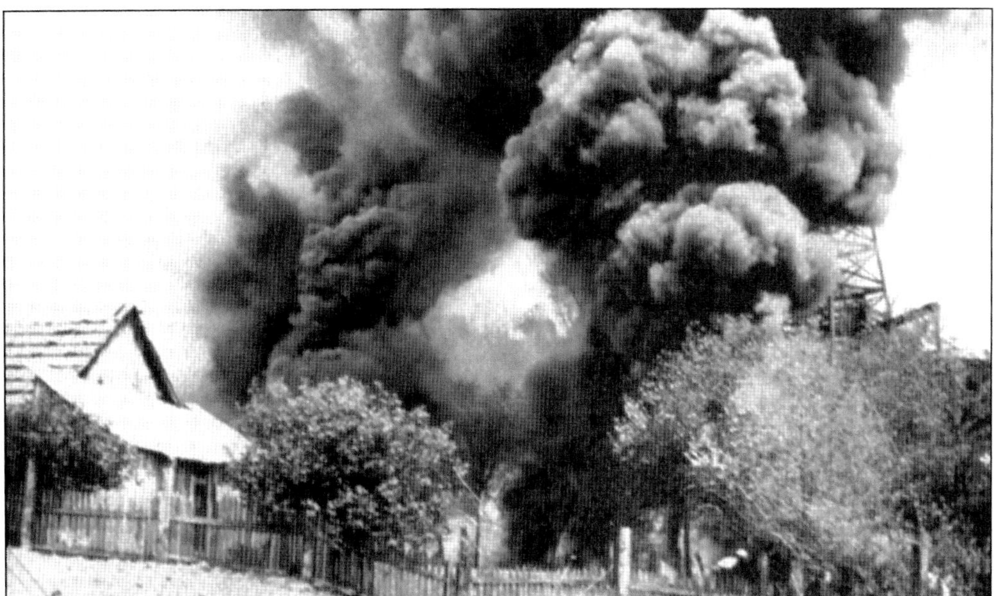

A fire scene taken in 1913 depicts the danger involved with oil and gas wells. Black smoke billowed from this well that had been drilled quite near a dwelling located at Hammack, later known as Stringtown, located off U.S. 119 south of Spencer. (Courtesy of David Boothe and David Freshwater.)

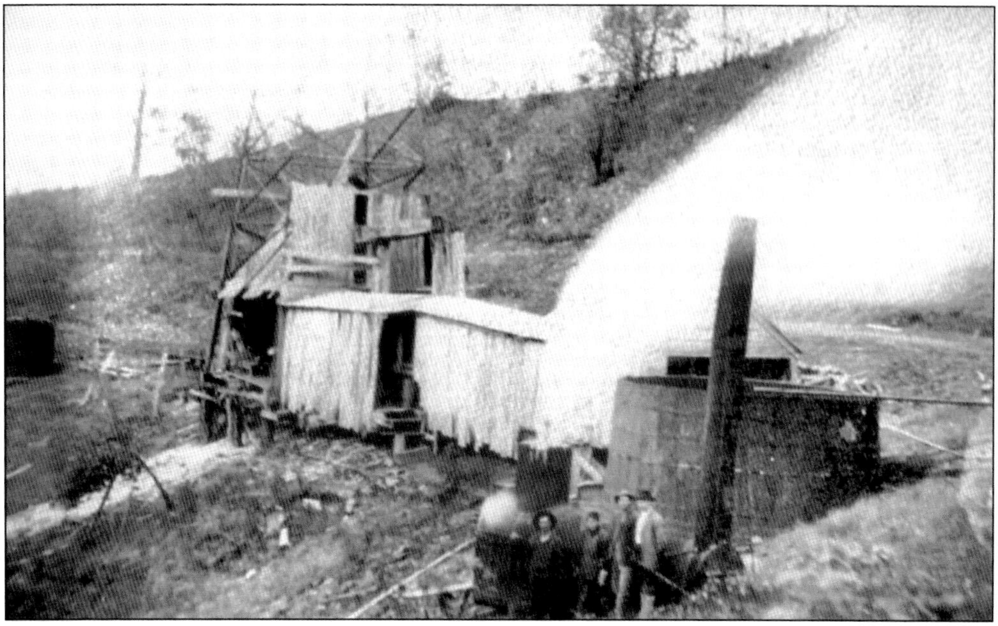

Boiler tanks were equipped with a relief valve in the event of excess pressure in the system. Wood fires heated the water to make steam that drove the engine and ran the drilling rig. Upon completion of the drilling process, this steam would operate the pump on this Chambers Well No. 5 in the Clover oil field. (Courtesy of David Boothe and David Freshwater.)

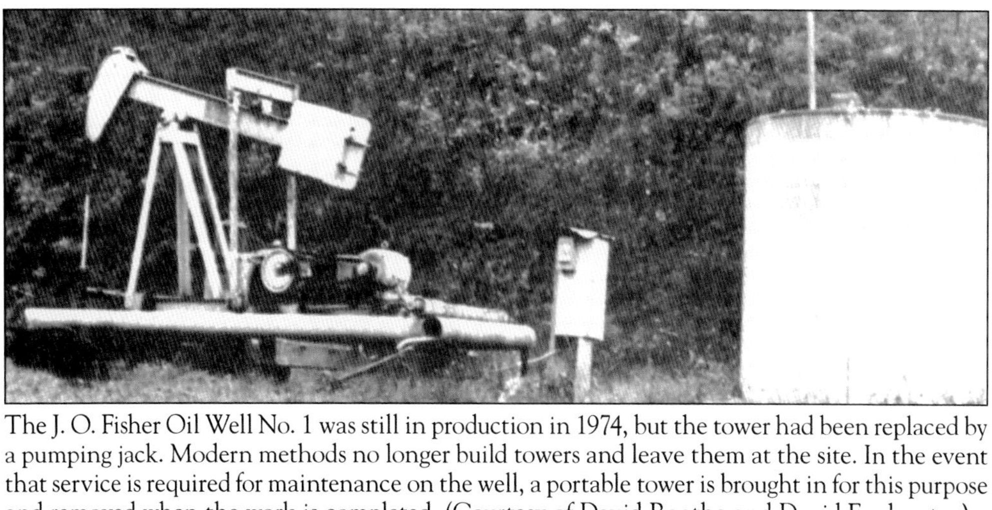

The J. O. Fisher Oil Well No. 1 was still in production in 1974, but the tower had been replaced by a pumping jack. Modern methods no longer build towers and leave them at the site. In the event that service is required for maintenance on the well, a portable tower is brought in for this purpose and removed when the work is completed. (Courtesy of David Boothe and David Freshwater.)

Four

Roads and Transportation

Prior to the year 1850, there were no all-weather roads within what is now Roane County. An act by the General Assembly of Virginia was enacted that year for the construction of "a turnpike road" from a point in the Staunton Turnpike in Gilmer County to run through Ripley and continue on to the Ohio River at Pomeroy. This dirt road, which was a minimum of 15 feet wide, was completed about 1853 from Weston to Ripley, without a bridge in the whole stretch. Tolls were placed on its use until about 1860 and were discontinued because of its bad condition. This road was designated as the Gilmer, Ripley, and Ohio River Turnpike. Beginning in 1870, bridges of wood were constructed to permit travel when deep waters made fording of streams impossible. Covered bridges were constructed at Reedy and Walton before 1900. The first steel bridge in the county was built in 1897 to span Spring Creek at the intersection of Main and Court Streets in Spencer. About 1906, a steel bridge was constructed across Big Sandy Creek at Newton and across the Pocatalico River at Walton. The first bridge to be constructed of reinforced concrete in Roane County was at the intersection of State Route 36 and U.S. 119 at the south end of Spencer.

Road improvements came slowly for the next 20 years after the construction of the turnpike. The war had taken a heavy toll on the condition of the roads, but a network was being formed to connect the island communities within the county. New settlers brought more wagons as the move westward continued. It was soon recognized that an organized plan for improvement would be necessary, and the construction of a rock base on existing wagon trails began by 1880 and slowly expanded from the villages toward the farmlands. About the beginning of the 20th century, a major effort to improve the dirt roads to the more rural areas was being made throughout the county. The paving of streets began in Spencer in 1907 with a good thick surfacing of concrete overlaid with hardest brick. Farming and the growth in commerce and industry throughout the county would require an improvement in the transportation system.

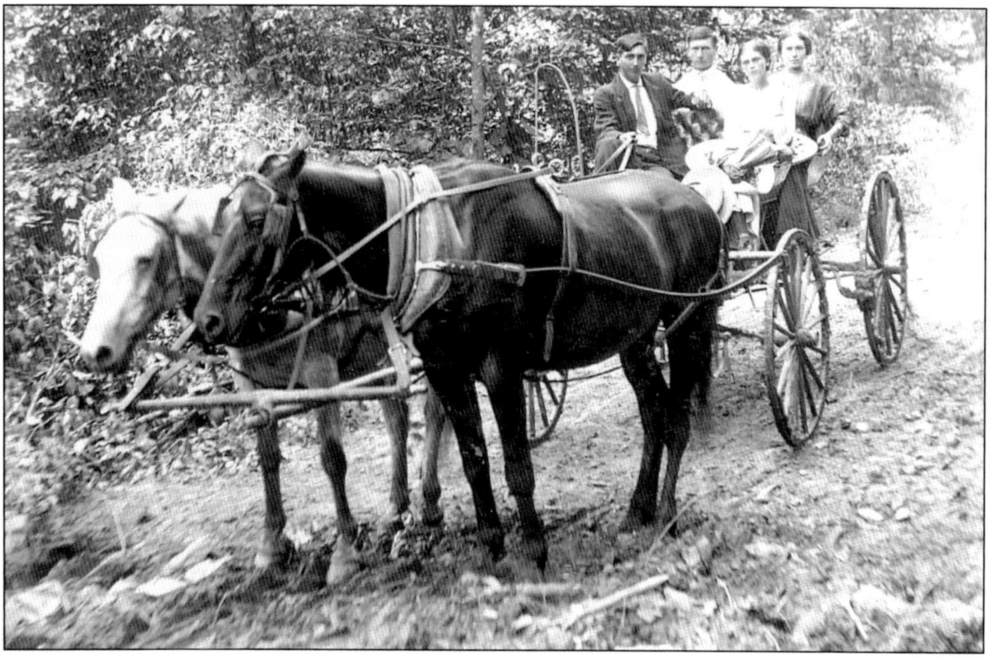

This was the common transportation for going to church around 1900. The motorcar would slowly replace the horse and buggy in the early years of the 20th century. These couples are unidentified, but they were probably of the Walton area. (Courtesy of Jane [Taylor] George.)

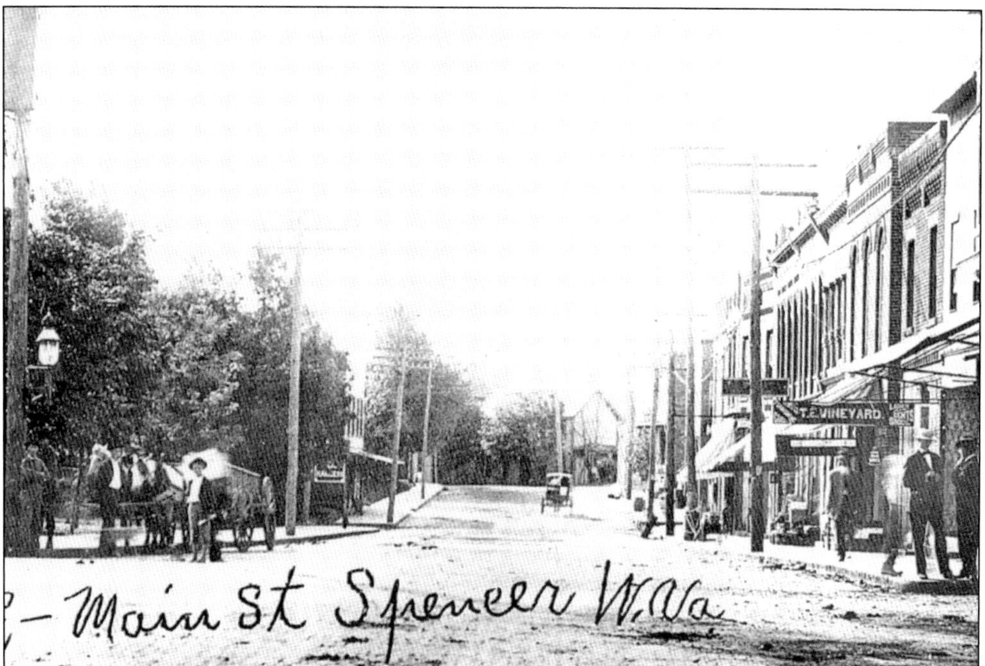

Main Street in Spencer was the town's primary business center around 1900. The courthouse was surrounded by business establishments to serve the main industries of timber, oil, and gas. (Ralph Nester Collection courtesy of Mark Sergent.)

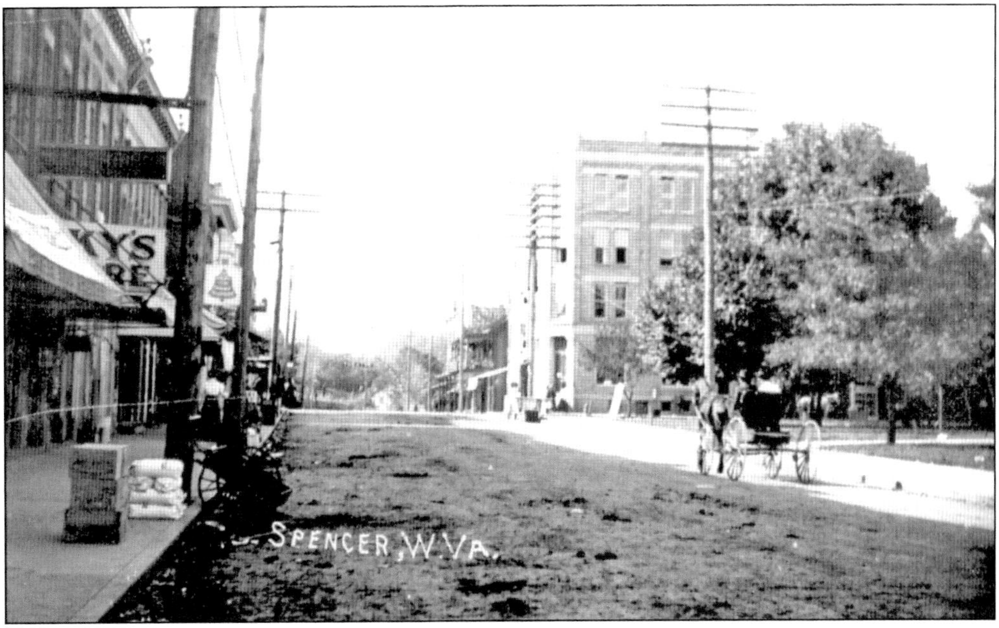

This view of Main Street looks west, probably in 1907 as the streets were starting to be paved. The condition of the streets during the winter months was generally deplorable, and it was a daily task for men to pry their stalled wagons out of mud holes. Paving began at the railroad tracks with Market Street and Main Street being the first completed. (Ralph Nester Collection courtesy of Mark Sergent.)

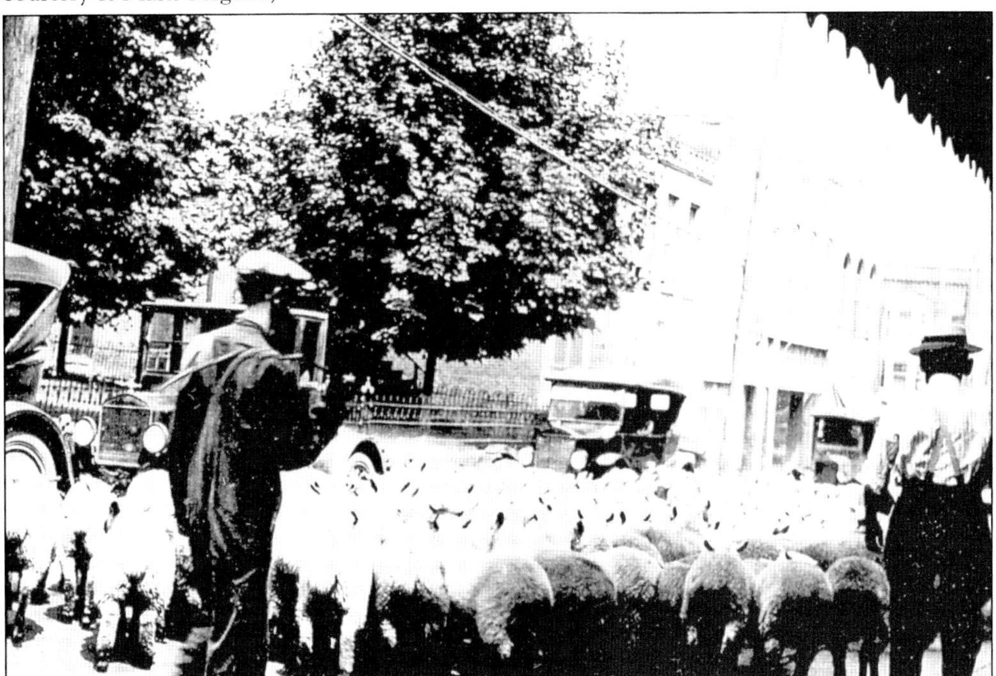

A flock of sheep was often driven to market in Spencer by the farmer, and they shared the streets with the motor vehicles in 1921. Cattle were also brought to town for shipment to the eastern cities by way of the train. (Ralph Nester Collection courtesy of Mark Sergent.)

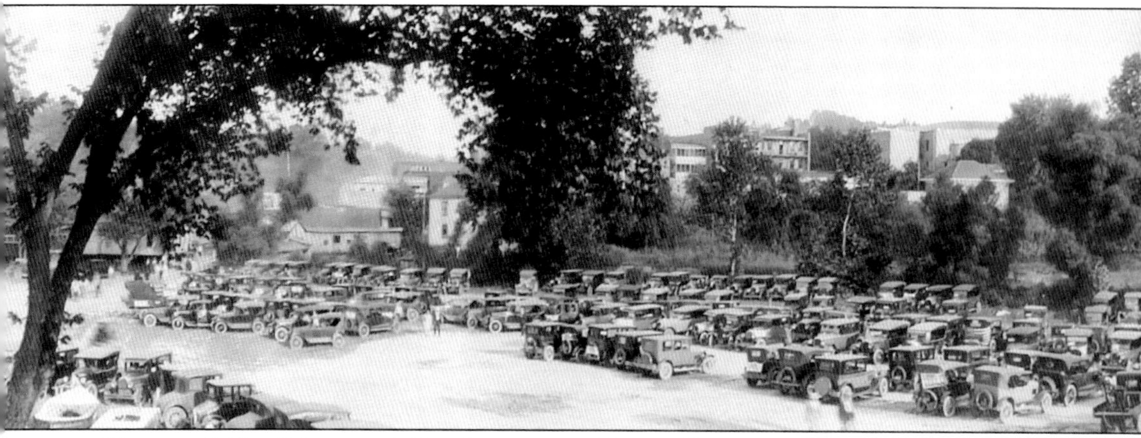

The year 1926 will be recorded in the history of Roane County as the period when the county listed its greatest progress in construction of highways, giving the county seat year-round highways north and south. The first celebration on July 15 marked the opening of a hard-surfaced highway between Spencer and Parkersburg via Reedy, Elizabeth, and Mineral Wells. A motorcade estimated at 500 cars started at Parkersburg and proceeded to Elizabeth for the first part of the celebration.

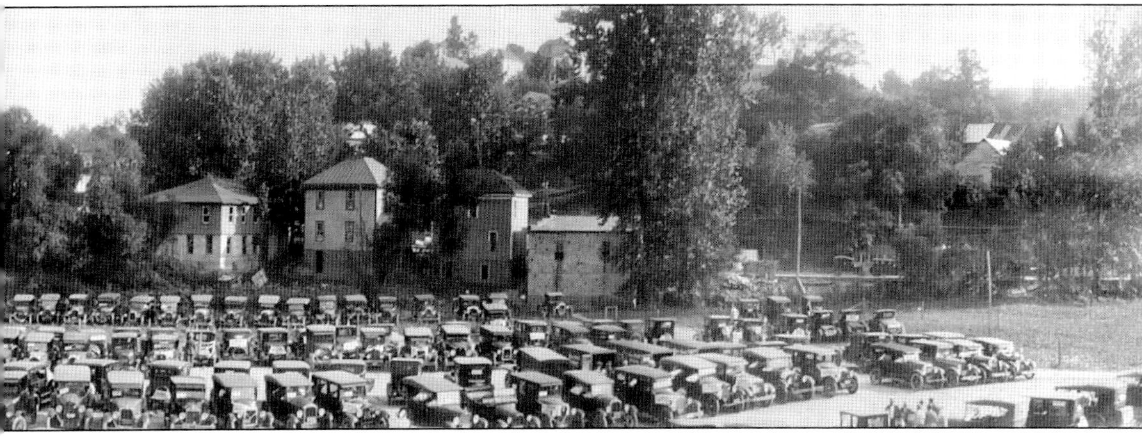

Then it continued to Reedy for another phase and finally on to Spencer for the principal program. The motorcade arrived at Spencer about 4:00 p.m., where E. J. Harris, mayor of Spencer, presided as master of ceremonies over a program that included speeches by many dignitaries. (Courtesy of Roane County Historical Society.)

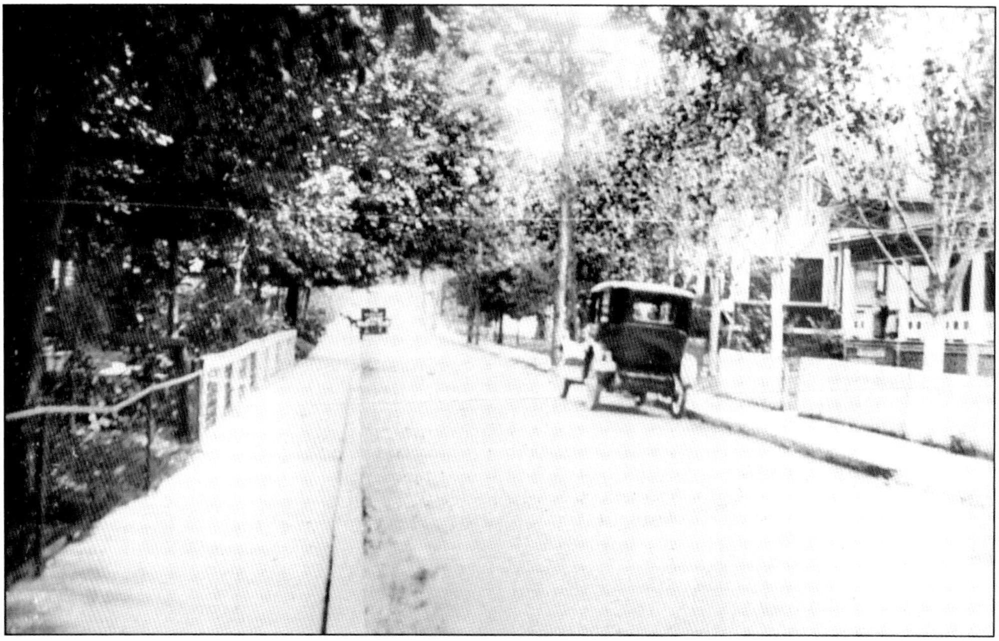

Dr. Harry Camp Sr. lived on Church Street in Spencer in 1919, and his automobile in the foreground is a Packard. In 1912, an ordinance required automobiles to have lights and respect certain speed limitations on the streets of the town. Another ordinance was passed in 1916 that levied a tax of $2.50 for every license issued. (Courtesy of Spencer Newspapers, Inc.)

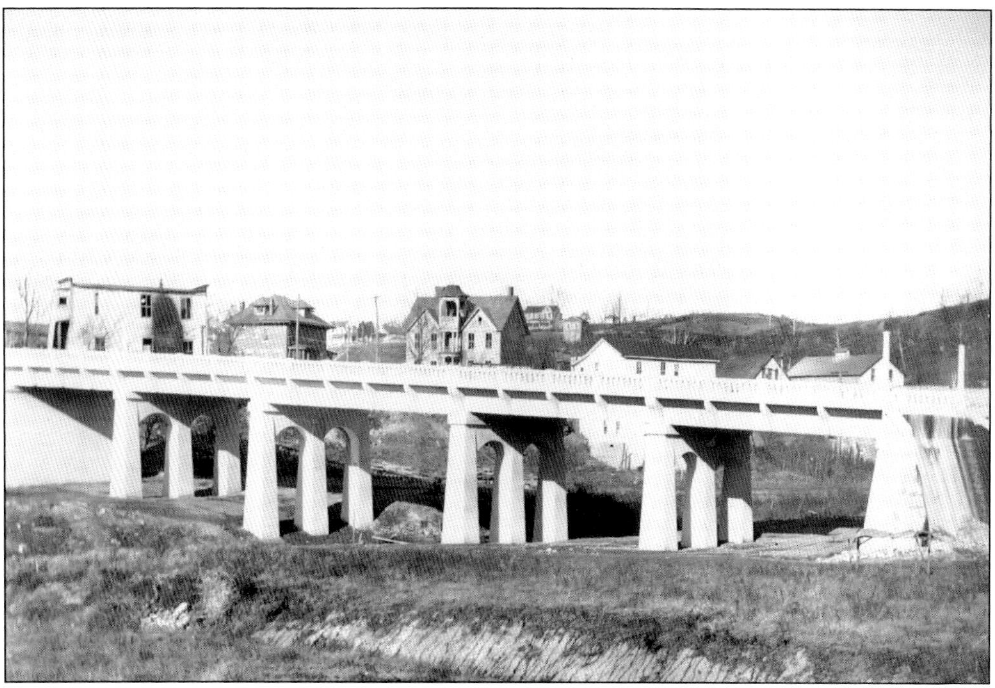

This bridge was built in 1932 across Spring Creek near the center of town. It is now called the Ruby Bradley Bridge and is scheduled for a replacement in the near future. (Courtesy of Dr. Harry H. Camp Sr. family.)

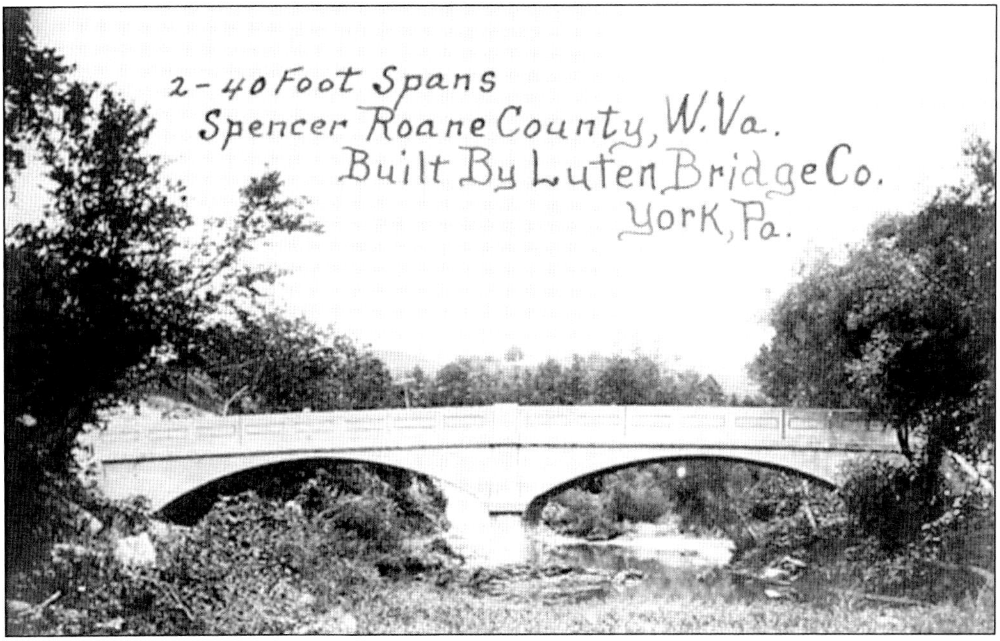

This 80-foot-long bridge spans Spring Creek in Spencer near the old railroad station. It was built by the Luten Bridge Company of York, Pennsylvania. The year of construction is not known. (Courtesy of Jack Nida.)

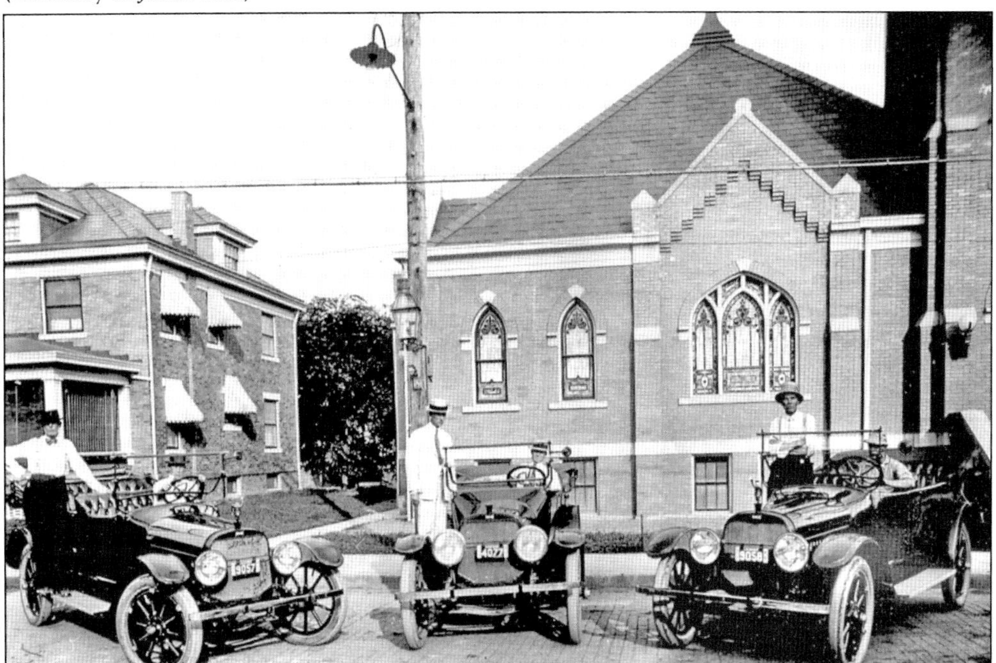

One of the early automobile agencies in Spencer was owned by Howard Simmons. Here are three of his new Chandler cars displayed in front of the Methodist Episcopal church and parsonage in 1915. From left to right are P. C. Adams, his son Hubert, Kenna Simmons, Sam Simmons, Howard Simmons, and DeWitt Edwards. (Ralph Nester Collection courtesy of Mark Sergent.)

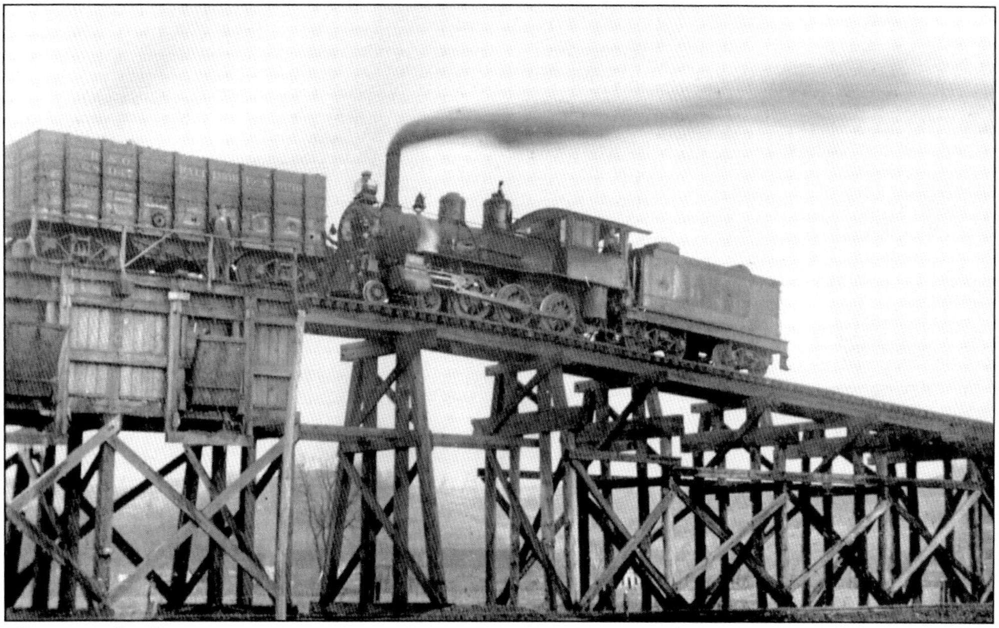

This was the first steam engine to arrive in Spencer. In 1886, the Ravenswood, Spencer, and Glenville (RS&G) Railroad was chartered. In 1889, the bonds of districts and county were issued and sold in aid of construction of this railroad from Spencer to Ravenswood by way of the town of Reedy. It was completed to Spencer in 1892. The line was never completed to Glenville. (Ralph Nester Collection courtesy of Mark Sergent.)

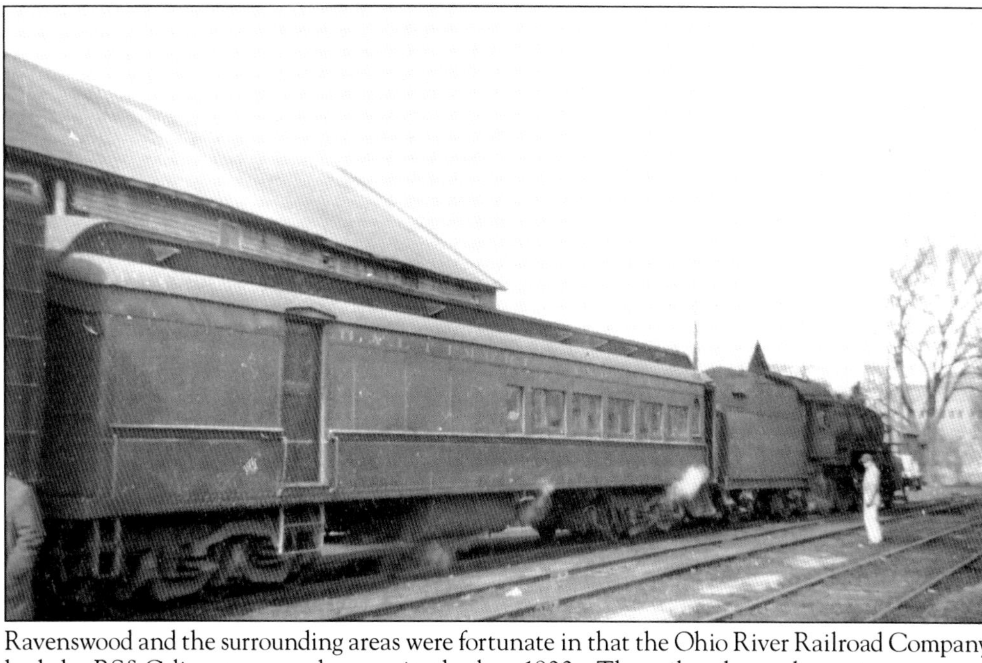

Ravenswood and the surrounding areas were fortunate in that the Ohio River Railroad Company had the RS&G line to serve the area in the late 1800s. The railroad was the major source of transportation for livestock and merchandise in the beginning of the 20th century. Cattle and sheep were shipped via the railroad from the Spencer Livestock Auction until the line was closed. (Ralph Nester Collection courtesy of Mark Sergent.)

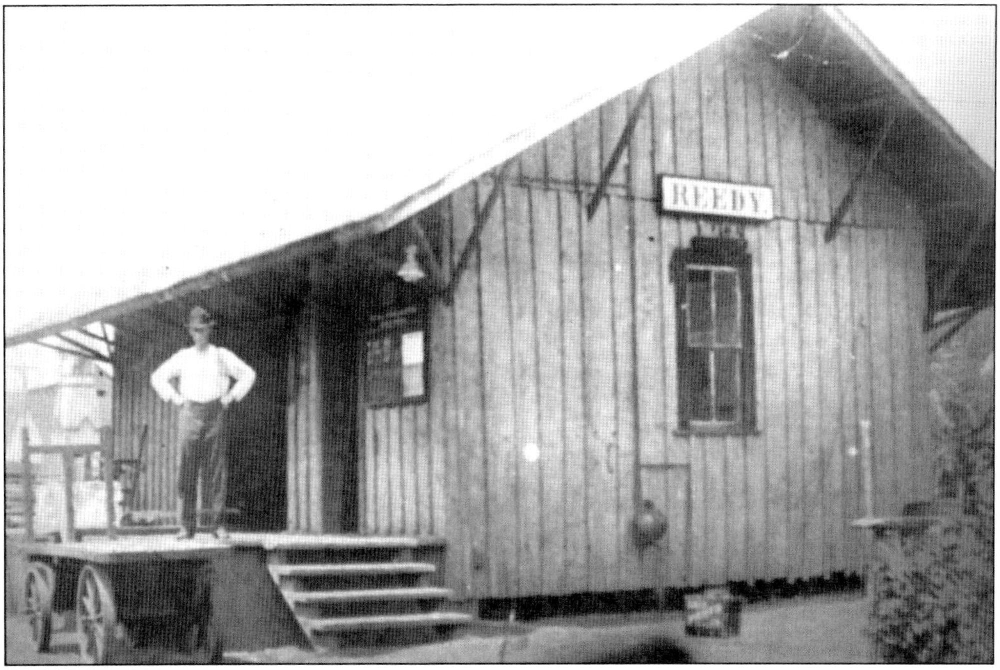

The Reedy train depot of the early 1920s was located at the intersection of Liverpool Road and Seaman's Fork. The old RS&G was now owned by the Baltimore and Ohio Railway Company, and people utilized the train for transportation and business. The agent shown is A. S. Brown, who was agent for many years; Homer Knowlton was agent at the time the depot was closed. (Courtesy of Fred Craig.)

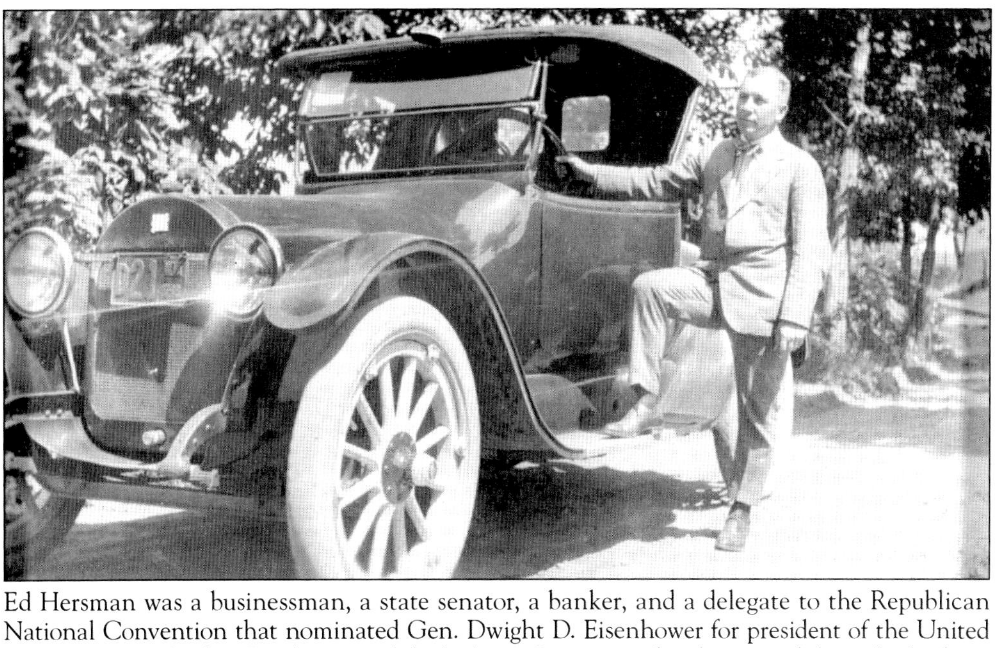

Ed Hersman was a businessman, a state senator, a banker, and a delegate to the Republican National Convention that nominated Gen. Dwight D. Eisenhower for president of the United States. He was the first Buick automobile dealer in Spencer and is shown with his vehicle about 1912. (Ralph Nester Collection courtesy of Mark Sergent.)

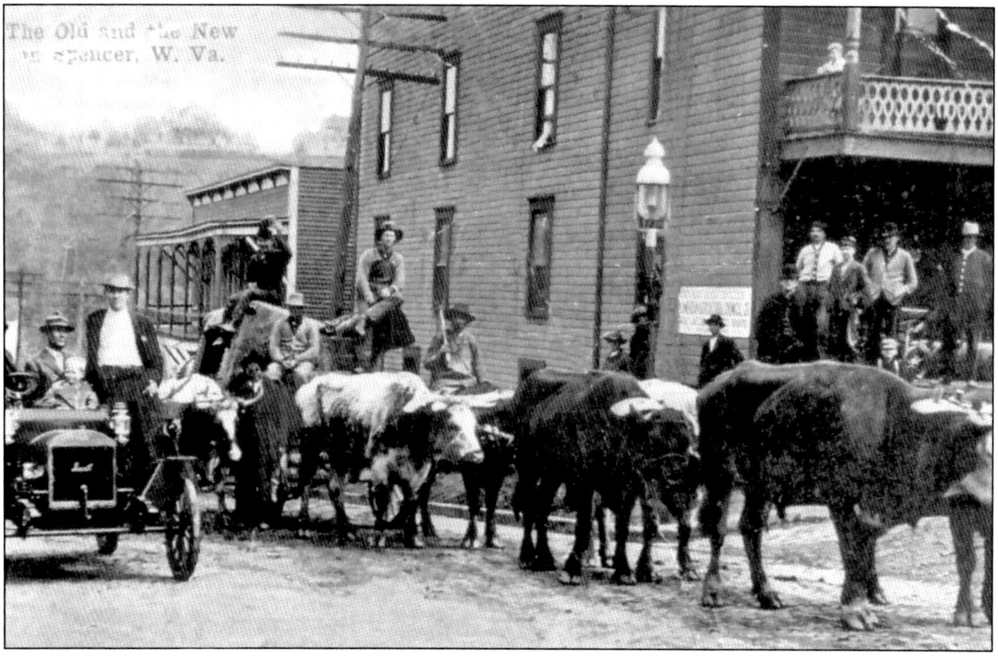

This postcard image was labeled "The Old and the New in Spencer in 1912" and shows the intersection of Market and Court Streets. Ten oxen are hauling a boiler from the B&O depot to one of the oil fields. The new mode of transportation shown on the left is one of Howard Simmons first automobiles. (Courtesy of Donna Walbrown.)

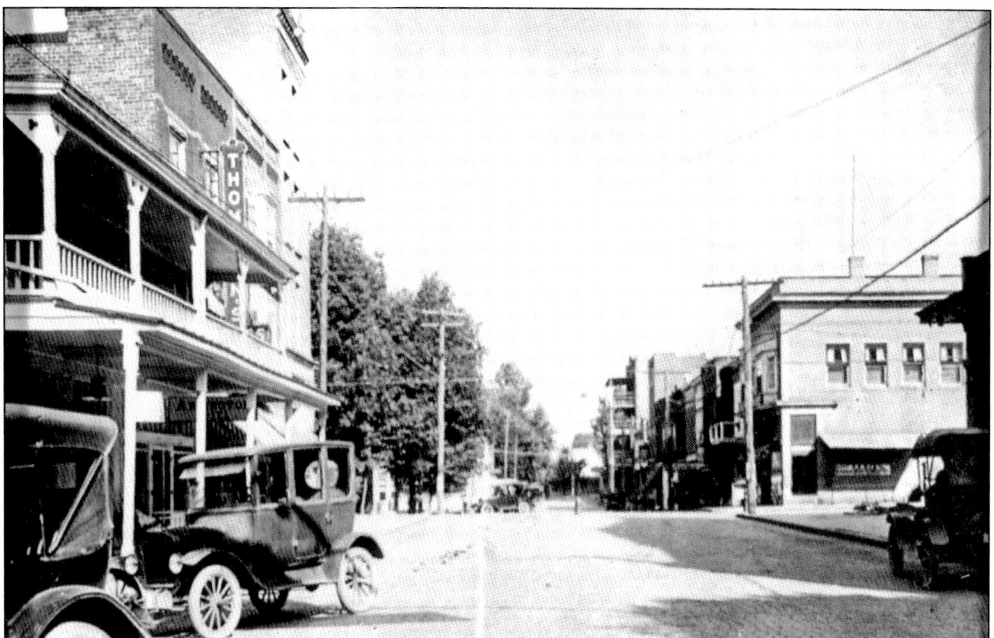

The Thompson Drug Store and the old Arlington Hotel are on the left, and the building in the right foreground housed the McMahon-Diehl Company about 1917. Upon buying out his partners in the Spencer Drug Store about 1916, Ronald E. Thompson founded a chain of drugstores beginning about 1916 and managed these until his death in 1945. (Courtesy of Spencer Newspapers, Inc.)

Five

Community Activities

At the end of a hard day of work, the early settlers would finish the family chores and be off to bed for a good night's sleep, as they were usually awake long before sunrise. This routine was quite common for most and continued until the Sabbath, as did the same routine of their forefathers primarily from old Virginia. They had brought with them books of arithmetic, grammar, geography, and spelling that were discussed around the fireside in the evenings. There were also books of poems, science, music, and physics to study. The pioneer was religious and supported organized worship to keep its beacons burning through the study of the Holy Bible. From this Holy Bible, a code of ethics was learned, and the church members were instrumental in administering a judgment for those who disobeyed them. They were bound by the understanding that they were to love their neighbor and would be at their side in time of need.

There were other social activities such as baseball, hunting, horse racing, picnics, wrestling, family reunions, and outdoor activities to keep the children busy. The Appalachian influence in Roane County was evident by those who were born to play music, sing, and dance. This heritage came with the immigration of their ancestors from Europe to America and was handed down to the children from one generation to the next. Dancing was a favorite pastime but was often forbidden by the church on Sunday. *History of Roane County West Virginia, 1774–1927* by William Henry Bishop states, "Preachers were of heroic stuff, and fearlessly warned or advised and fostered, and kept in the hearts of the people, consciences given to tender sympathies and love of justice."

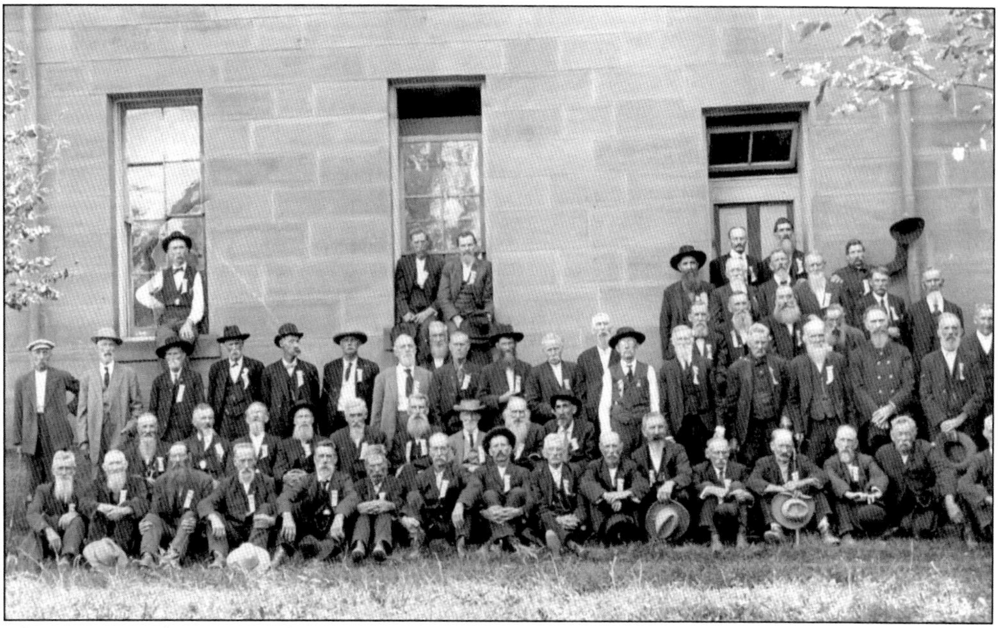

This reunion of Veterans of '62 United in Defense of the Flag took place in Spencer on August 25, 26, and 27, 1908. By the spring of 1862, the fortunes of war had shifted in favor of the Union. Their troops were blocking the strategic mountain approaches to the northwest portion of the state, and the Confederates were unable to mount a campaign of retaliation. (Courtesy of Joyce Higginbotham.)

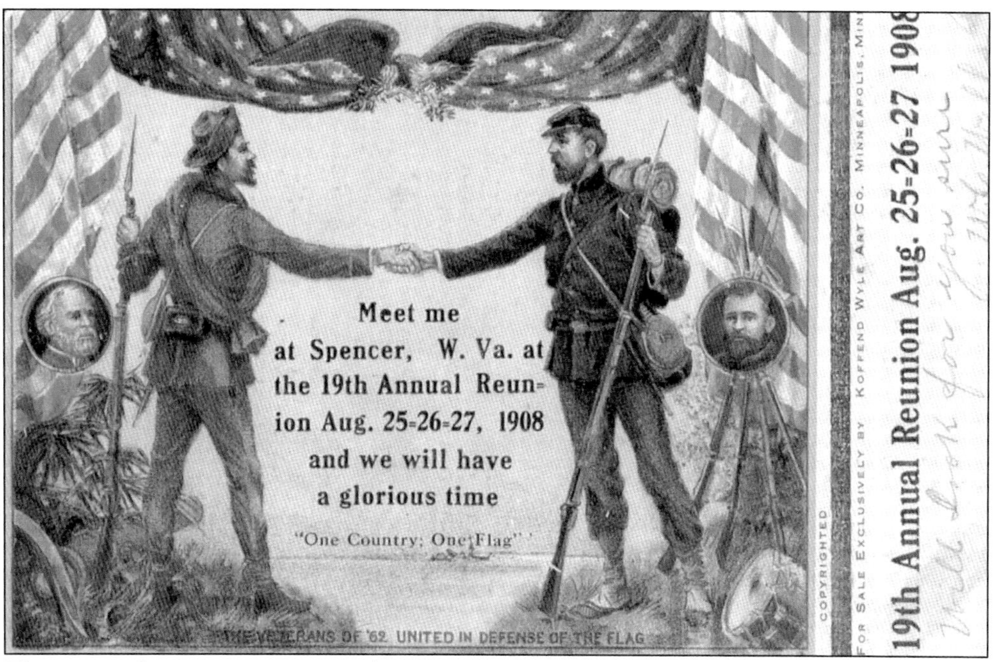

This postcard was an invitation to the Spencer reunion of Veterans of '62 United in Defense of the Flag. (Courtesy of Joyce Higginbotham.)

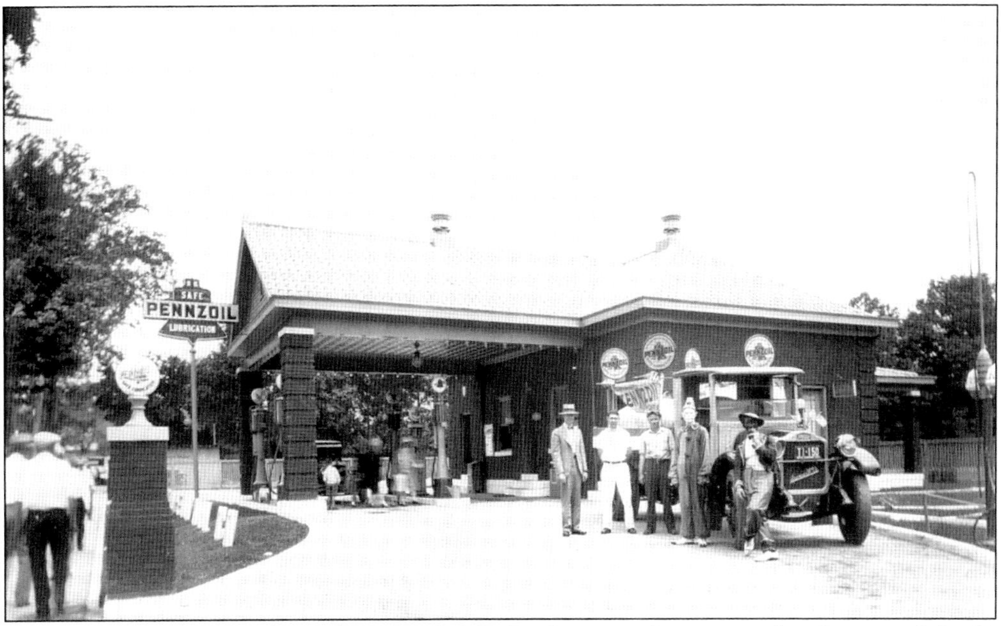

This service station was located on South Market Street and was owned and operated for 34 years by James W. Board until 1968. Dee Anderson was the last owner of this station before it was torn down and an office building for Pennzoil was constructed on this site. (Courtesy of Dr. Harry H. Camp Sr. family.)

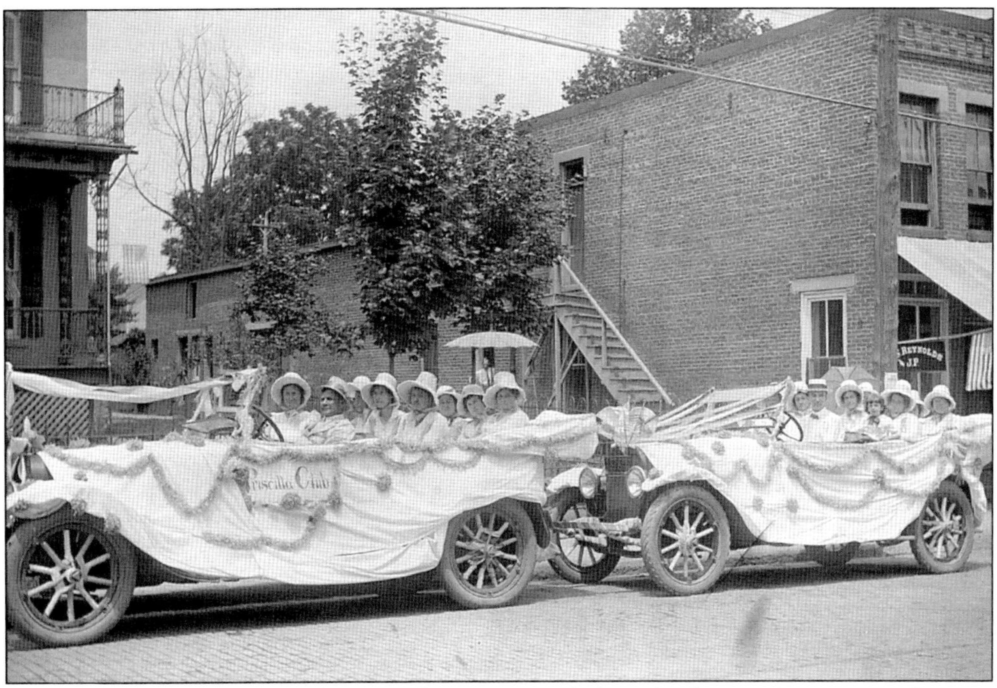

These highly decorated old vehicles of the 1920s were believed to be in a Spencer parade, quite possibly for the celebration of the opening of a new highway. (Courtesy of Dr. Harry H. Camp Sr. family.)

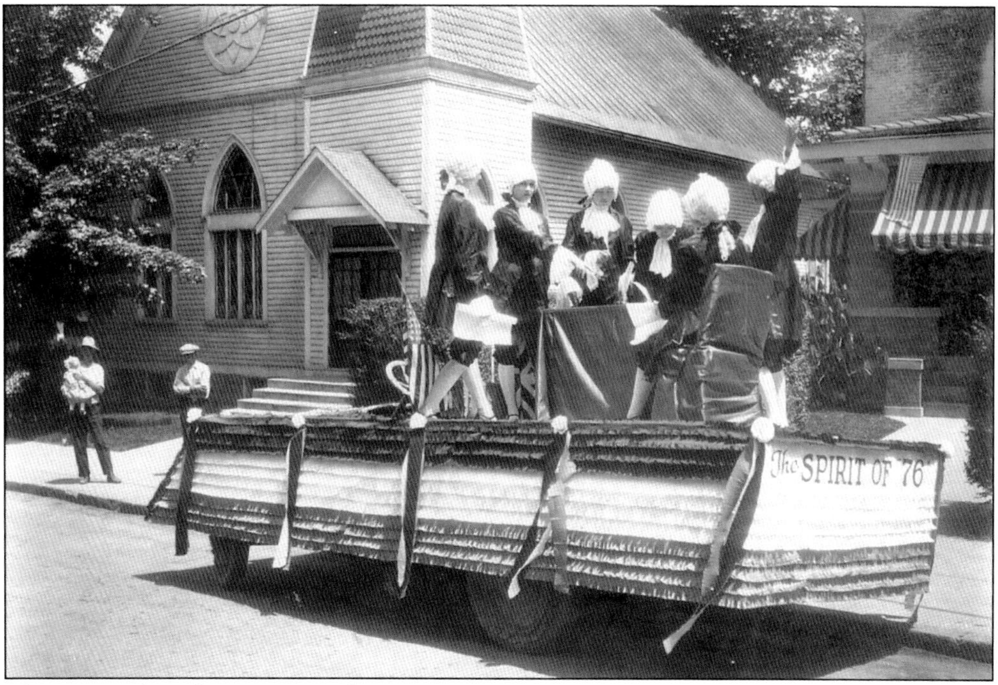

This Spirit of '76 float is pictured on Main Street with the First Baptist Church of Spencer in the background. (Courtesy of Dr. Harry H. Camp Sr. family.)

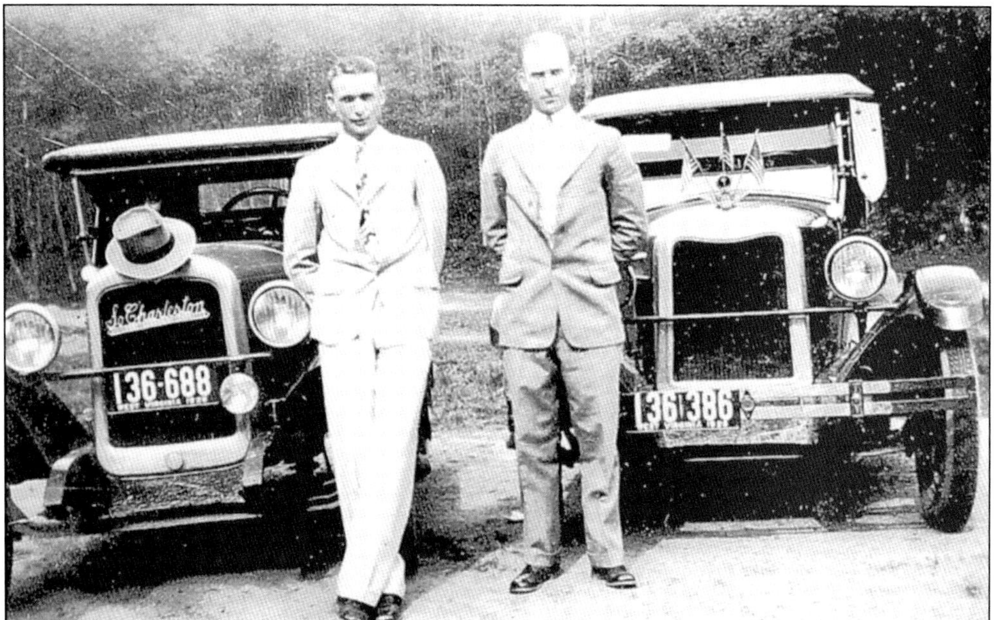

Brothers John E. (left) and Roy J. Nida are shown with their new, late-1920s model vehicles. Each of them worked for only one company in their lifetime: John was employed by Union Carbide Corporation in South Charleston, West Virginia, and Roy was employed for 43 years by United Fuel Gas Company, a division of Columbia Gas System in Roane and Kanawha Counties. (Courtesy of Jack Nida.)

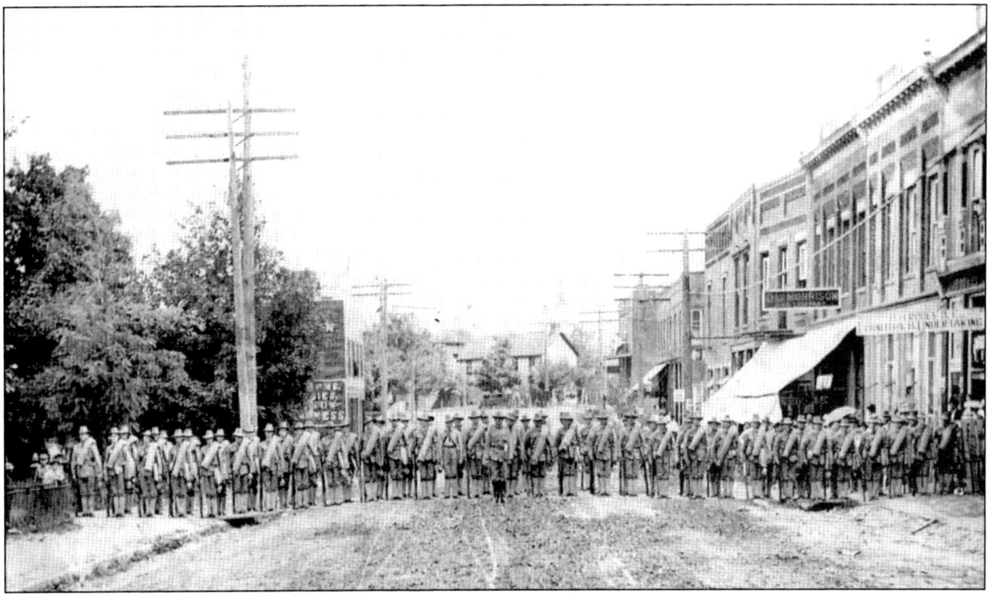

Capt. H. J. Simmons Sr. organized Company D for the U.S. Army in Spencer about 1906. Total deaths of U.S. military personnel during World War I were 116,708. Thirty-one of those casualties were from Roane County. (Ralph Nester Collection courtesy of Mark Sergent.)

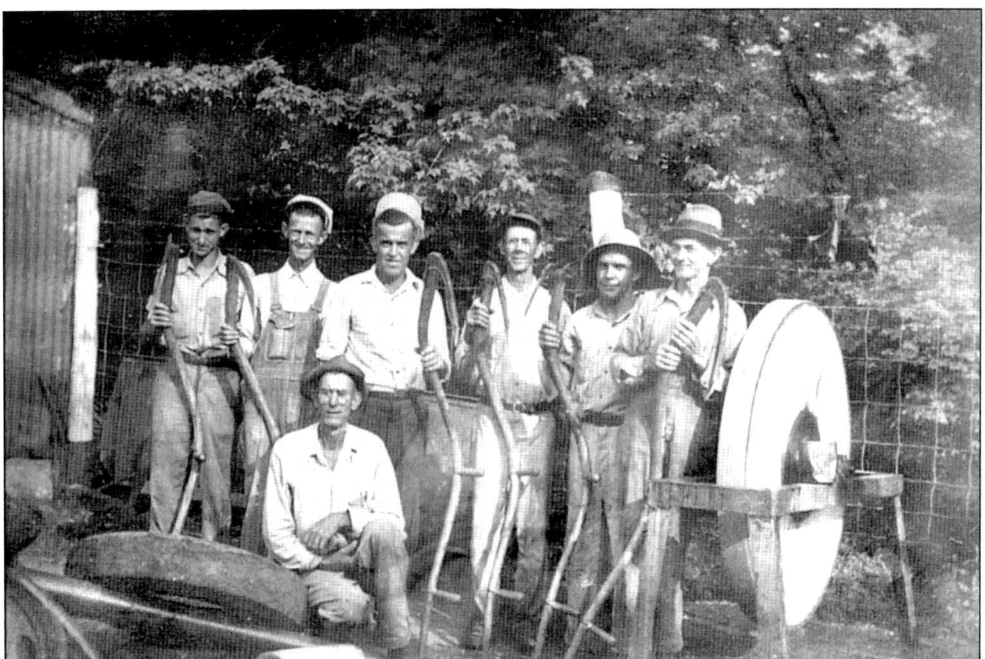

This group of unidentified men is prepared for a hard day's work in the field with their scythes. Mowing of grass and weeds by this method was very common in the days before power mowers came into existence. (Courtesy of Donna Walbrown.)

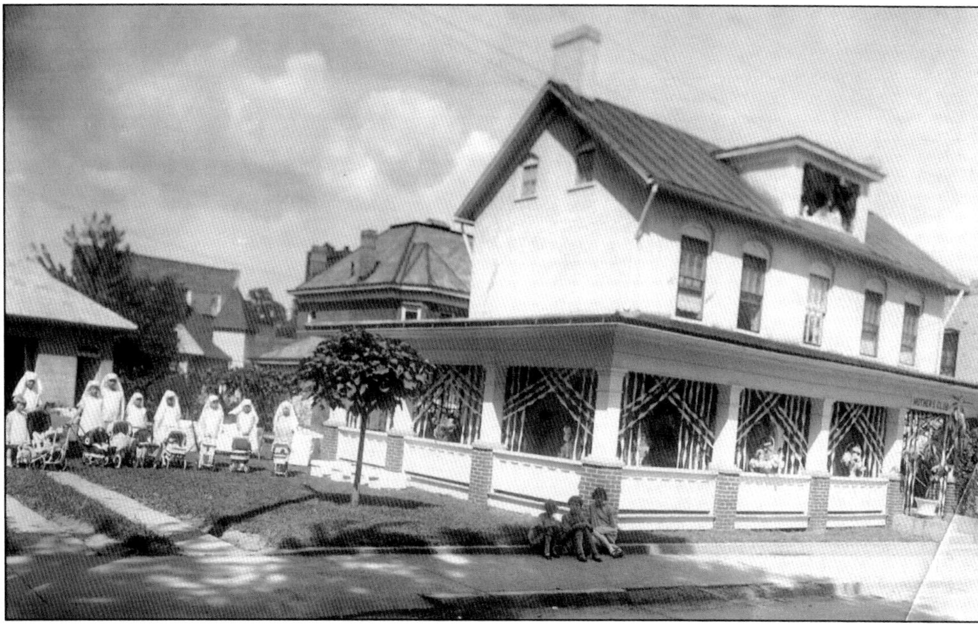

The residence of Grace Holswade, formerly the home of Dr. A. G. Bailey on Church Street, is decorated for the grand opening of State Road 14 on July 15, 1926. The Spencer Mothers Club on the lawn is represented by young girls with dolls in their carriages. (Courtesy of Dr. Harry H. Camp Sr. family.)

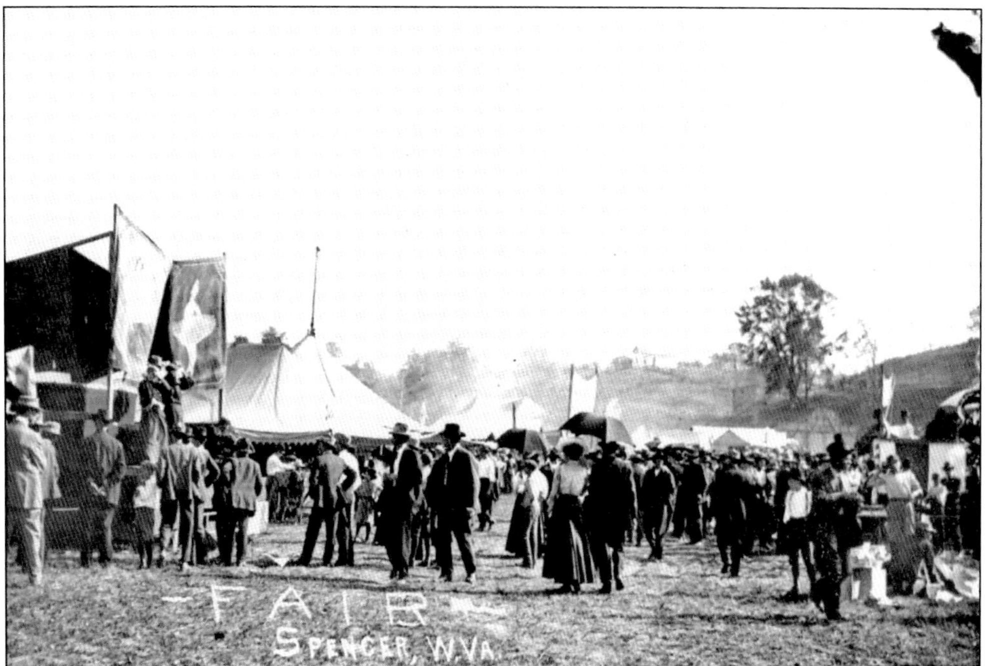

The Roane County Fairgrounds were located in Alvord, which was a separate community from Spencer in the early years. The tremendous success of the fair, held September 27–30, 1910, is shown in this image. The half-mile racetrack was considered to be one of the finest in the state. (Ralph Nester Collection courtesy of Mark Sergent.)

Everyone loves a parade, and the people of Spencer were eager to accommodate them. This scene from July 1926 shows a portion of the motorcade that came from Parkersburg in celebration of the opening of the newly paved highway between these cities. It was designated as State Route 14. (Ralph Nester Collection courtesy of Mark Sergent.)

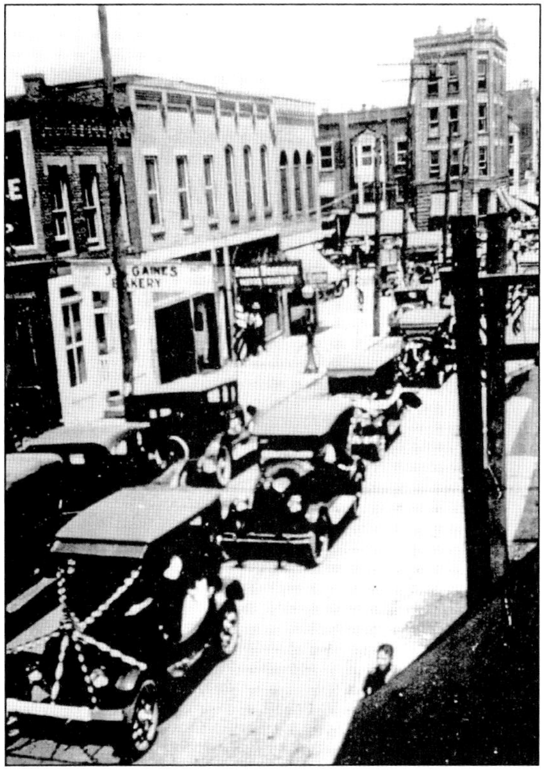

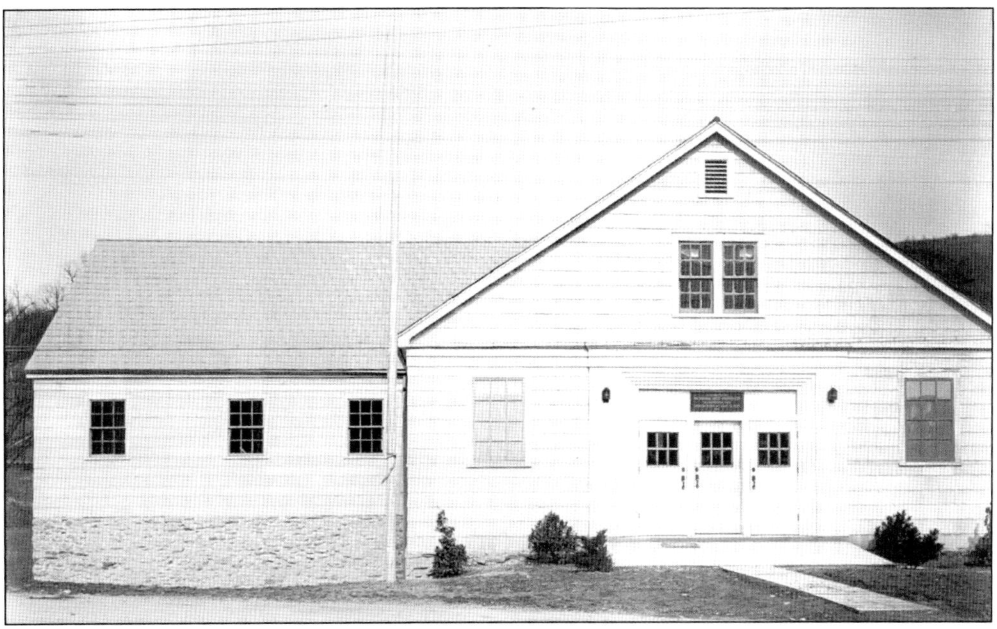

The American Legion building shown was built in 1940 and later burned. Spencer became a city in 1921, and many service organizations were soon established. The undisputed leader was the Rotary Club, organized in 1921. In 1922, the Women's Club was organized, and in 1923, the West Virginia National Guard unit of Roane County was established. The American Legion Post No. 21 was formed in 1925. (Courtesy of Dr. Harry H. Camp Sr. family.)

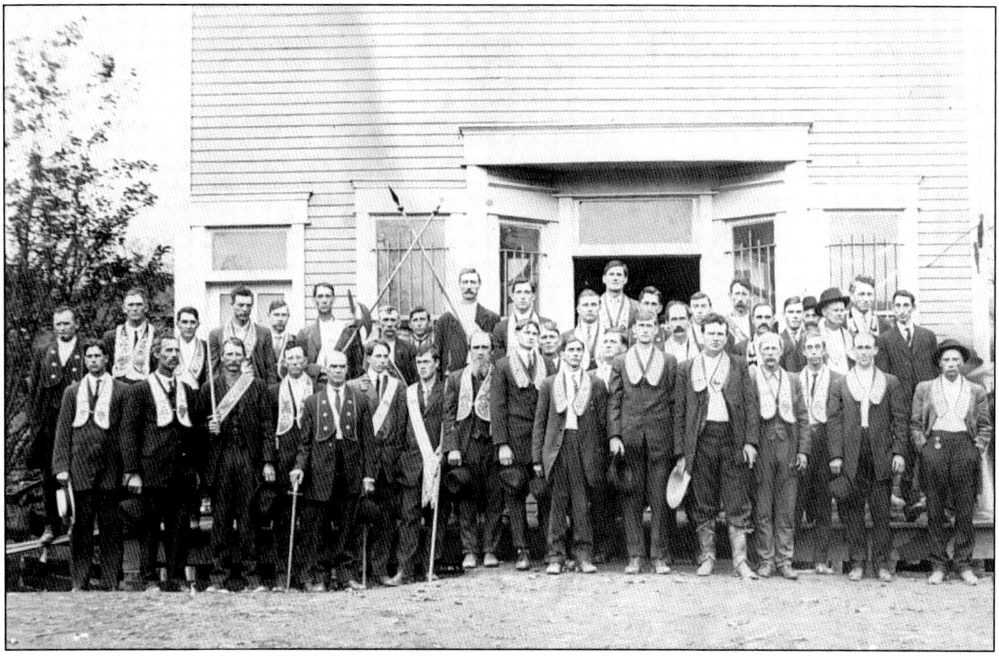

The Newton chapter of the Independent Order of Odd Fellows Lodge dates to before 1900. The first IOOF established in Roane County was in Spencer in 1887, and this lodge assisted in the organization of the Newton, Walton, Linden, Reedy, Red Knob, and Reedyville lodges. (Courtesy of Marlin Morris.)

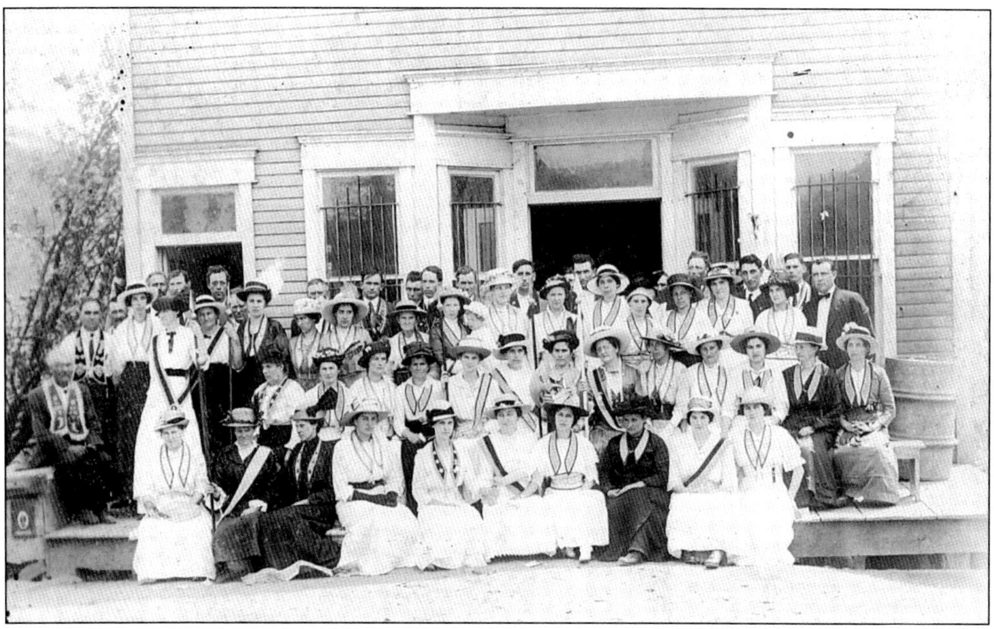

The Woman's Chapter of the IOOF Lodge is the Rebecca Lodge. This is the Newton chapter, and the ladies are joined by some members of the men's IOOF group, who share this meeting place in the general store. (Courtesy of Joyce Higginbotham.)

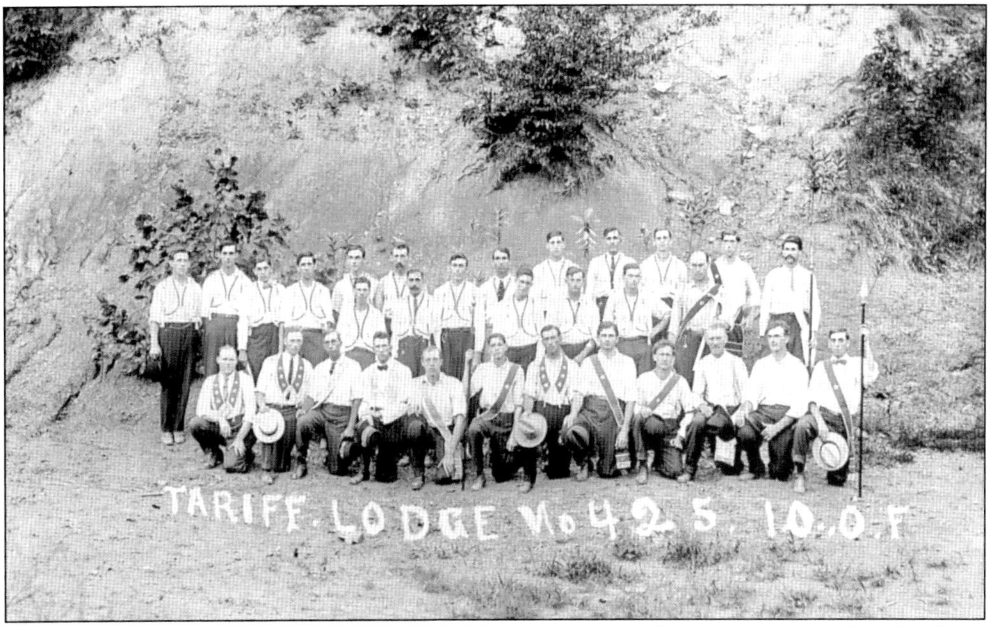

This early-1920s photograph was of the Tariff chapter of the Independent Order of Odd Fellows Lodge. (Courtesy of Marlin Morris.)

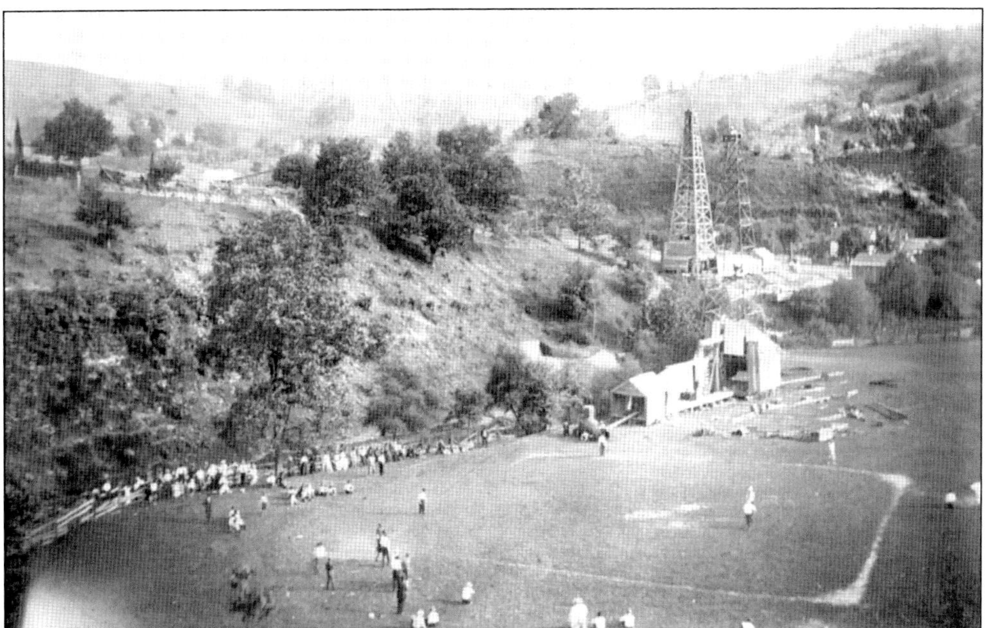

This field was on the Ott Kincaid farm at Stringtown. Baseball was a favorite activity on Sunday afternoons in the summer and was enjoyed by the entire family. Two oil derricks can be seen—the wooden one has been completed, and the other steel rig is under construction. (Courtesy of Mark Sergent.)

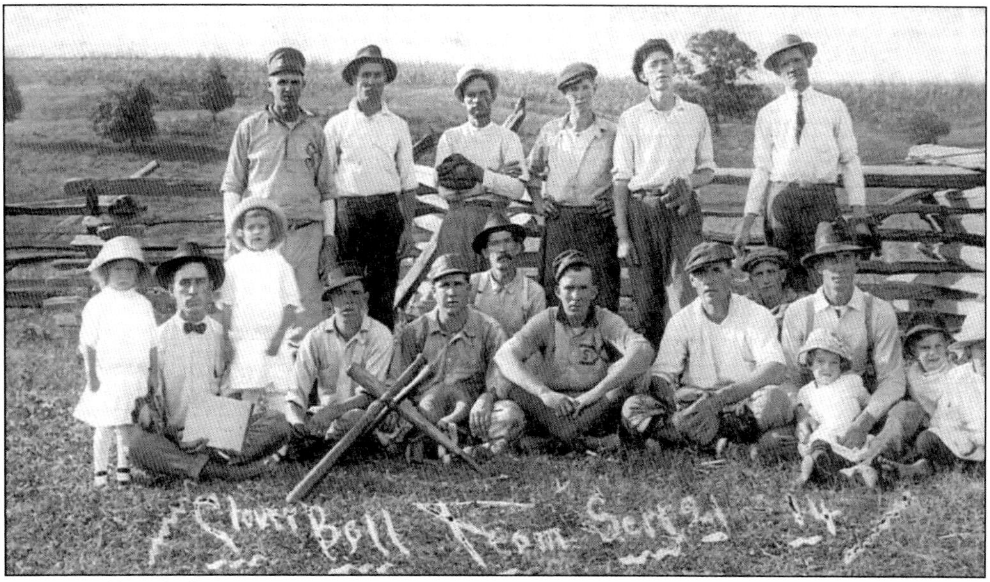

Organized baseball teams came to Roane County around 1910. This Clover team of 1914 played against the men of nearby villages, and the local newspaper provided details of the game each week. A county league was formed within a few years and included as many as eight teams that competed for the championship. (Courtesy of Donna Walbrown.)

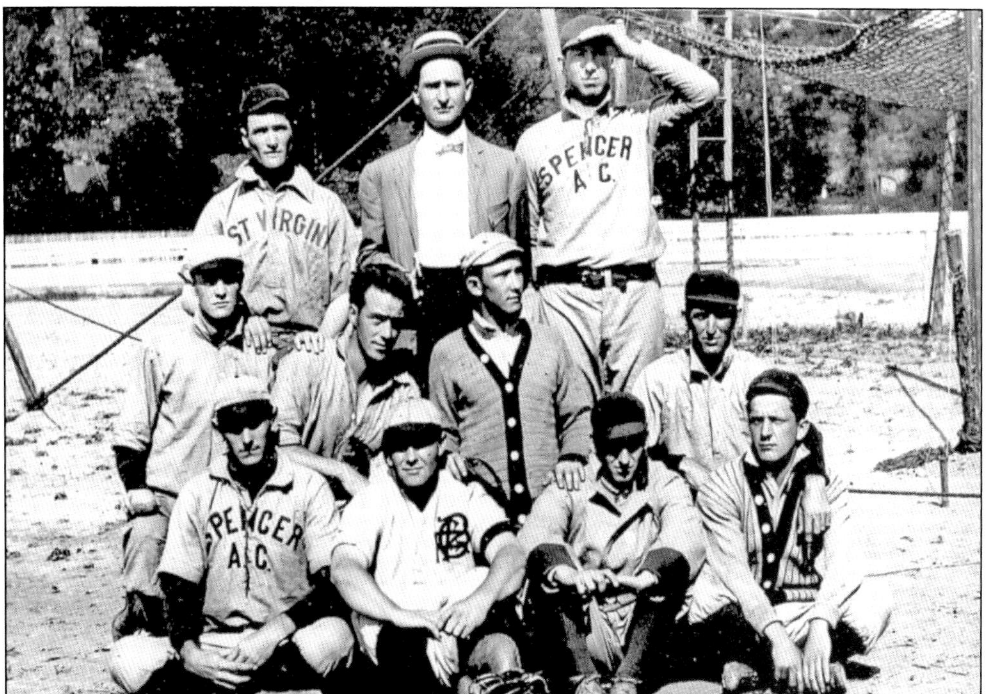

The Spencer baseball team of 1910 was fortunate to have partial uniforms. An effort was initiated each year to find local businesses to help sponsor the costs incurred by the ball team. It was commonplace to have the name of the local business sewn on the back if they donated the cost of a uniform. (Ralph Nester Collection courtesy of Mark Sergent.)

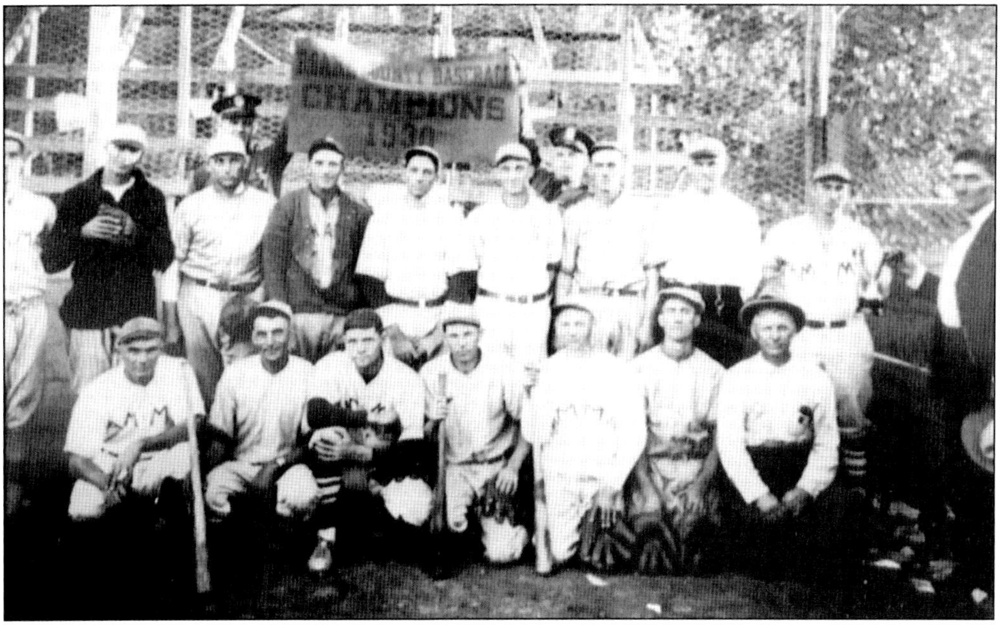

It was advertised in the Spencer newspapers as the Little World Series with over 1,000 in attendance for each of the three-game playoff series in 1930. This team from Amma won the series 2-1 with Roy J. Nida as manager. There were eight teams in the league with an 18-game schedule during the summer. A silver loving cup was awarded to the manager by Congressman Harry C. Woodyard. (Courtesy of Jack Nida.)

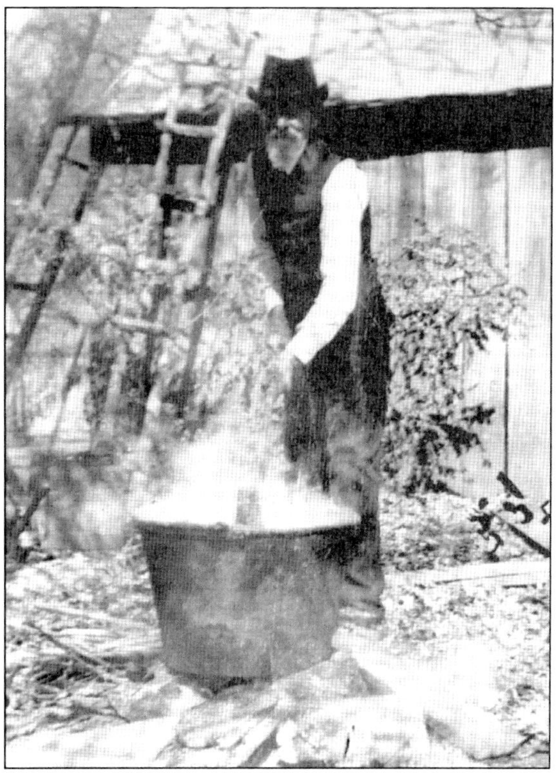

Jesse Starcher is practicing the tradition of making apple butter that has been handed down for many generations. A large kettle, generally made of copper, is placed over a fire, and a small amount of water is added to prevent burning. Peeling, coring, and slicing prepares the apples before they are placed in the hot kettle. About six hours of constant stirring is necessary. (Courtesy of Evelyn [Bissell] Starcher.)

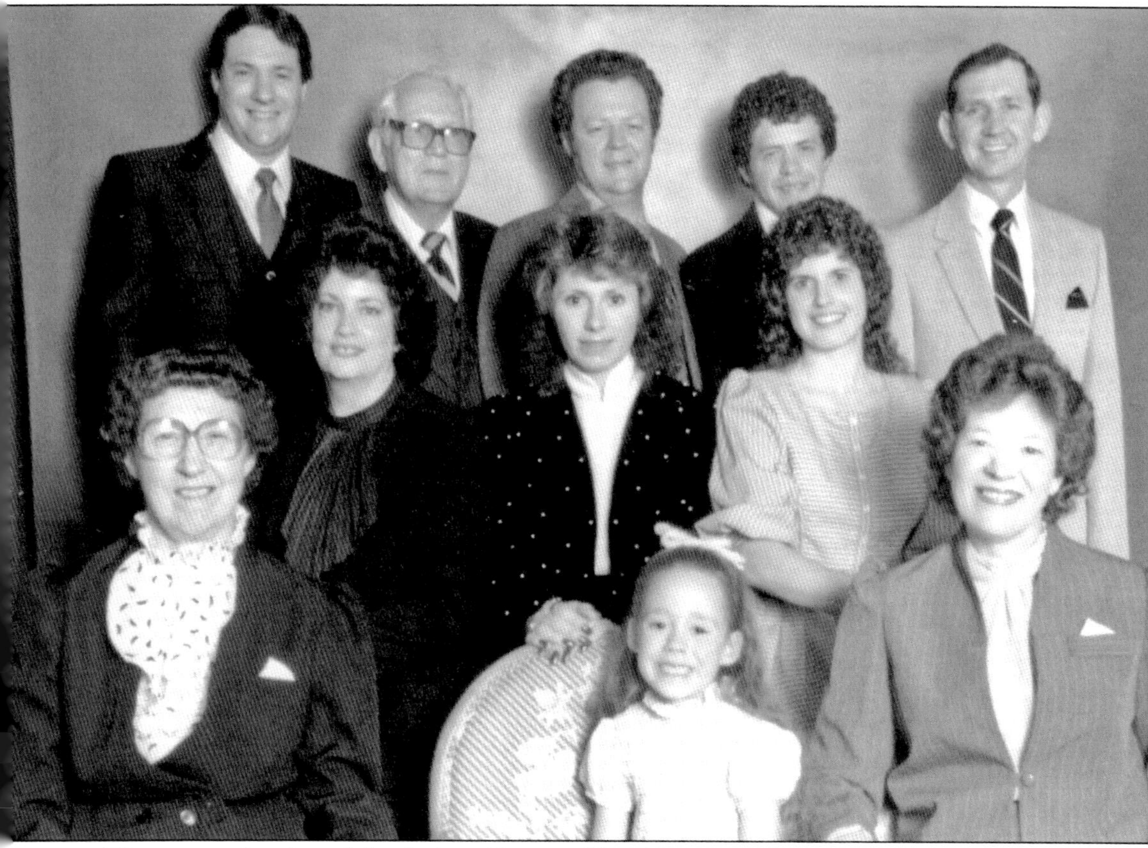

This extremely talented family from Newton, West Virginia is the Squire Parsons Sr. family in 1982. From left to right are (first row) Maysel Parsons, Sarah Parsons, and Carolyn (Parsons) Fisher; (second row) June Parsons, Linda Parsons, and Cynthia Parsons; (third row) Squire Parsons Jr., Squire Parsons Sr., Virgil Parsons, Tom Parsons, and Ron Fisher. Squire Sr. and his wife, Maysel J. (McCune) Parsons, were married in 1937 and have lived on Hollywood Road in Newton since 1947. They joined the Newton Baptist Church and were very active in church functions. Carolyn played piano for church services and quartets before leaving home for school and work. She married Ron Fisher, and he later became the pastor of Newton Baptist Church. Virgil began singing with a young quartet at Newton Baptist Church before enlisting in the U.S. Army. He married June Simpson and by 1970 was singing with brother Squire Jr. and the Calvarymen Quartet. Virgil sings with the Brighterside Quartet and is now devoting much of his time to a new Newton Baptist Church project of building a Christian school. The youngest son, Tom, also began singing at an early age and played in the Spencer High School Band. He has written several gospel songs and joined brother Virgil with the Brighterside Quartet in the late 1990s. Tom is also an accomplished pianist. (Courtesy of Virgil Parsons.)

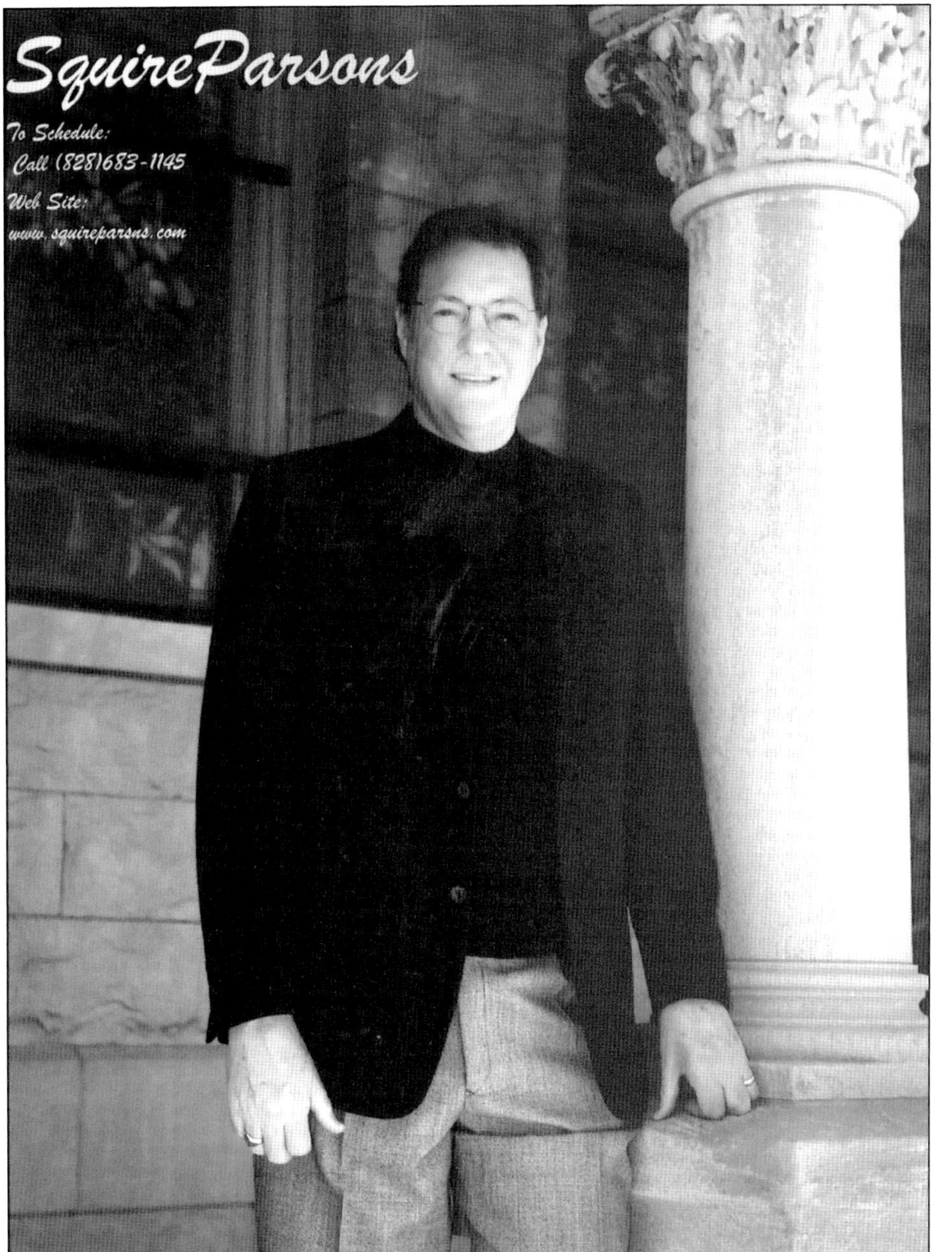

Squire Parsons Jr. attended school and church in Newton where he was active in both with his music. He is an outstanding pianist and sang in quartets during his high school years at Spencer and sang in the West Virginia All State Choir. He graduated from West Virginia Institute of Technology and majored in music. He became an accomplished songwriter with such hits as *Look for Me at Jesus' Feet*, *Master of the Sea*, *Sweet Beulah Land*, and many others. In 1975, he moved to Asheville, North Carolina, and was singing with the Kingsmen Quartet. In 1979, he began a full-time ministry that would allow him to assist churches where he felt that God was directing him. He is often seen as a participant in the television productions of Bill and Gloria Gaither and their Homecoming Friends. (Courtesy of Squire Parsons.)

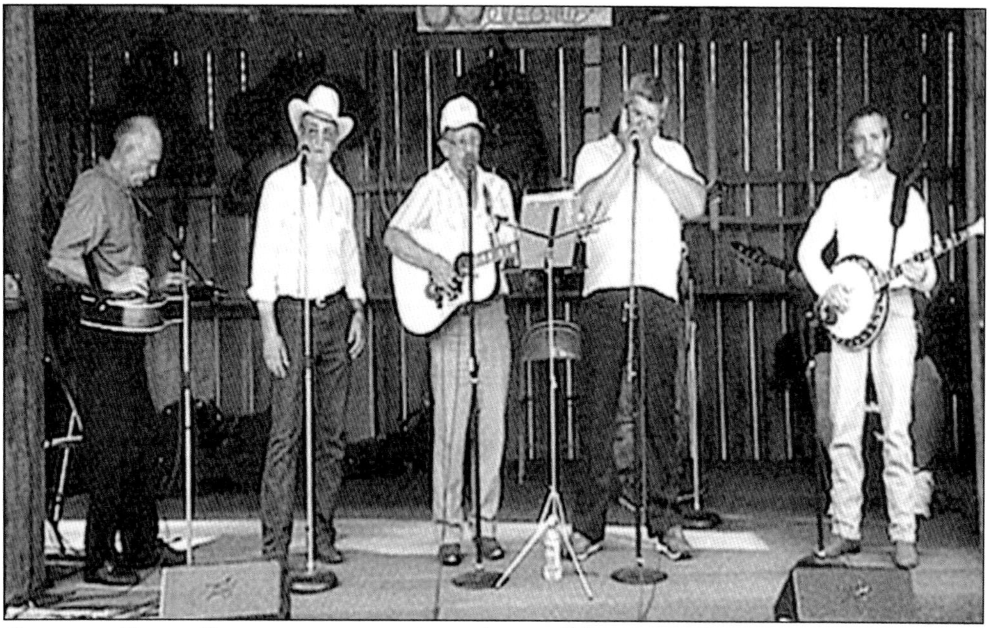

One native Roane Countian carries on the tradition of bluegrass and country music today. He is Bud Keen of Country Mix. This performance was in Amma at Joe Shafer's Trail Ride. From left to right are (first row) Jack Nida (dobro), Paul Harold (tenor vocalist), Bud Keen (lead vocalist and guitar), Lowell Harold (harmonica and baritone vocals), and Rad Lewis (banjo); (second row, partially hidden) Jimmy Harold (bass guitar) and Denny Dobbins (mandolin). (Courtesy of Jack Nida.)

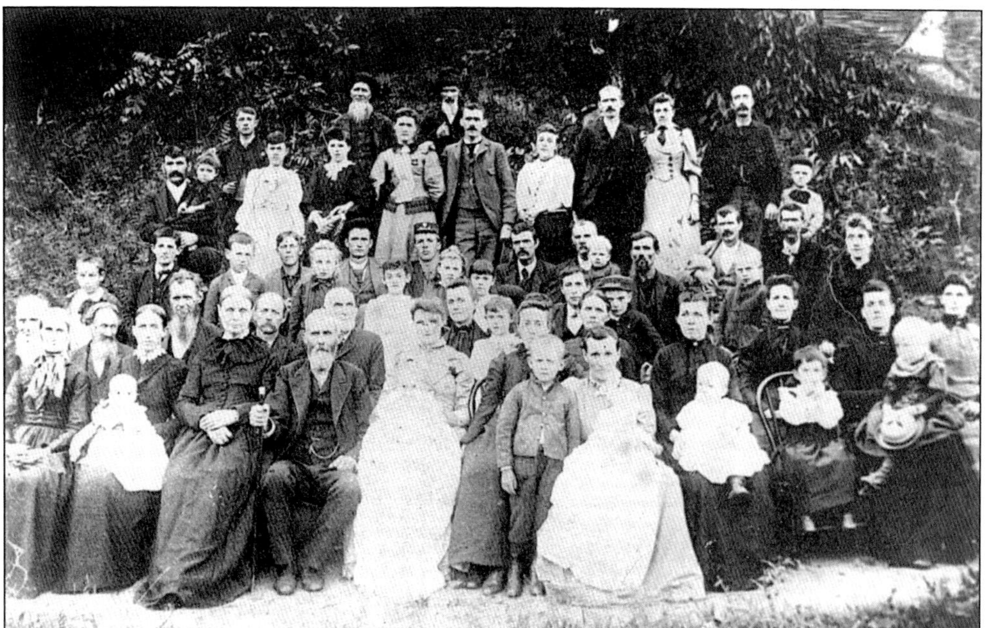

This is the last-known photograph of the Jordan McMillan family before Jordan moved to Washington, D.C., where he lived until his death in 1898. The family reunion was held on September 7, 1892, at his home at Otto. He is seated in the first row, fourth from left, holding a cane. (Courtesy of Evelyn [Bissell] Starcher.)

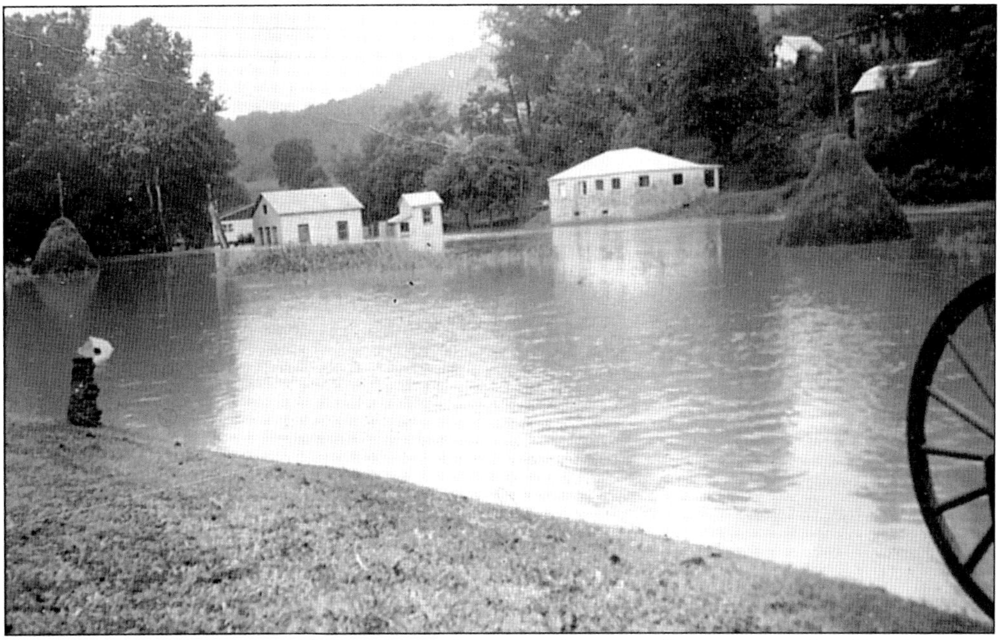

The flood of 1959 was very damaging to Amma and surrounding areas on Big Sandy Creek. Pictured from the front yard of the Roy J. Nida home is the Jonathan and Maggie (Honaker) McCune house and the United Fuel Gas Company pumping station. (Courtesy of Jack Nida.)

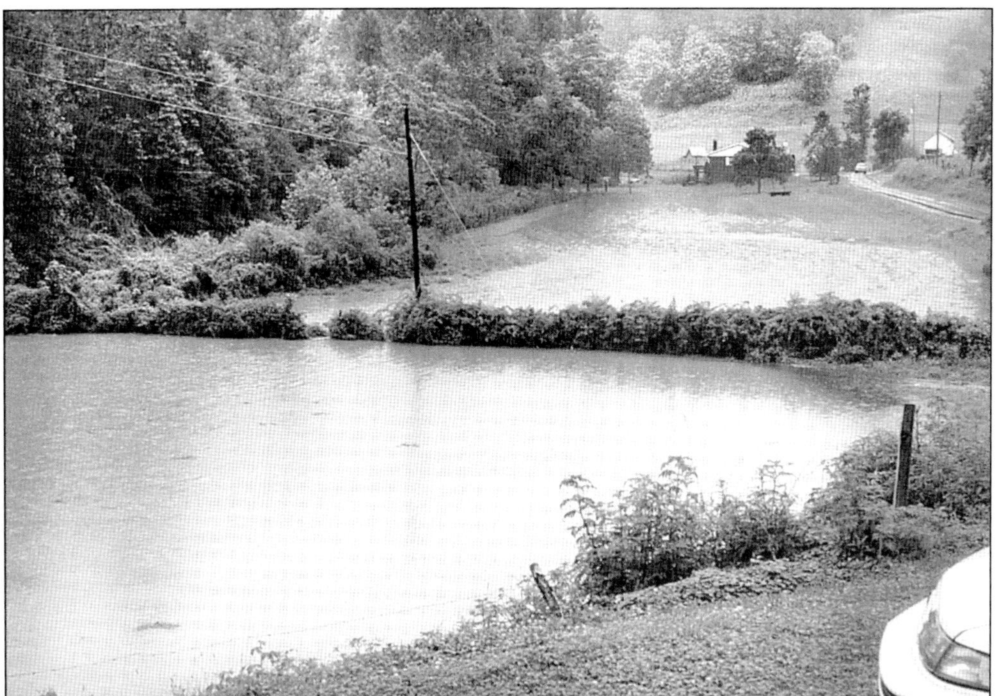

This flood in 2004 was in the headwaters of Big Sandy Creek. The water covered the bottomlands on the middle fork of this creek near Uler and Newton. (Courtesy of Ruth Harold.)

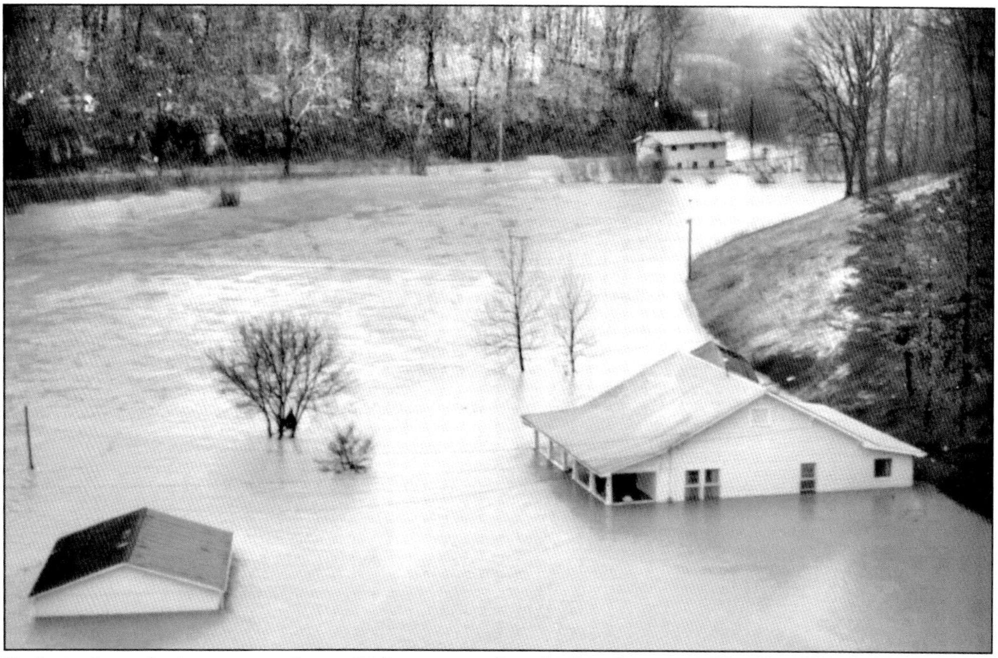

Eight inches of rain came within a 10-hour period to the headwaters of Big Sandy Creek on March 1, 1997. The result was the most severe flooding of the Newton, Amma, and Clendenin areas that has ever been recorded. The National Guard assisted in hauling the ruins of this disaster to landfill areas to assist the victims of the flood. (Courtesy of Jack Nida.)

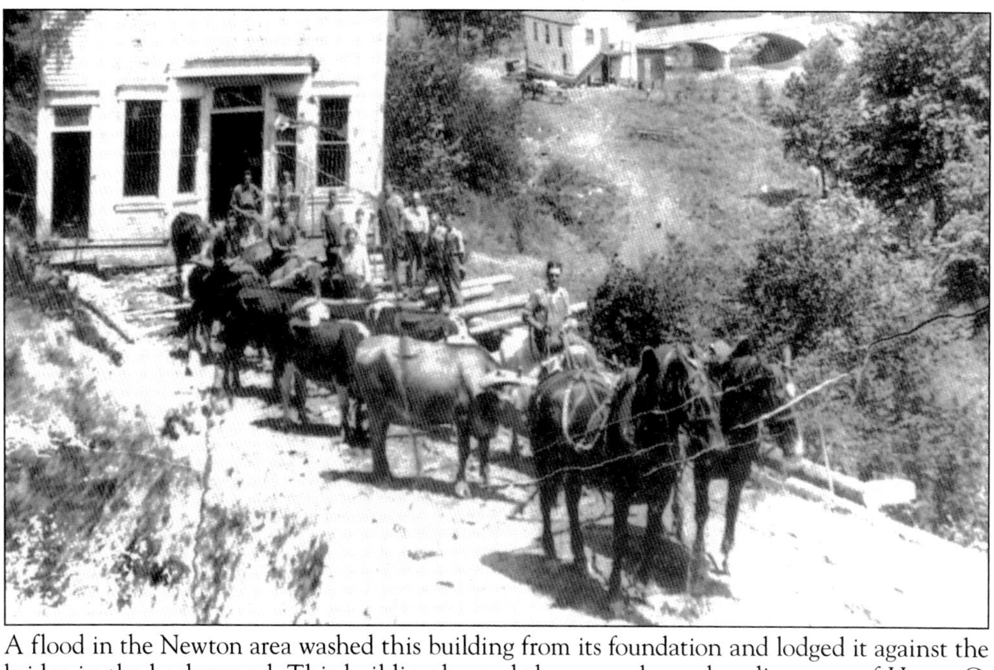

A flood in the Newton area washed this building from its foundation and lodged it against the bridge in the background. This building housed the general merchandise store of Henry C. Looney in 1914. With the assistance of oxen and horses and using logs for skids, the building was moved from the flooded location and relocated about 200 yards to the west on State Route 36. (Courtesy of Paul Harold.)

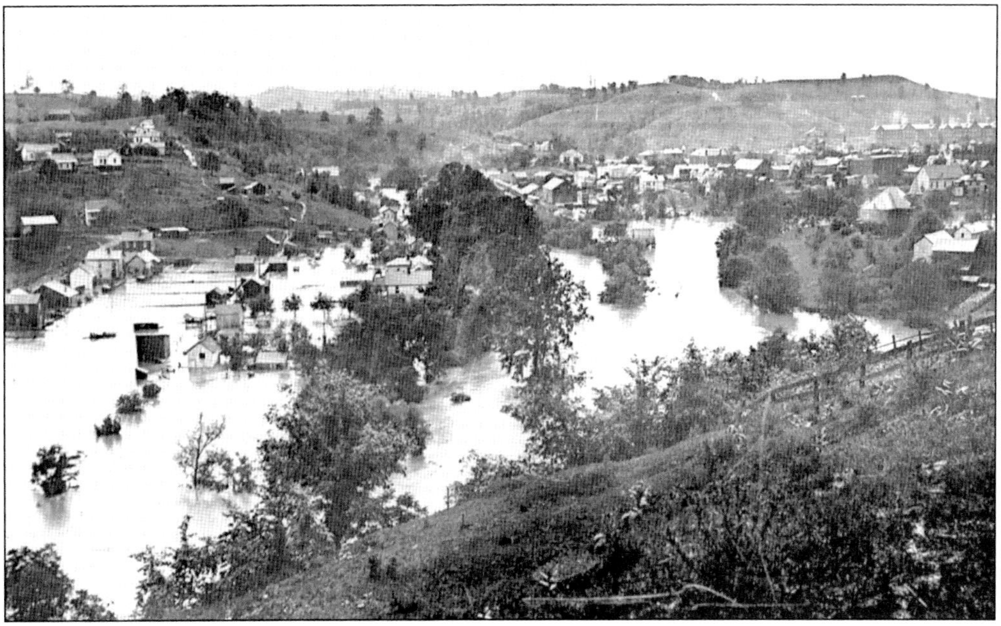

One of the worst floods in the history of Spencer occurred in the spring of 1901. On the upper left is the Alvord hill, sparsely settled at that time. The floodwaters covered the lowlands of what was to become the Fairview Addition and the high school athletic field. The B&O Railroad tracks are completely covered by swollen Spring Creek. (Ralph Nester Collection courtesy of Mark Sergent.)

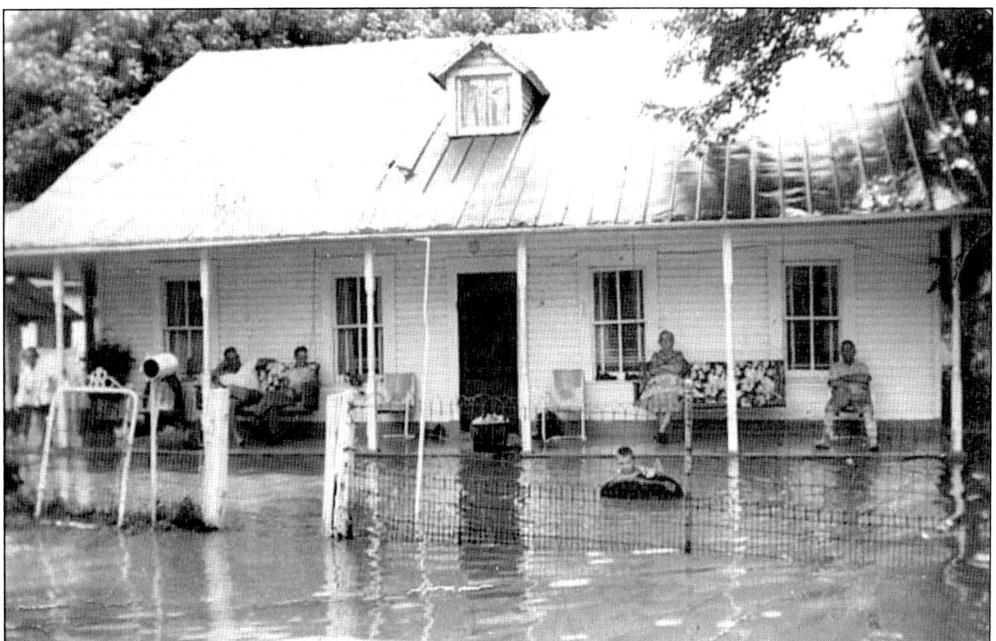

The home of Nelson and Junie Carper was flooded by the Big Sandy Creek in 1958. They operated a general store just across the road from their home in Amma for many years. On the porch and observing the rising of the water were, from left to right, Melda Carper, Raymond Cook, Frank Carper, Junie Carper, and Chilt Byrd. (Courtesy of Jack Nida.)

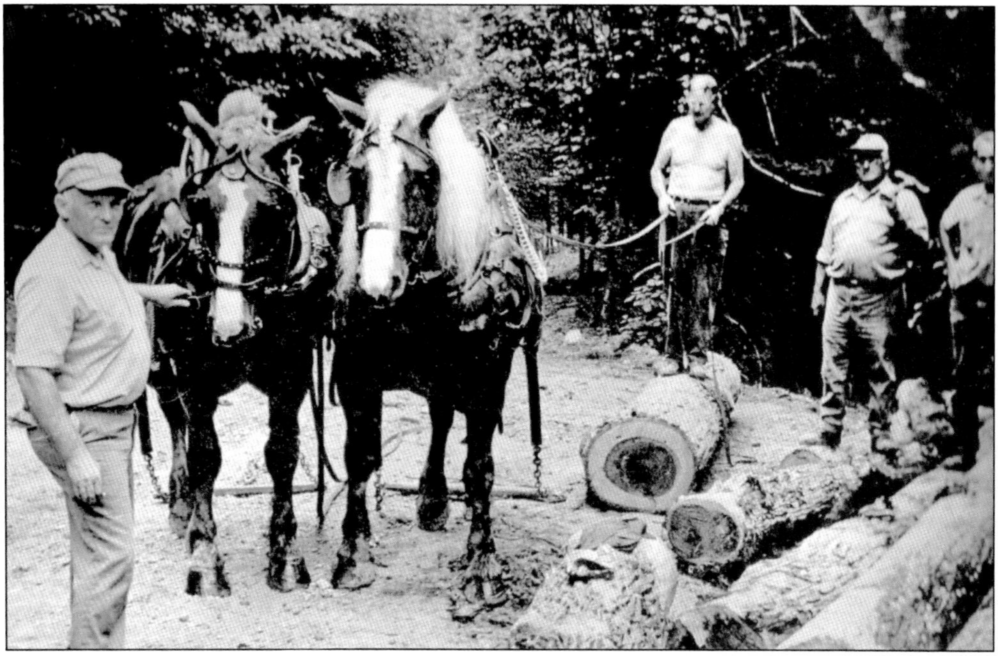

Joe Shafer was a merchant and businessman, but his first love was horses. He retired to his farm at Amma and established an annual wagon ride featuring local bands with breakfast and dinner for his guests. This two-day event included a 9-mile wagon ride of 20 or more wagons being pulled by horses, mules, or donkeys. (Courtesy of the Shafer family.)

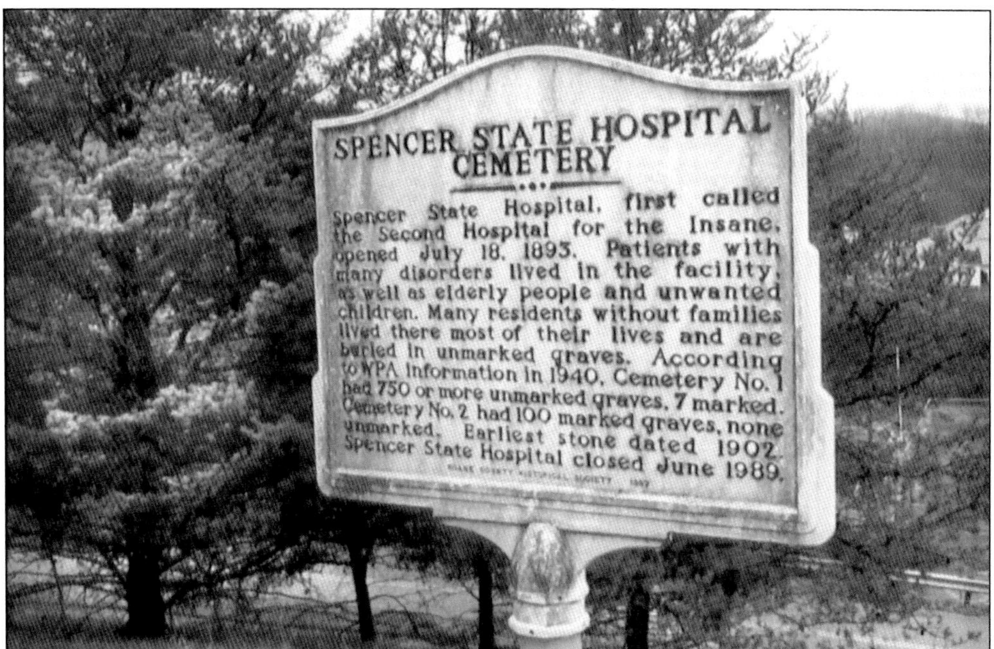

This marker was installed in May 1998 to mark the site of the Spencer State Hospital cemetery. All of the old stones were removed after the property was sold, and no evidence of the former cemetery remains except this new marker. (Courtesy of Carol Board.)

Six

SCHOOLS AND CHURCHES

The first school that is recorded in the county was erected in 1866 near Little Spring Creek in Spencer. The pioneers subscribed to the theory handed down to them that civilization is dependent upon three basic institutions: the home, the church, and the school. The first schools were generally started in the home, and as the need increased in the village because of its growth, a landowner donated a piece of land for the construction of a school building. Frank G. Timmel, a graduate of one of Germany's finest schools of higher learning, taught several terms in the community of Spencer. He was also an artist and musician and had been an instructor in a college at Columbus, Ohio, for several years before coming to this area. He organized and trained the first brass band in Spencer and also trained a band for Ravenswood and other river towns. In 1864, the first county school superintendent was elected, and the Roane County Board of Education was established. Their offices were housed in the county courthouse until about 1940, when their new administration building was erected during the term of Orton R. Karickhoff as county superintendent.

Careful study of history leads to the conclusion that the early settlers of our county, like their contemporaries in other sections of the westward movement, relied mostly on three implements: their guns for protection against the beasts of the forest and the marauding Native Americans, their axes to clear the wilderness and hew out the logs for their cabins, and their Bibles to bring solace and peace to their minds. The evidence is conclusive that without belief and faith in God by our early settlers, the brilliant history of development and progress of our county would not have been recorded. Early churches began in the homes until a building could be erected for their services. The first recorded sermon that was preached in Roane County was at Tanner's Cross Roads, now Spencer, about 1817, with the religious movement spreading outside the village as more settlers arrived.

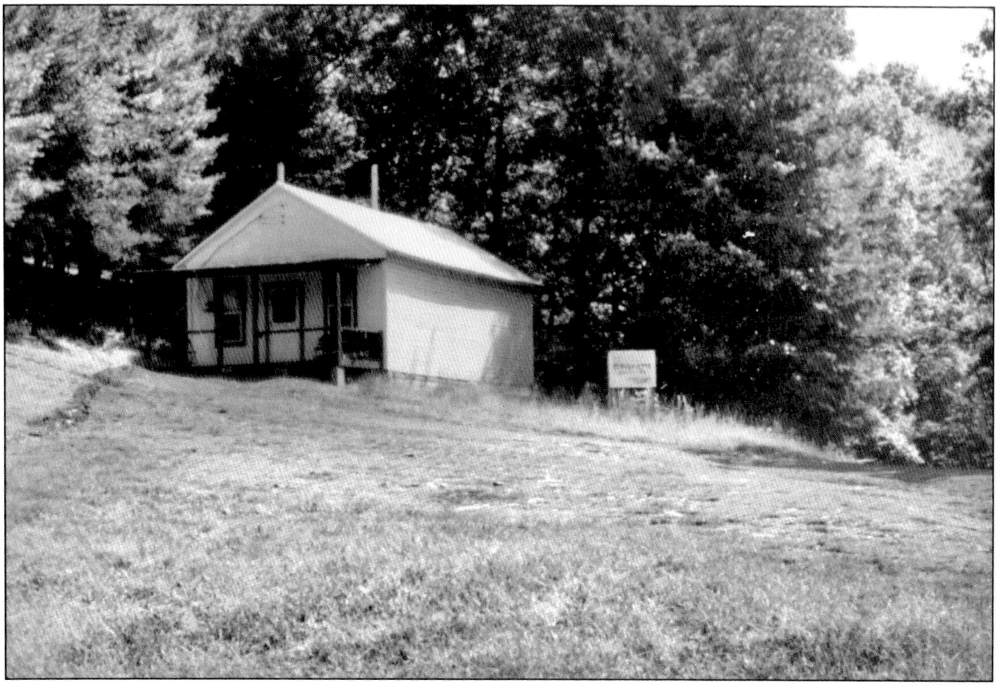

The Otto School building served the village for many years. Since its closing, the building has been converted to the Clover-Otto Community Building. (Courtesy of Donna Walbrown.)

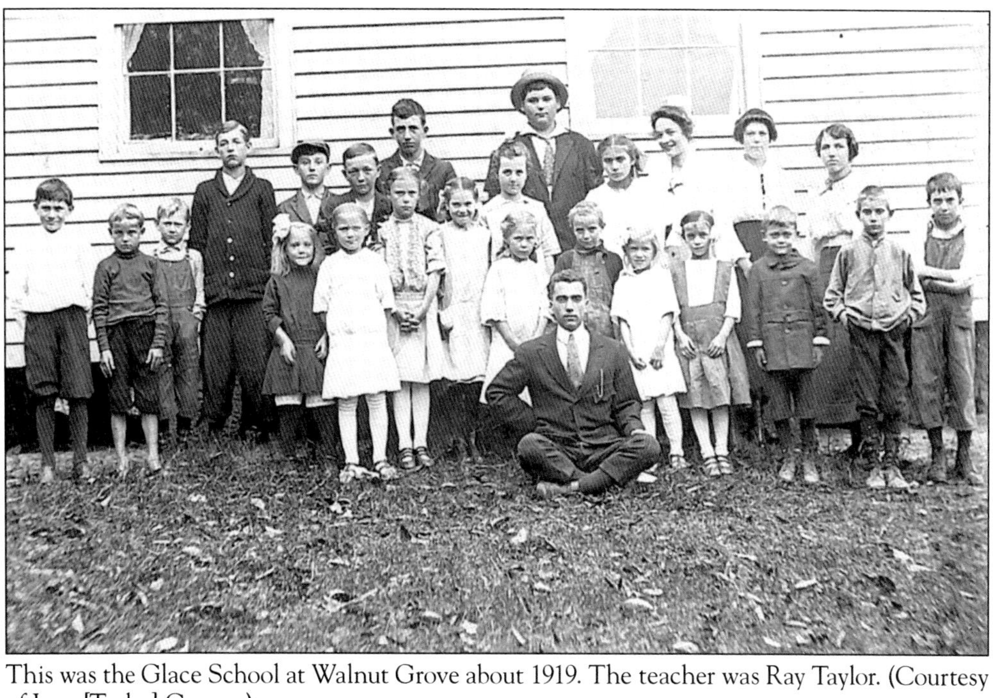

This was the Glace School at Walnut Grove about 1919. The teacher was Ray Taylor. (Courtesy of Jane [Taylor] George.)

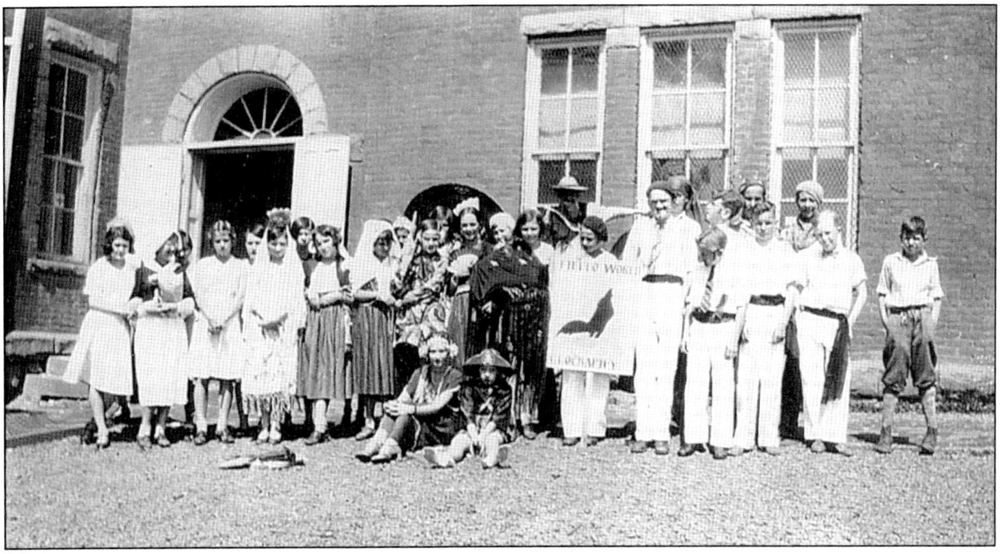

This was the Spencer Elementary School about 1930. This building on Schoolhouse Hill had served the community since 1895 and would continue to house the grade school students until 1949. (Courtesy of Jane [Taylor] George.)

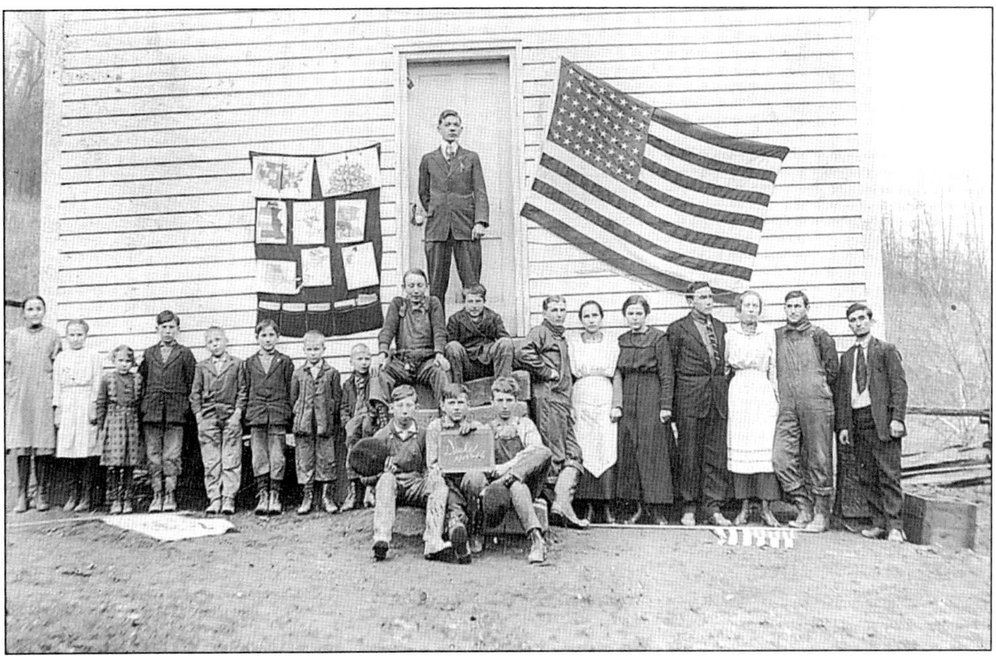

This was the Drake School, pictured in 1916. (Courtesy of Jane [Taylor] George.)

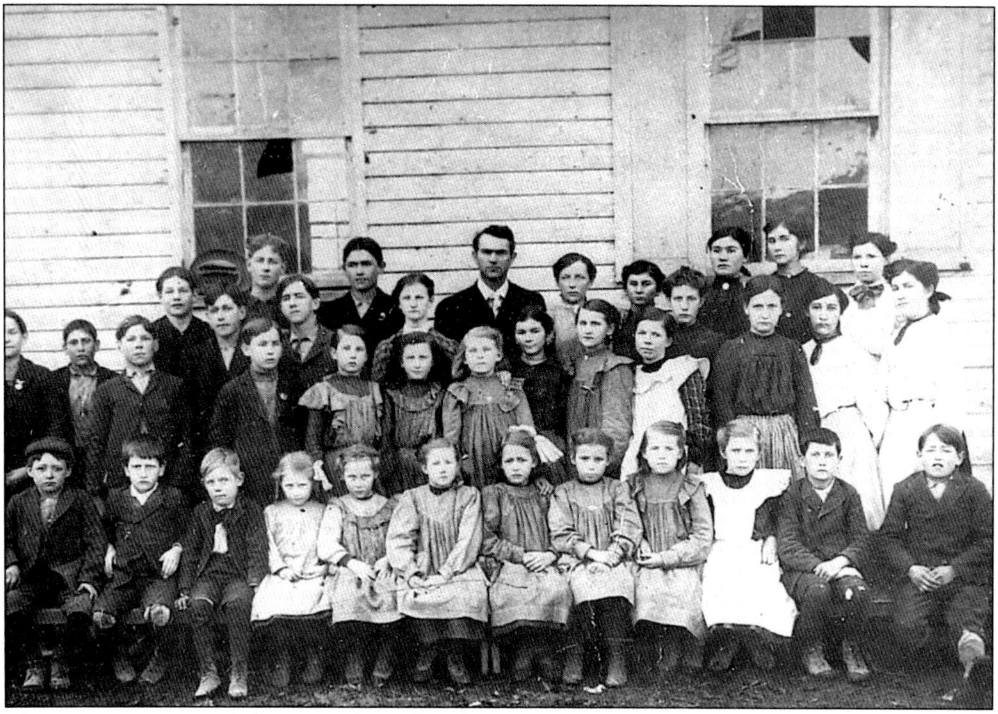

This was a picture of the Round Knob School and its students in 1904. (Courtesy of Jane [Taylor] George.)

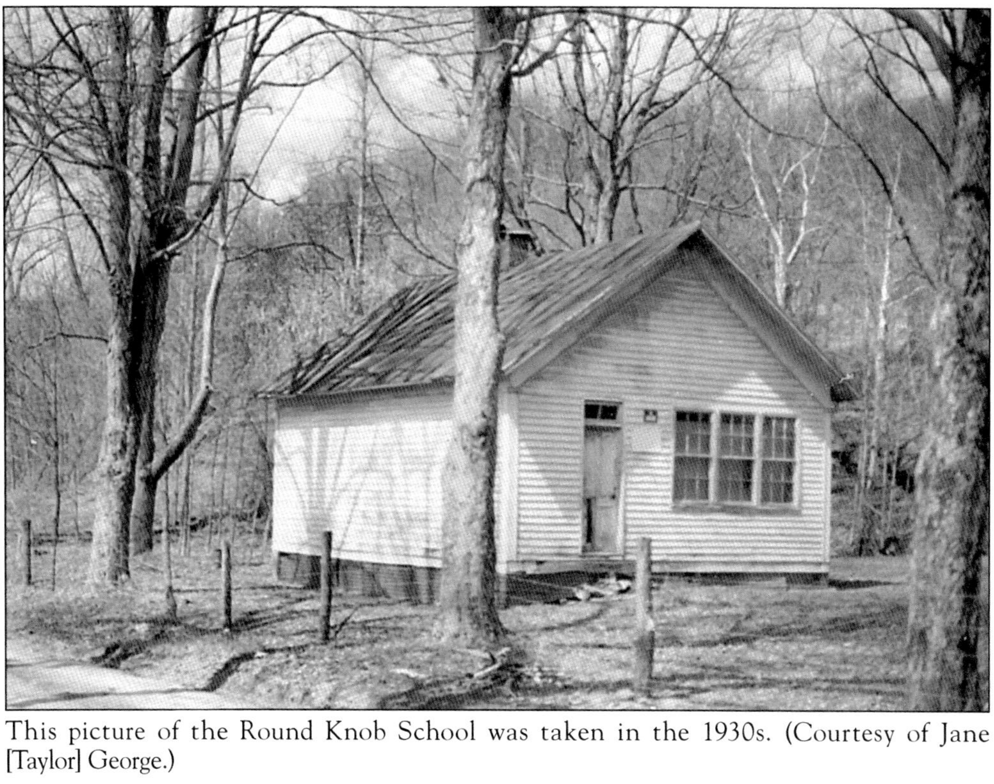

This picture of the Round Knob School was taken in the 1930s. (Courtesy of Jane [Taylor] George.)

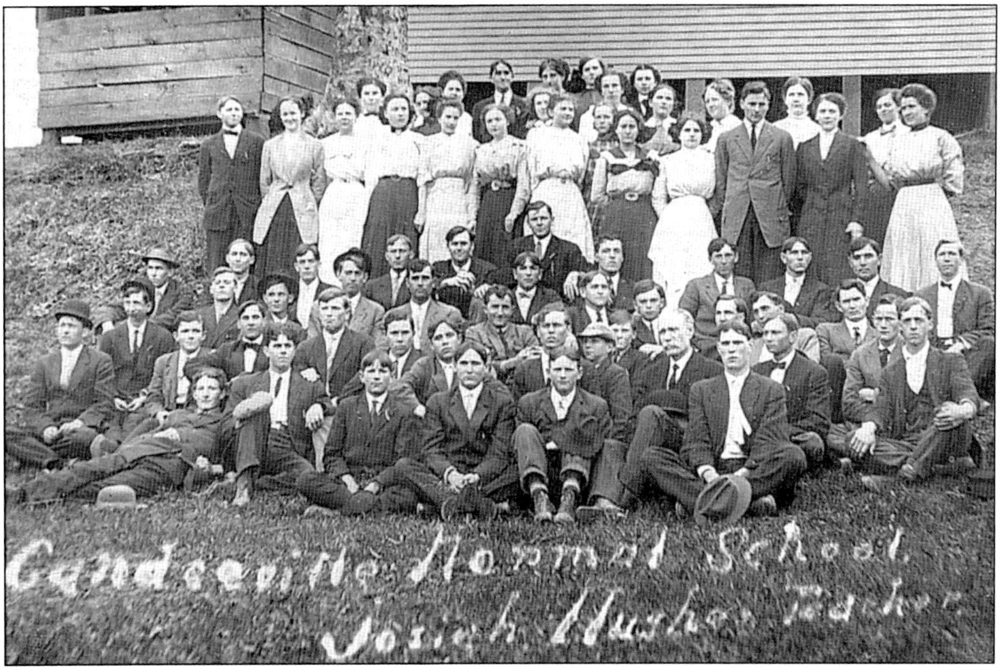

This group of young men and women were attending the Gandeeville Normal School with Josiah Hughes as their teacher. The summer normal or summer schools were designed to prepare prospective teachers to pass the county examinations in order to qualify to teach in public schools. (Courtesy of Joyce Higginbotham.)

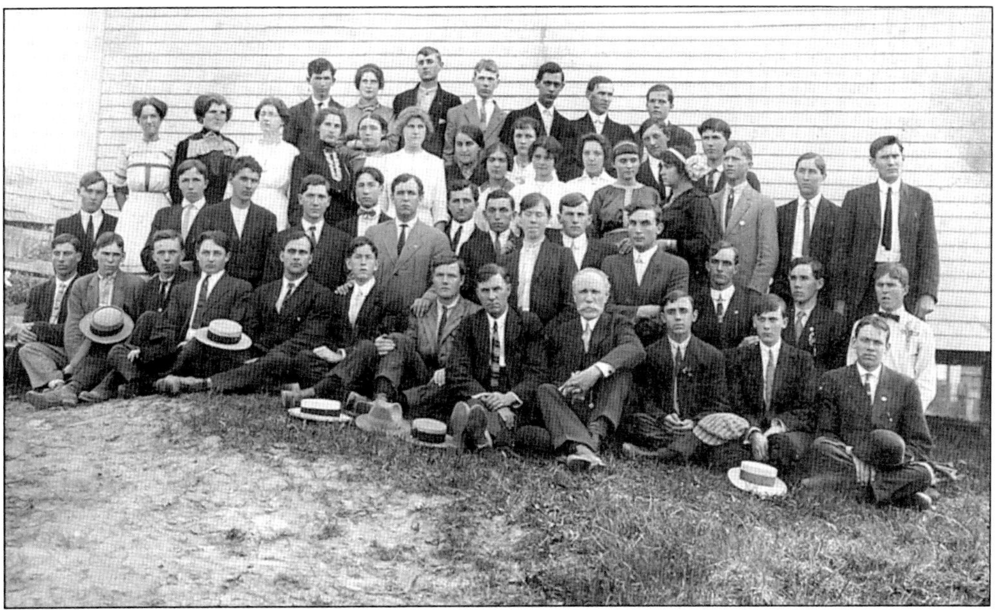

The Gandeeville Normal or Summer School provided the instructional education for local teachers to prepare for the county certification examination. These special schools required payment of a tuition, and the instructors were leading educators of the county. Records indicate that Roane County had at least 22 such schools from as early as 1875 in Walton through 1923 in Reedy. (Courtesy of Jane [Taylor] George.)

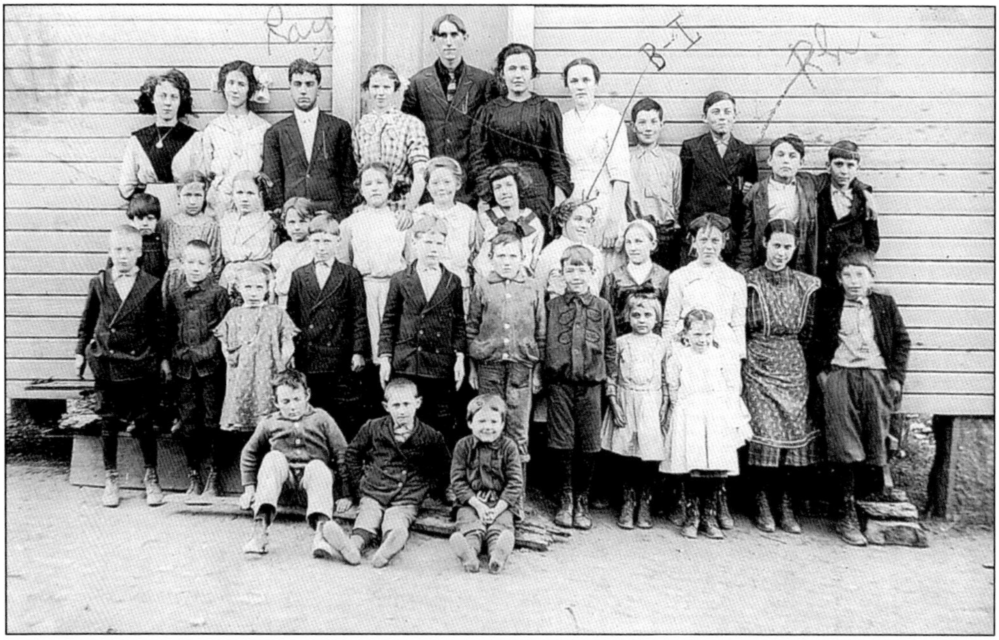

These children were students at the Stringtown School in 1912 with Ray Taylor as their teacher. (Courtesy of Jane [Taylor] George.)

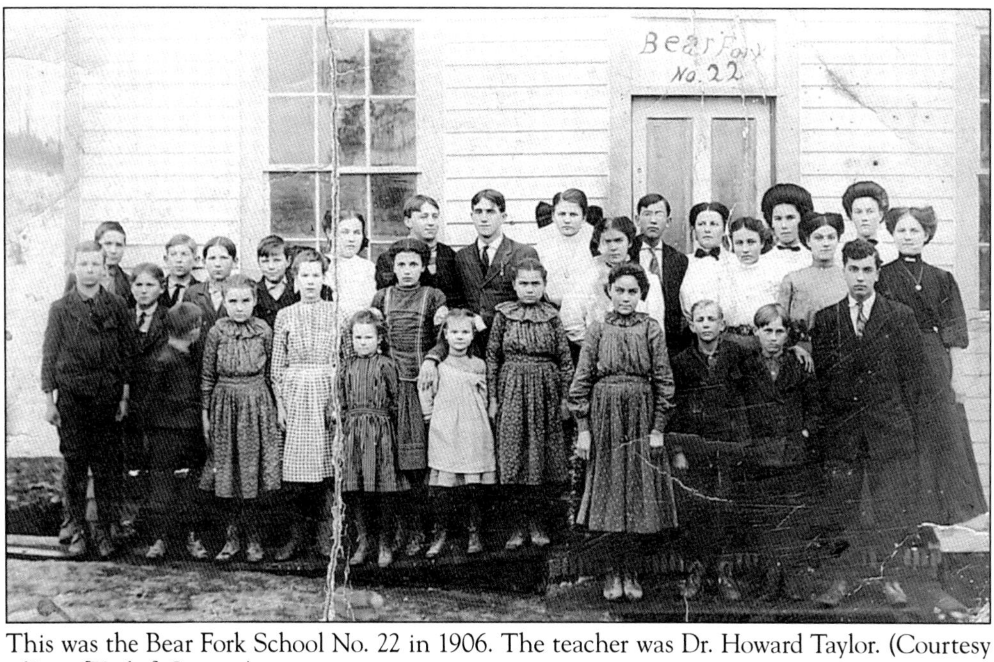

This was the Bear Fork School No. 22 in 1906. The teacher was Dr. Howard Taylor. (Courtesy of Jane [Taylor] George.)

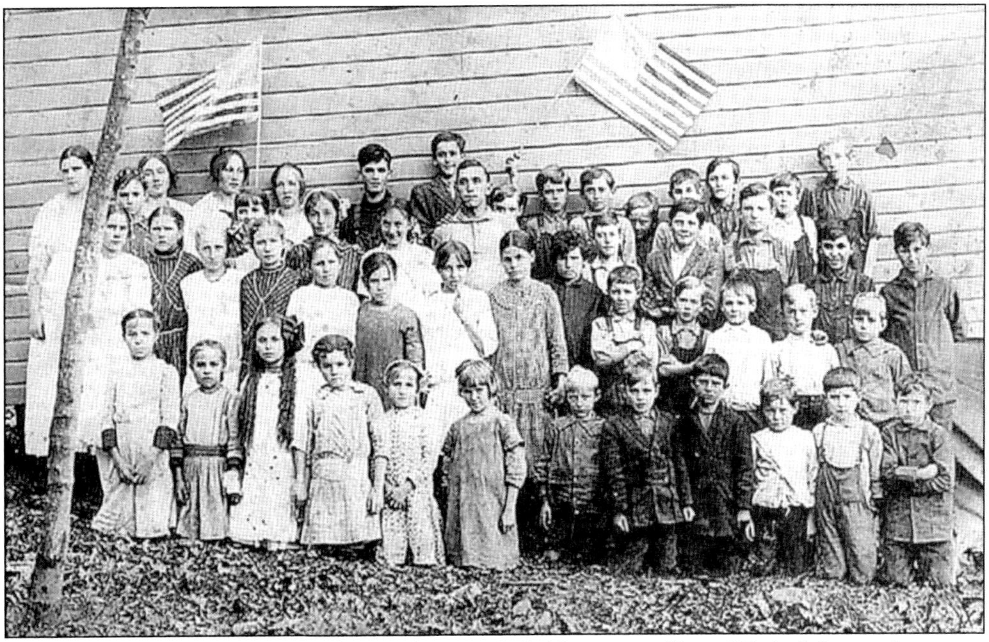

This picture of the Elana School was taken in 1915. (Courtesy of Jane [Taylor] George.)

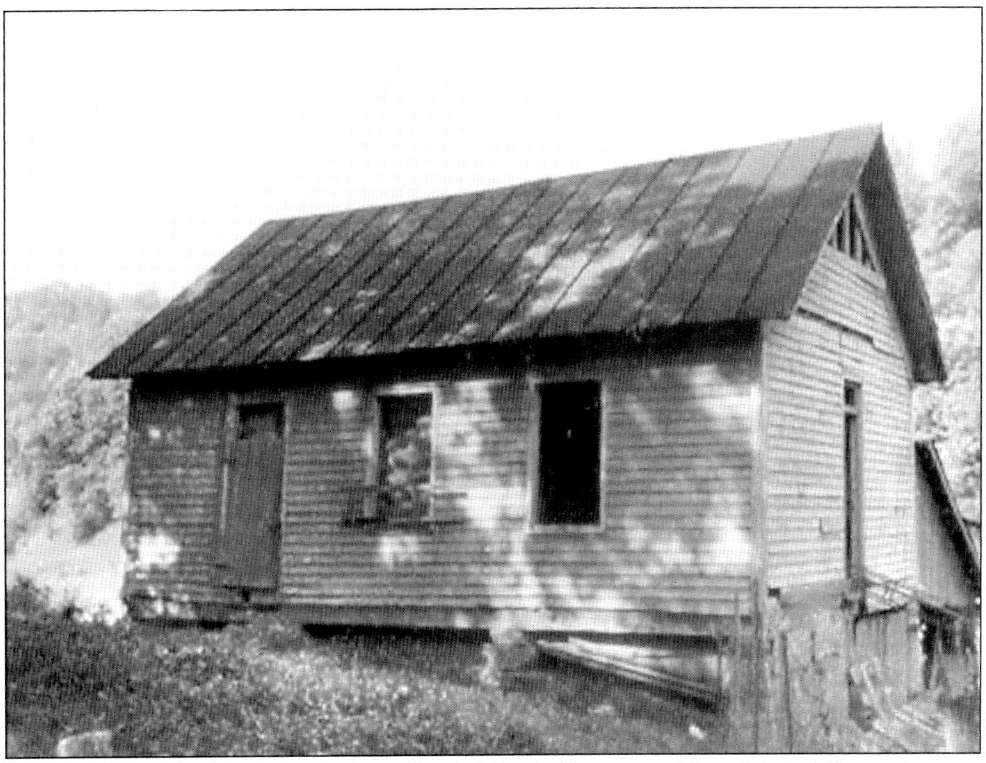

This abandoned building was the Dog Creek School. (Courtesy of Jane [Taylor] George.)

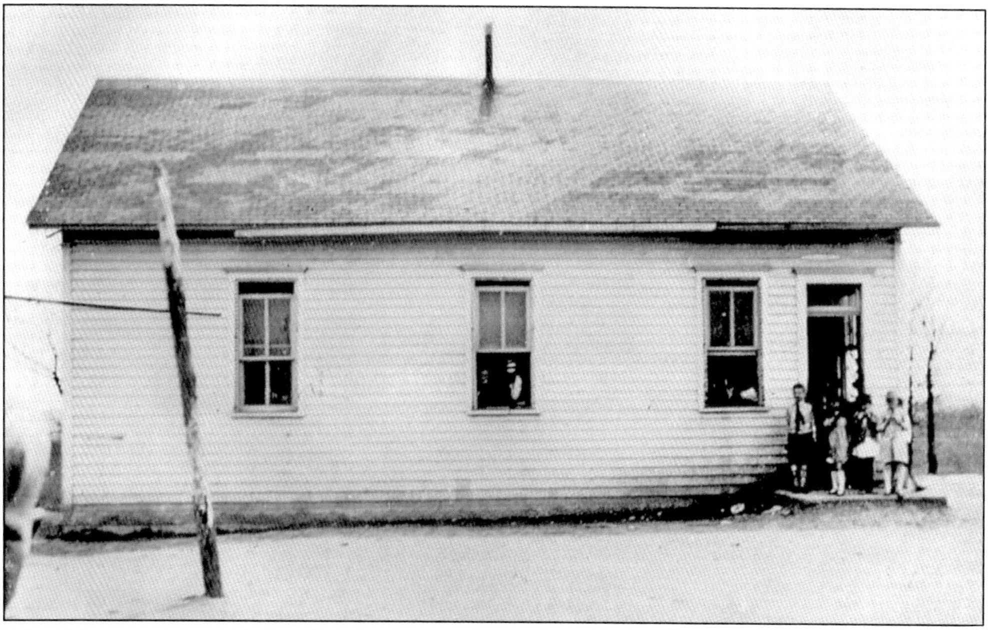

The Fairview School in Reedy District was located on Parkersburg Road. (Courtesy of Jane [Taylor] George.)

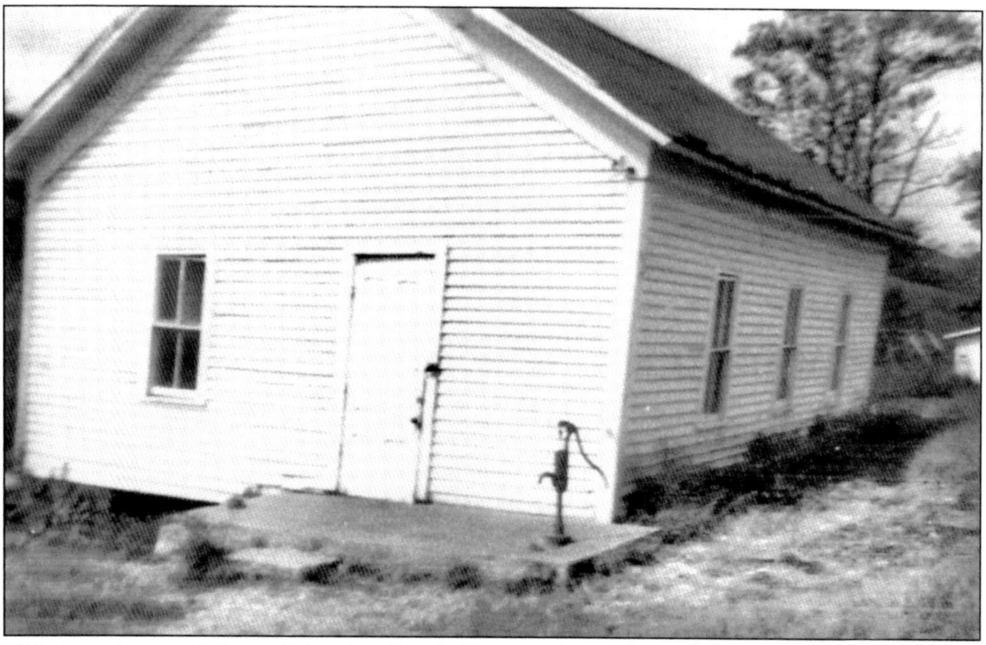

This is a picture of Grace School in Reedy District. It was located on Spring Creek near the Gilboa Baptist Church in the Grace community. The last term of school was in 1956, and the building was later torn down. (Courtesy of Ramona Wenmoth.)

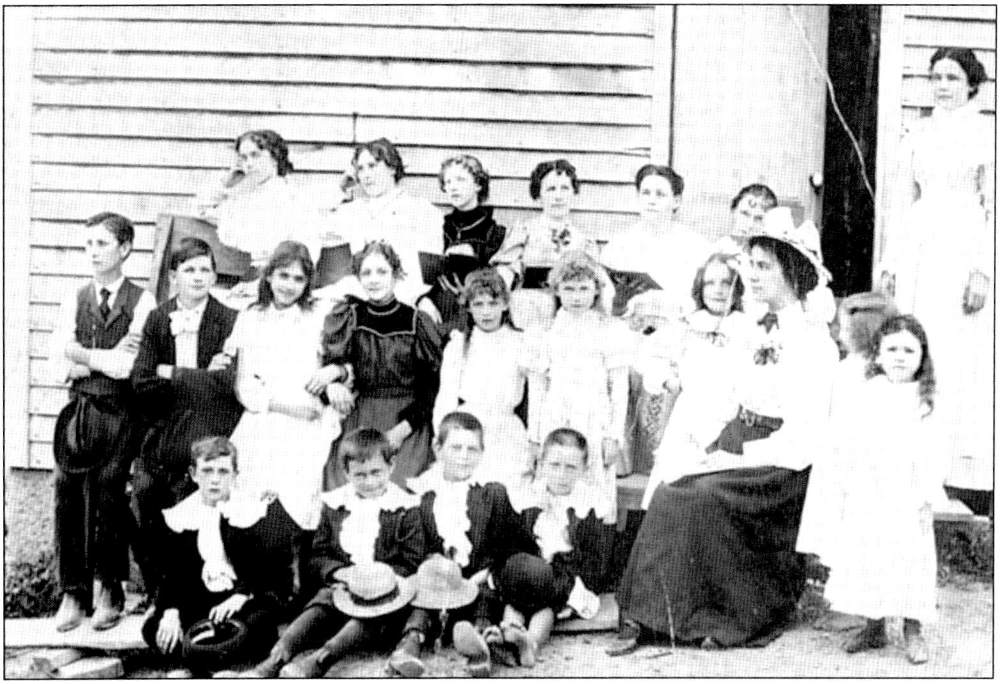

This was the Newton School class of 1897 and was in what is referred to as the "Old School." A new one was built in about 1929 near the mouth of Hollywood Creek, also known as the left fork of Big Sandy Creek. (Courtesy of West Virginia State Archives.)

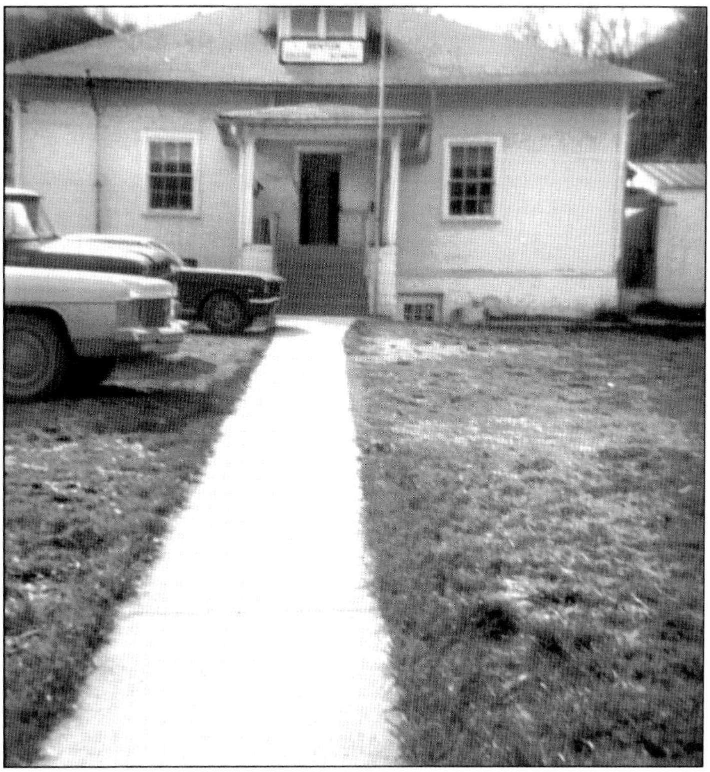

The new Newton School was a four-room, wood structure that would remain in use until the consolidation of rural area schools. It has been torn down. (Courtesy of Joyce Higginbotham.)

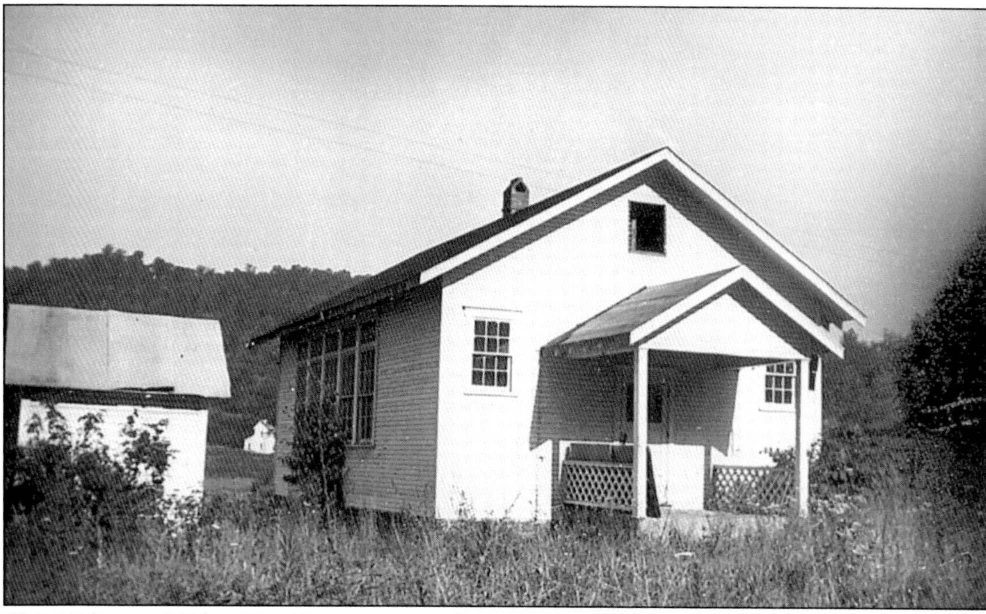

This Hollywood School building was torn down when the area schools were consolidated, and the children of Hollywood attended the Newton School. The land was deeded to Dick and Irene Reynolds in 1948. (Courtesy of Joyce Higginbotham.)

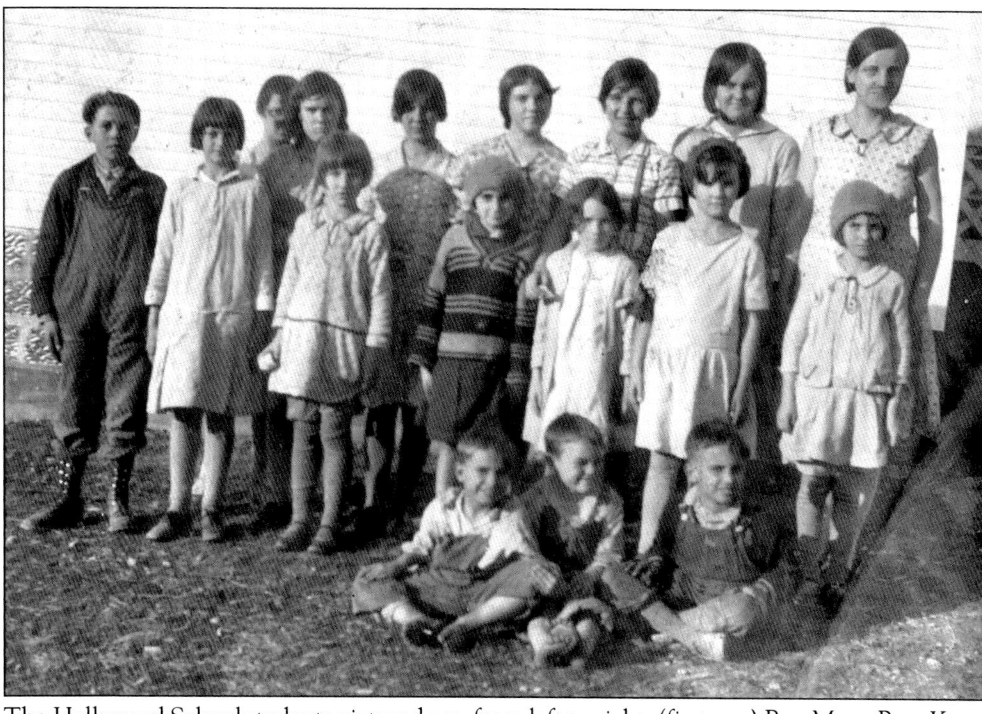

The Hollywood School students pictured are, from left to right, (first row) Rex Moss, Buzz Keen, and Forest "Kayo" Moss; (second row) Ronald Keen, Dicie Moss, Oreta Moss, Maxine Moss, Almeta Keen, Helen Keen, and Anna Keen; (third row) Sharlie Wright, Alberta Steorts, Arlene Surface, Irene Steorts, Geraldine Surface, Velma Moss, and Grace Smith. (Courtesy of Joyce Higginbotham.)

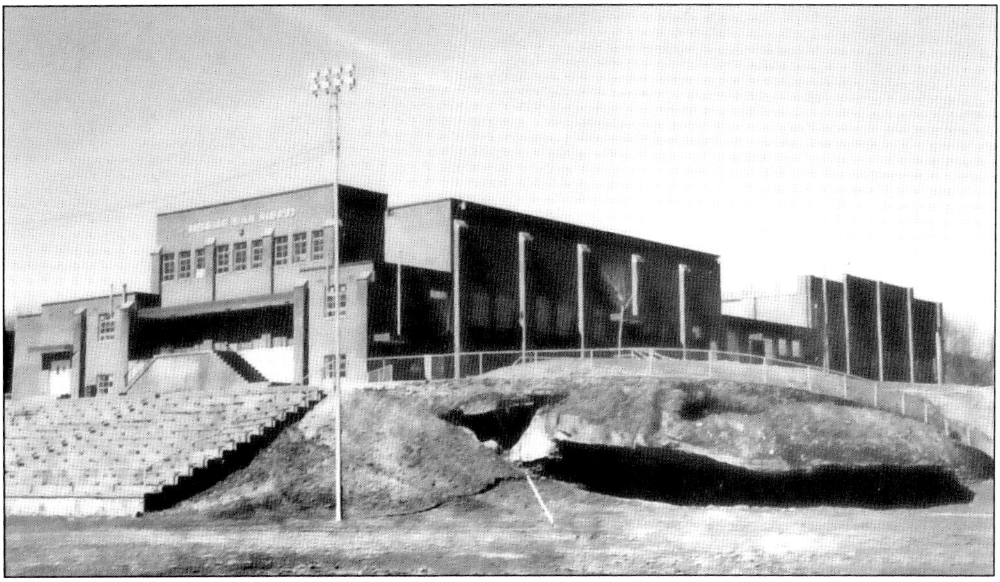

The Spencer High School building was completed in 1916 for a price of $29,000. This photograph was taken after several additions, and it is now the Spencer Middle School. The Spencer Summer School of 1920 was held in this building with D. M. McKown and Clarence White as instructors. The summer normal schools had an important role in the educational program of the county. (Courtesy of Donna Walbrown.)

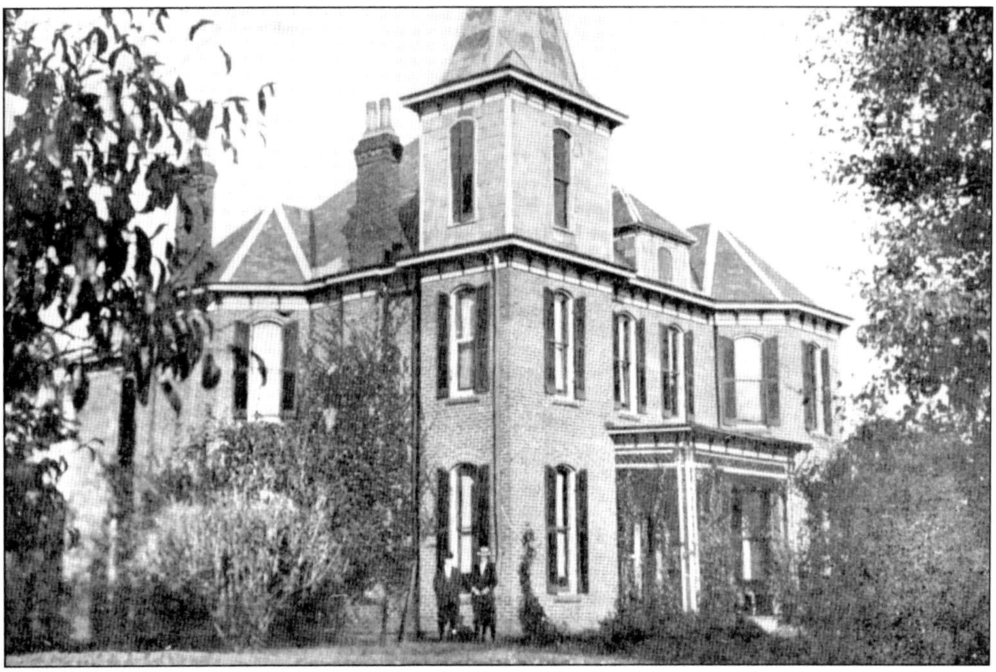

For many years, this was the home of Sen. William Woodyard. It was sold and remodeled for the establishment of the first high school. The first graduating class was in 1913; Marjorie Pfost was the only graduating member. In 1916, the new Spencer High School building was completed, and several new additions were later added. It now serves as the Spencer Middle School. (Courtesy of Dr. Harry H. Camp Sr. family.)

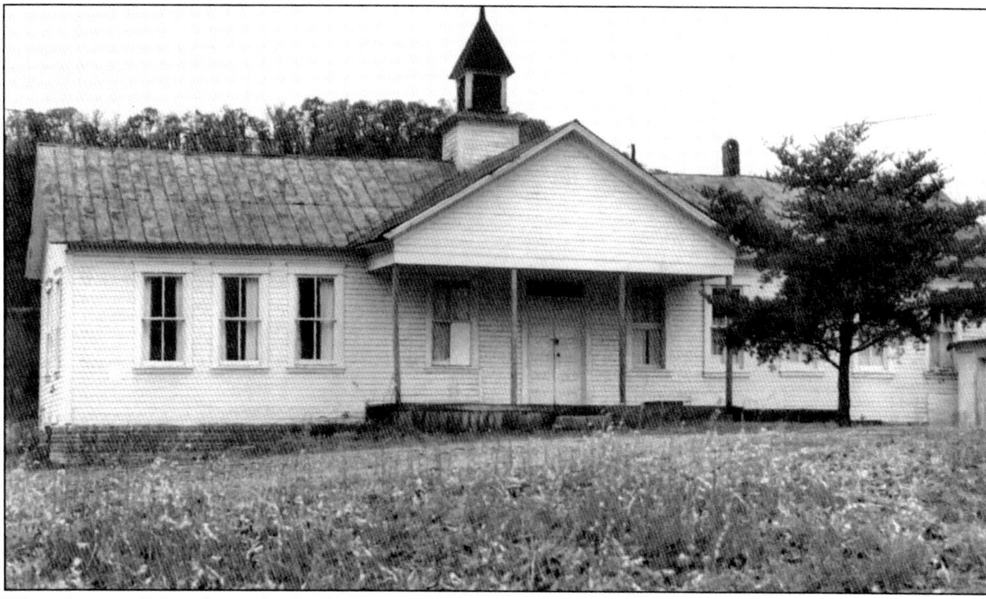

This Amma School was built about 1915 to accommodate the growing population of the area. The two restrooms were about 30 yards east of the building. Upon closing, the building served as a senior citizens and community building before being torn down around 2003. (Courtesy of Linda Drennen.)

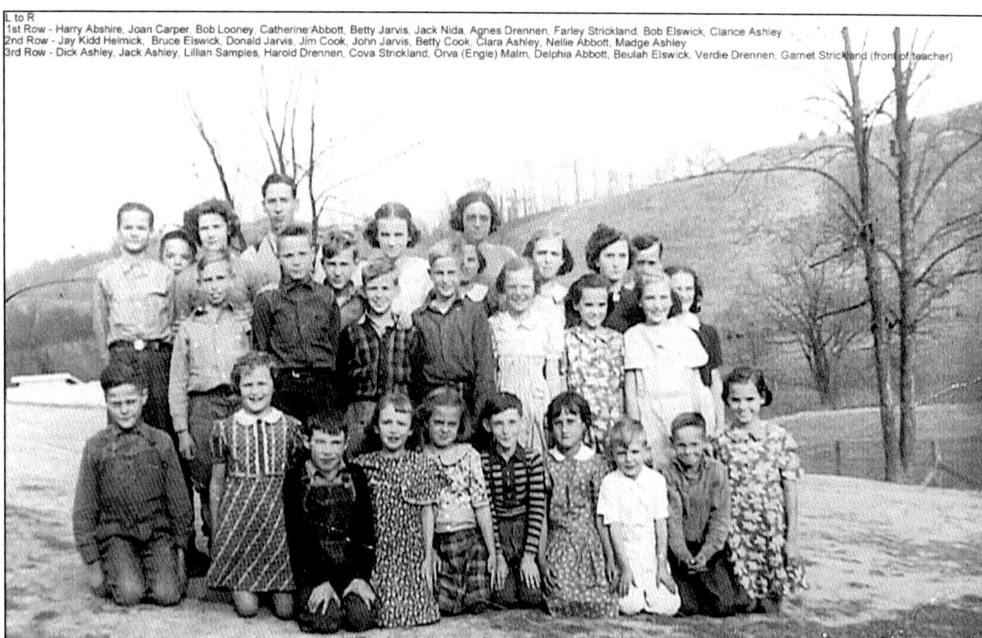

This 1937 photograph was of the Amma School students and teacher, Orva (Engle) Malm. (Courtesy of Jack Nida)

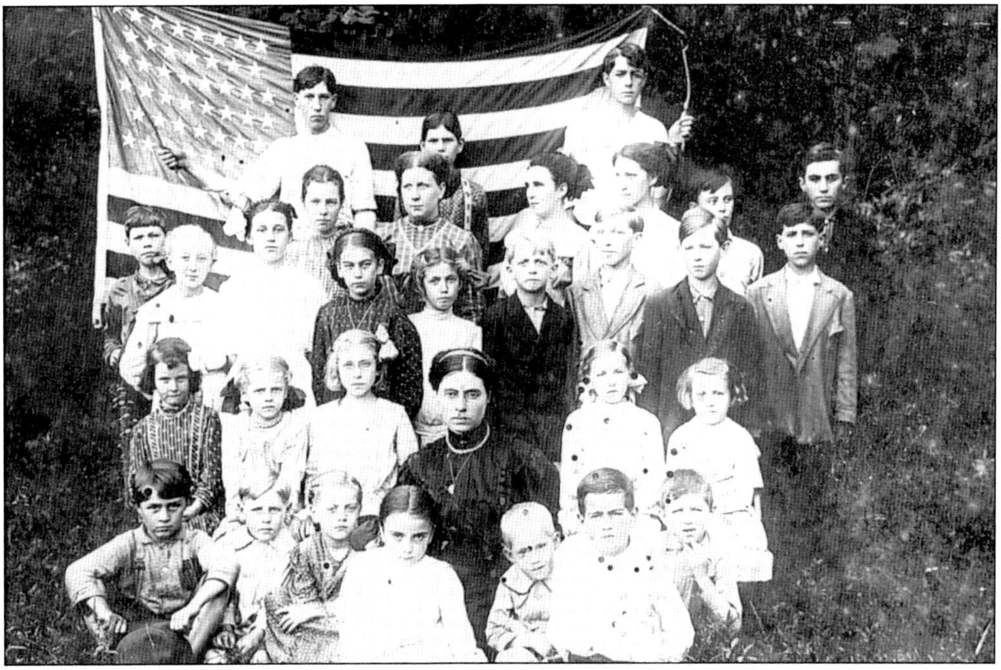

This class was of the Rocky Branch School near Walton. This school was established about 1890. The children were from the Sergent, Looney, Gandee, Vineyard, Nellis, and other families of the area. A teacher's pay was $30 to $37 per month during the early 1900s. (Courtesy of Mark Sergent.)

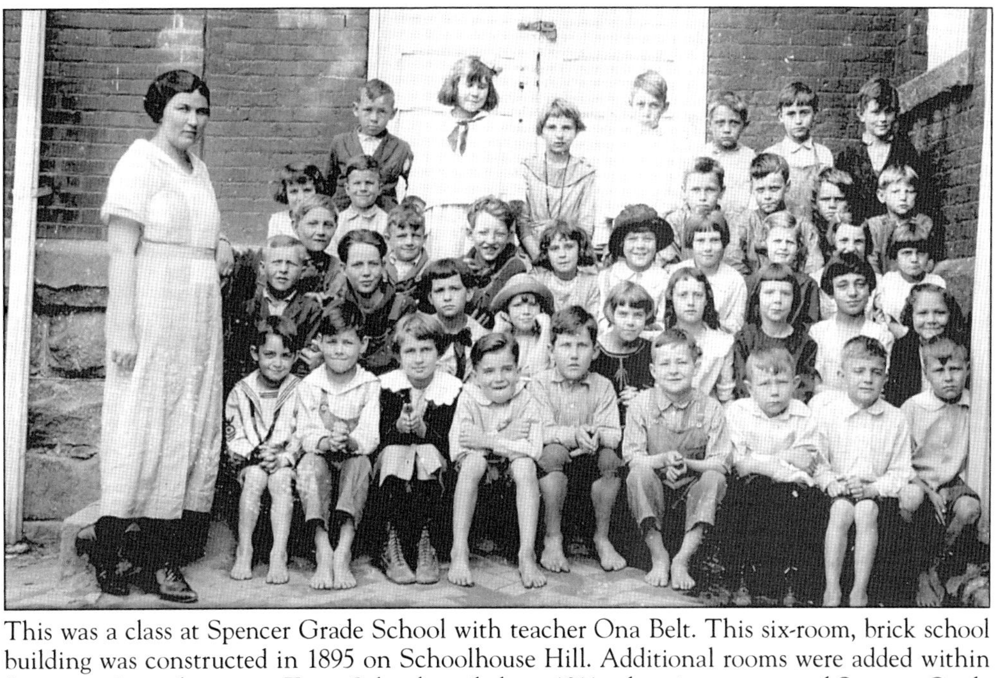

This was a class at Spencer Grade School with teacher Ona Belt. This six-room, brick school building was constructed in 1895 on Schoolhouse Hill. Additional rooms were added within five years. It was known as Town School until about 1911, when it was renamed Spencer Grade School. This building was also utilized for classes of Spencer Summer or Normal School until 1949. (Ralph Nester Collection courtesy of Mark Sergent.)

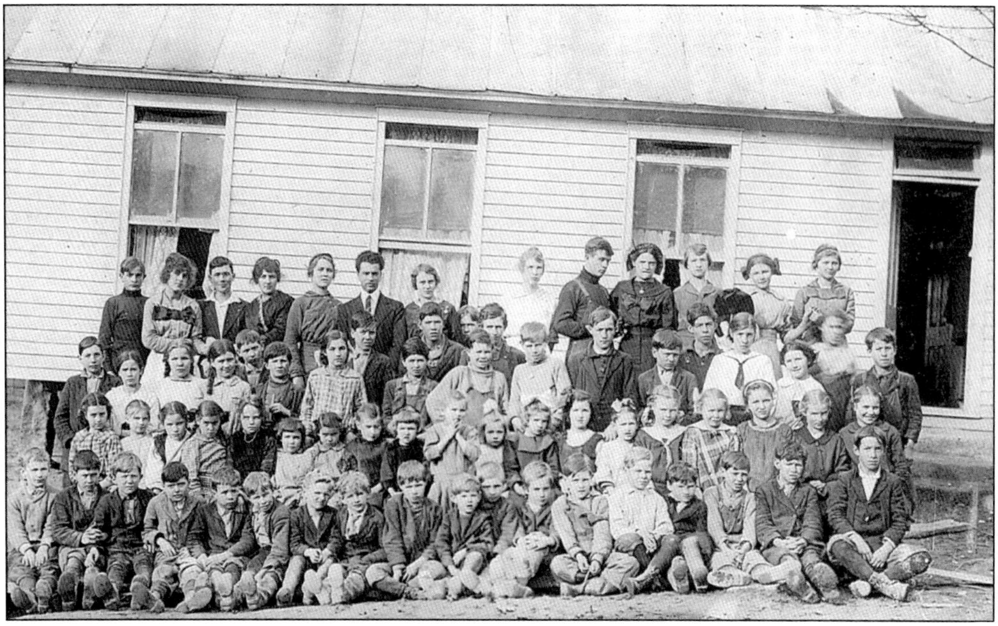

This school picture is of the Stringtown School. (Courtesy of Mark Sergent.)

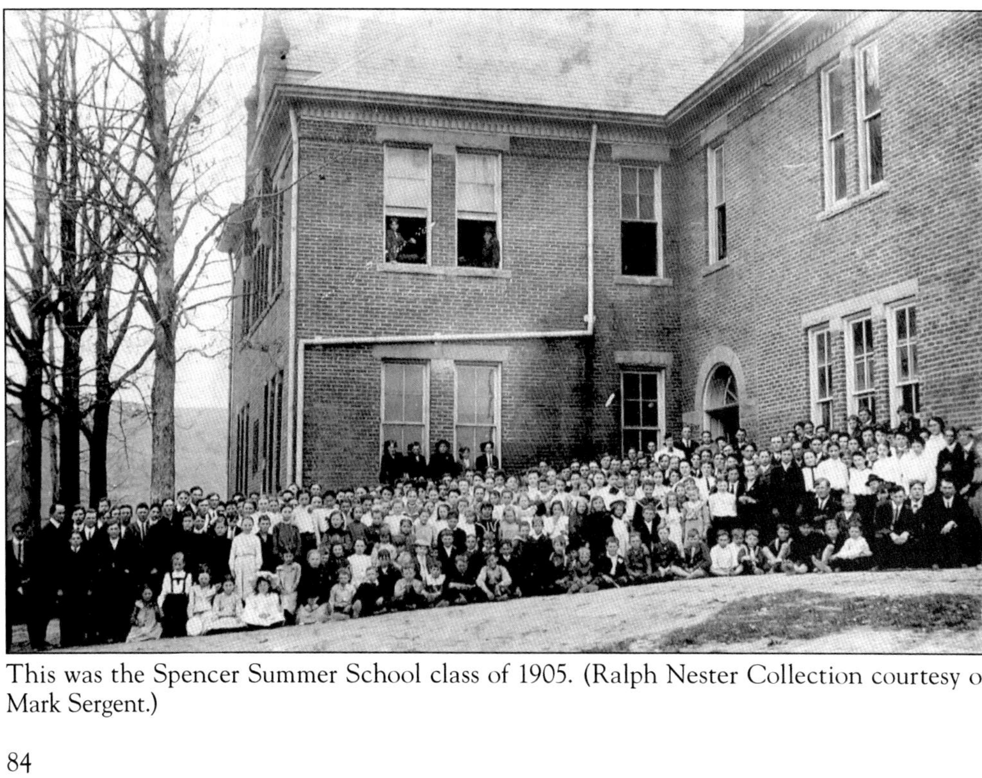

This was the Spencer Summer School class of 1905. (Ralph Nester Collection courtesy of Mark Sergent.)

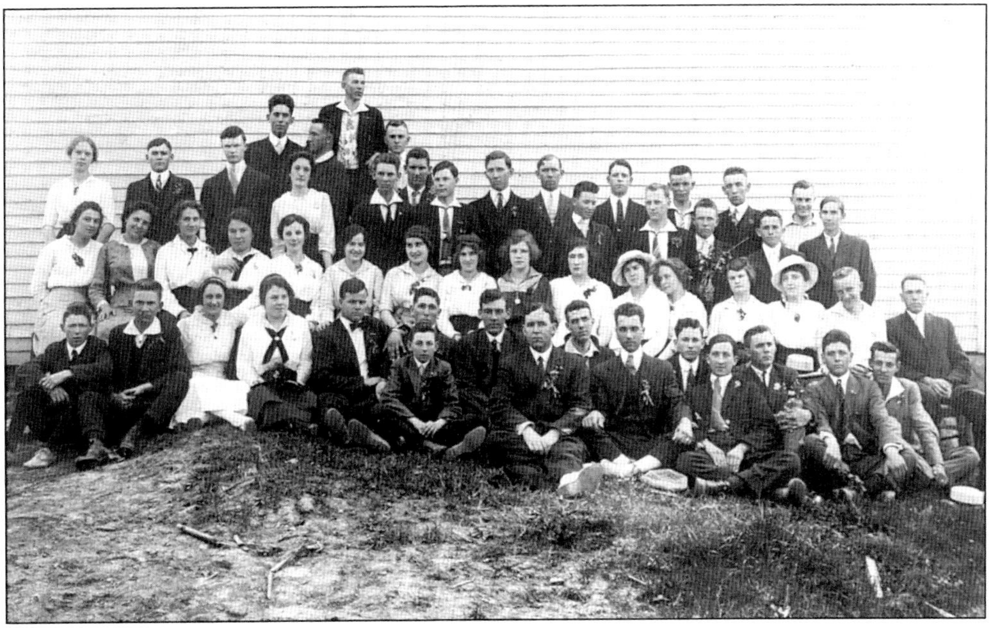

This Reedy Normal School class is preparing for the county board of examiners who administer the tests for teaching certificates in the county. (Courtesy of Jane [Taylor] George.)

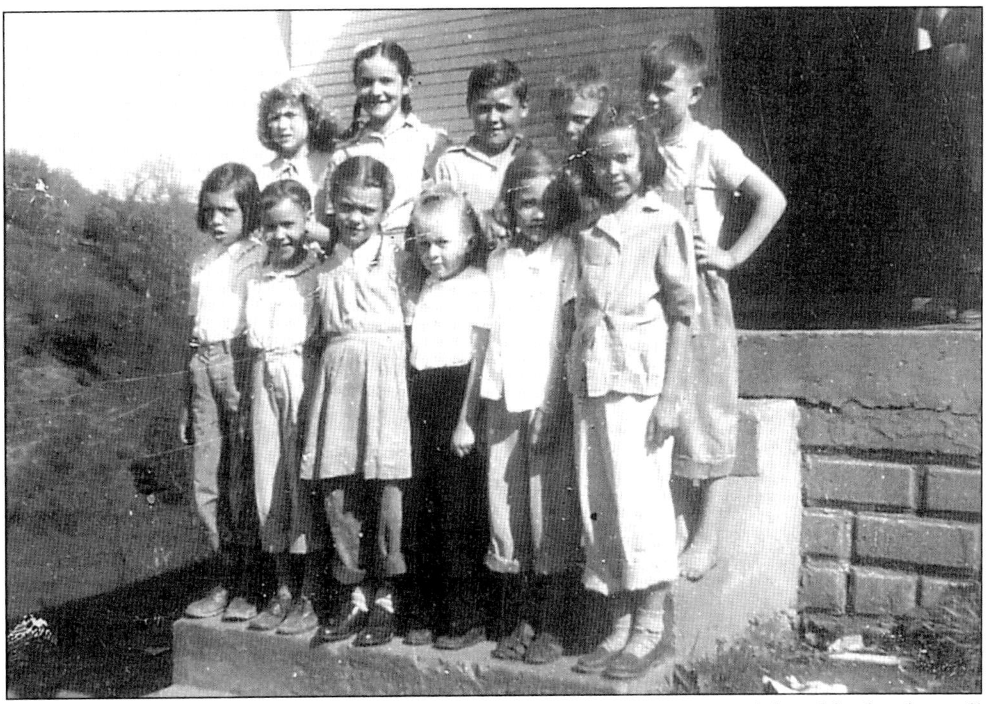

This picture of Beech Hill School students was taken in 1946. A part of the old school is still standing on Little Left Hand road about a mile from Amma. The students from left to right are (first row) Irene Payne, Ella Carper, Mabel Payne, Georgia Carper, Hazel Payne, and Minnie Carper; (second row) Ellen Drake, Betty Ann Carper, Richard Campbell, Howard Carper Jr., and Darius Hall. (Courtesy of Ella [Carper] Myers.)

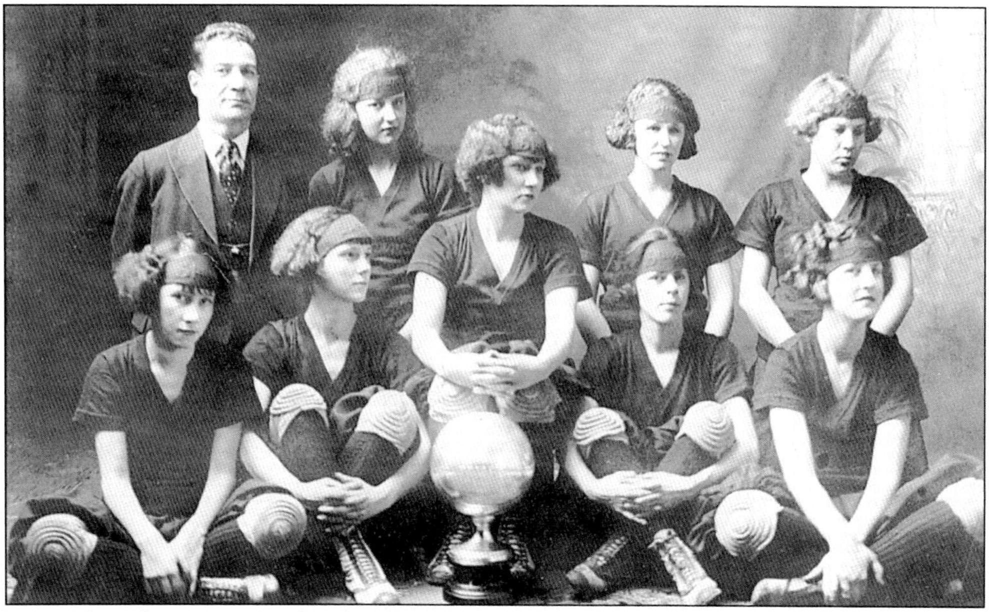

Pictured are the Spencer High School girls' basketball state champions in 1923. From left to right are (first row) Elsie Runnion, Geraldine Runnion, Orlie Runnion, Helen Dunaway, and Martha Rhodes; (second row) coach R. W. Shumaker, Virginia Smith, Elsie Hall, and Beulah Wolfe. (Courtesy of Steve Cooper.)

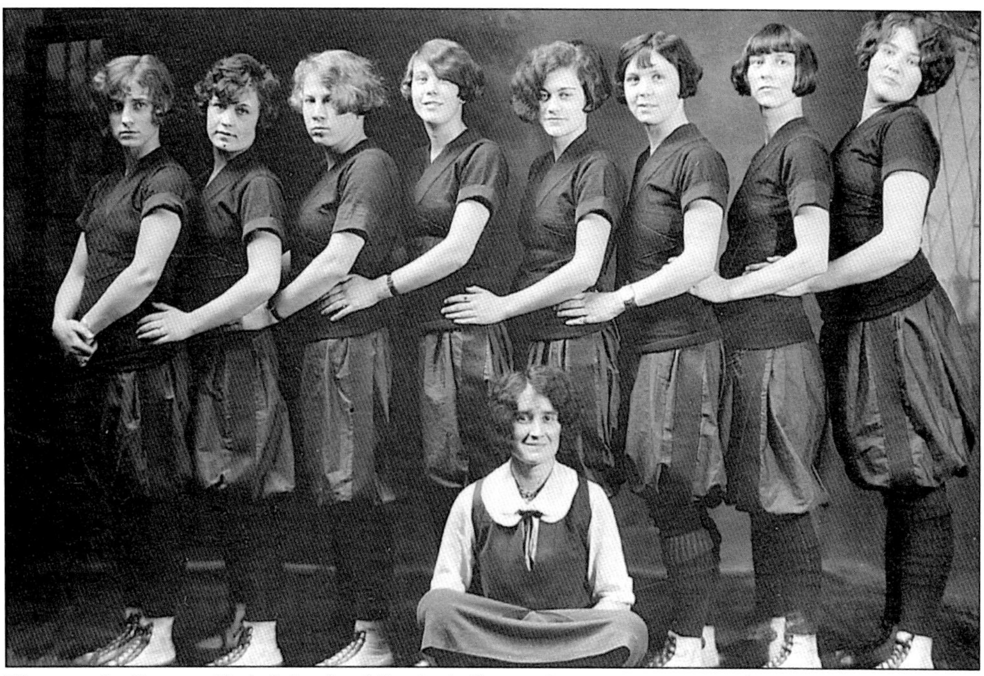

This was the Spencer High School girls' basketball state champions in 1926. They represented the state of West Virginia in the Westfield Cup National High School Girls Basketball Tournament held in Youngstown, Ohio. Nicknamed the "Wonder Six," the team was, from left to right, Frances Hutchinson, Pearl Bowers, Beulah Wolfe, Glenna Rader, Millie Nellis, Elsie Gandee, Geraldine Runnion, and Delphia Raines. The coach (seated) was Sylvia Burgun. (Courtesy of Steve Cooper.)

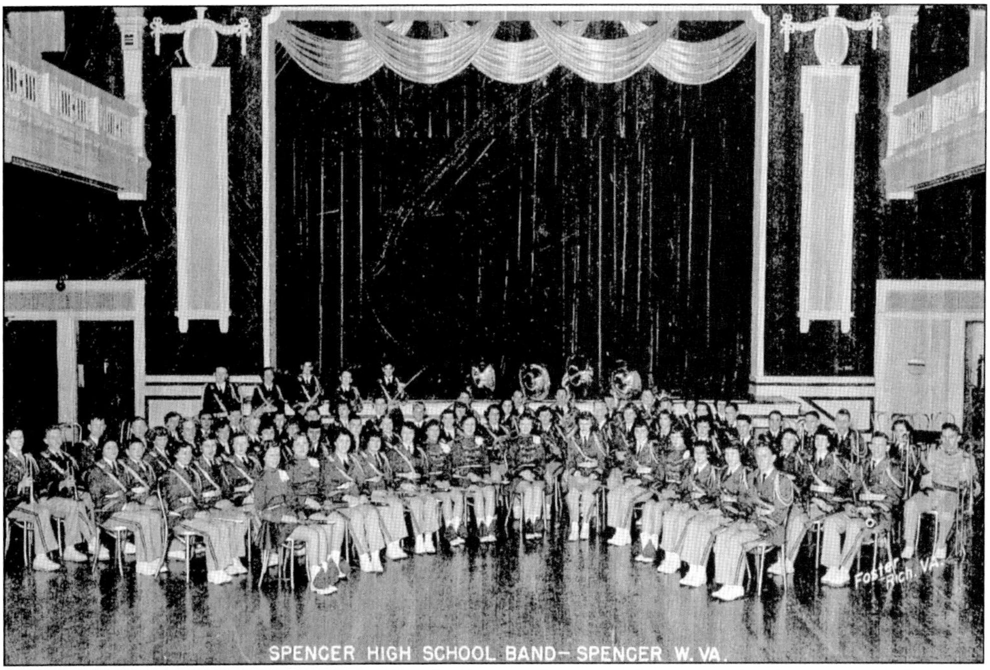

This Spencer High School Band played for the Eastern Regional Educator Conference in Richmond, Virginia, in 1951. Karl V. Brown was band director at this high school for many years. (Courtesy of Steve Cooper.)

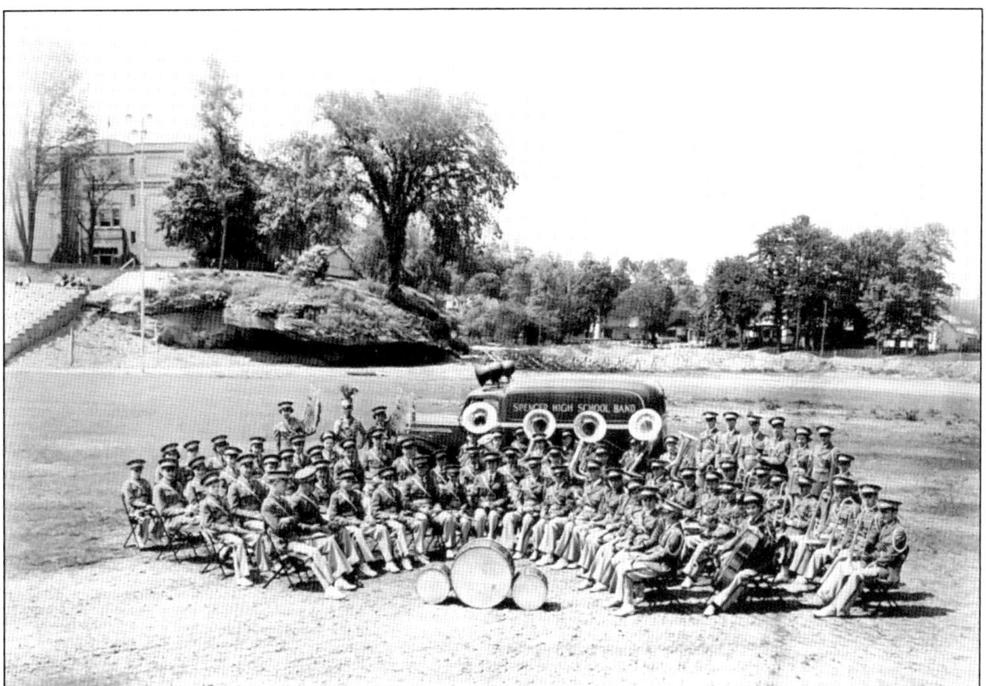

The Spencer High School Band in full uniform is shown on the school athletic field. (Courtesy of Dr. Harry H. Camp Sr. family.)

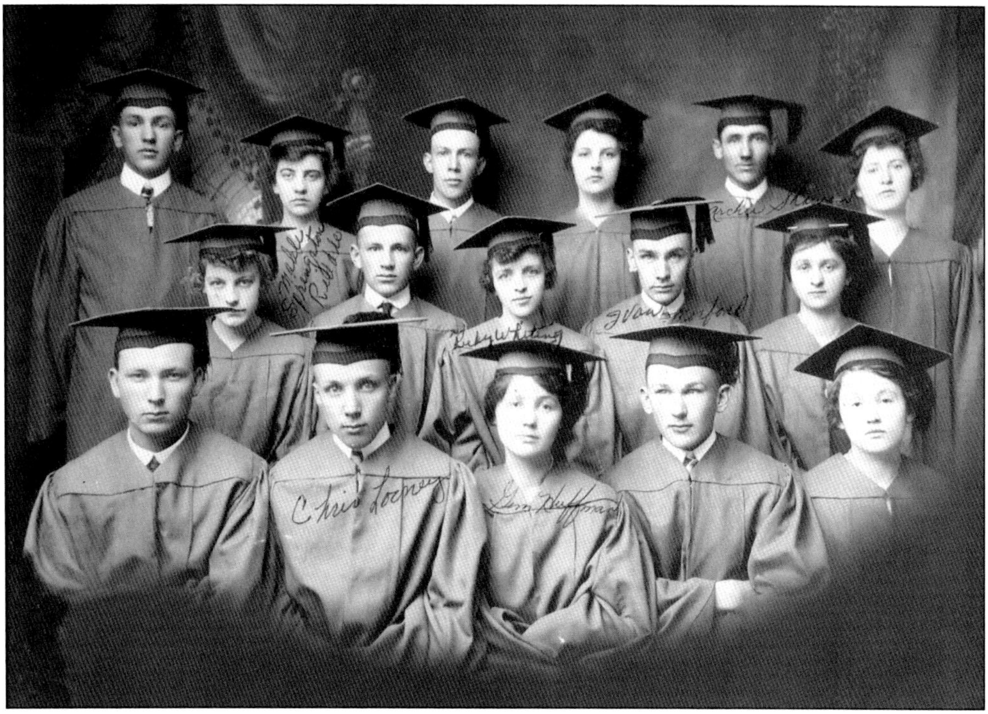

This was the graduating class of Spencer High School in 1916. They were unusually distinguished by the fact that they were the first graduates to wear caps and gowns. (Courtesy of Dr. Harry H. Camp Sr. family.)

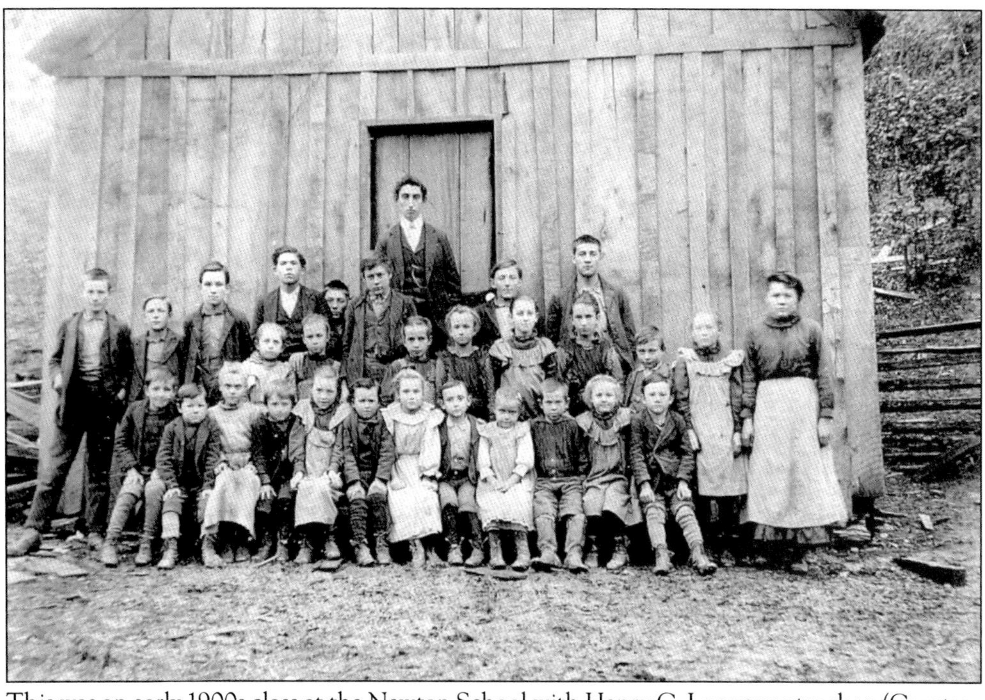

This was an early-1900s class at the Newton School with Henry C. Looney as teacher. (Courtesy of Jack Nida.)

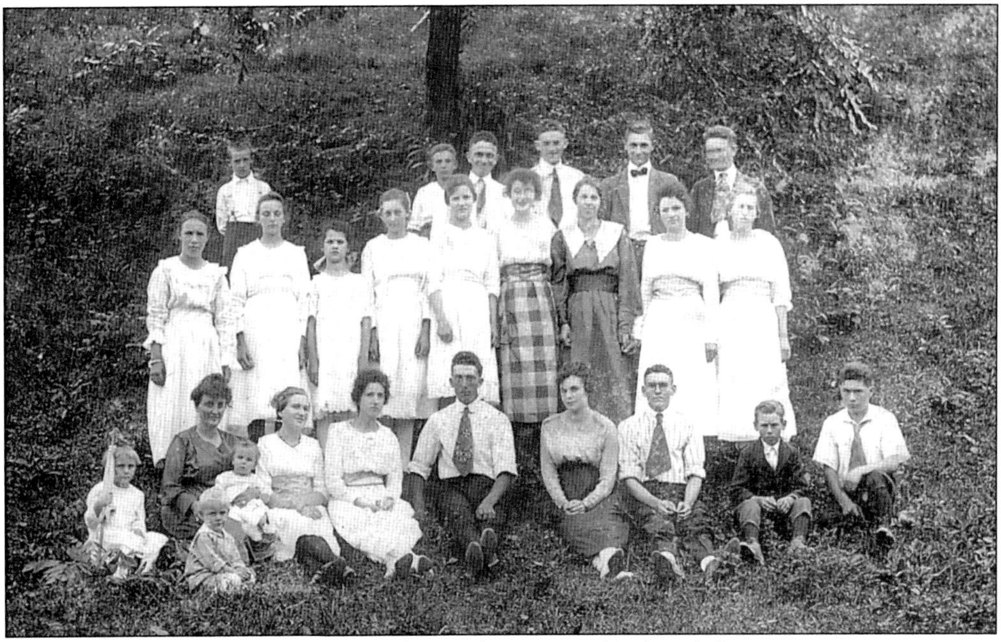

The Newton School, class of 1922, is shown. (Courtesy of Jack Nida.)

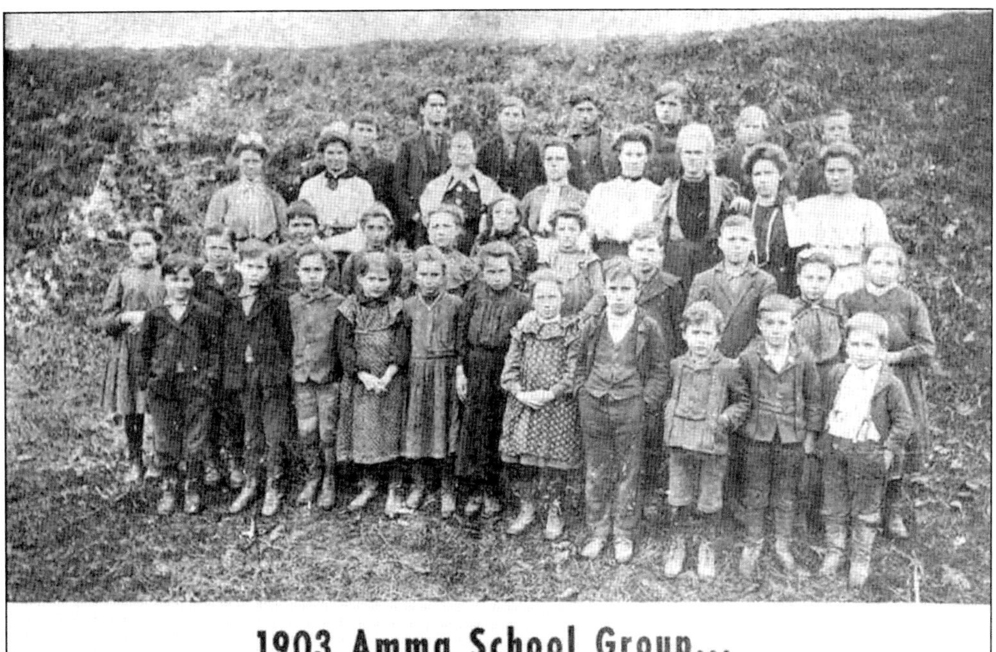

This 1903 picture of the Amma School students is presented in memory of Elsie Looney, who shared it with friends through the *Spencer Newspaper*. (Courtesy of Jack Nida.)

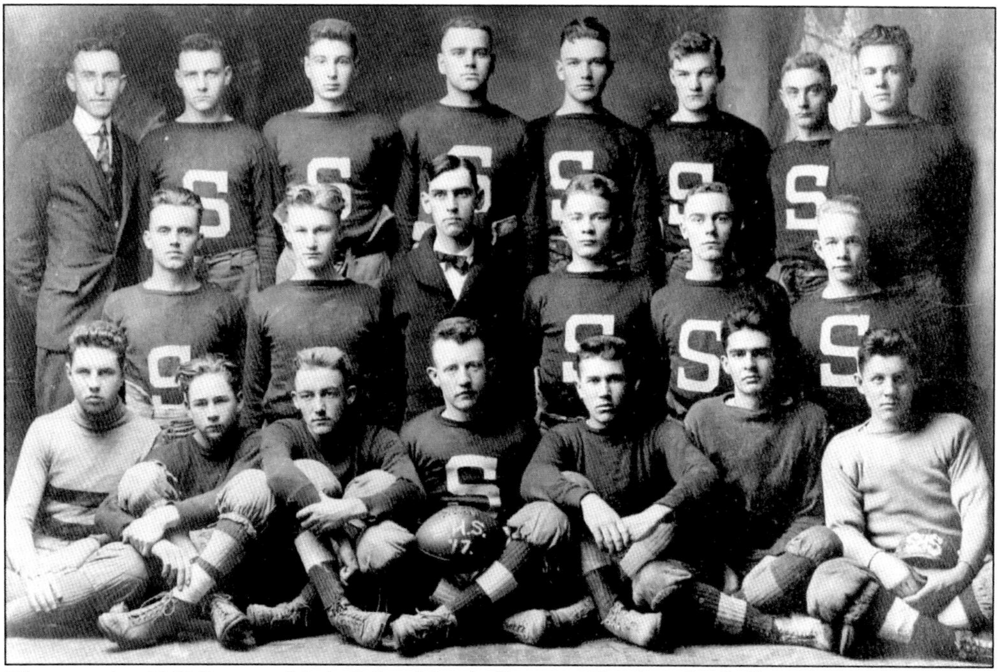

This was the 1917 Spencer High School football team. The first football team to represent the school was in 1914. (Ralph Nester Collection courtesy of Mark Sergent.)

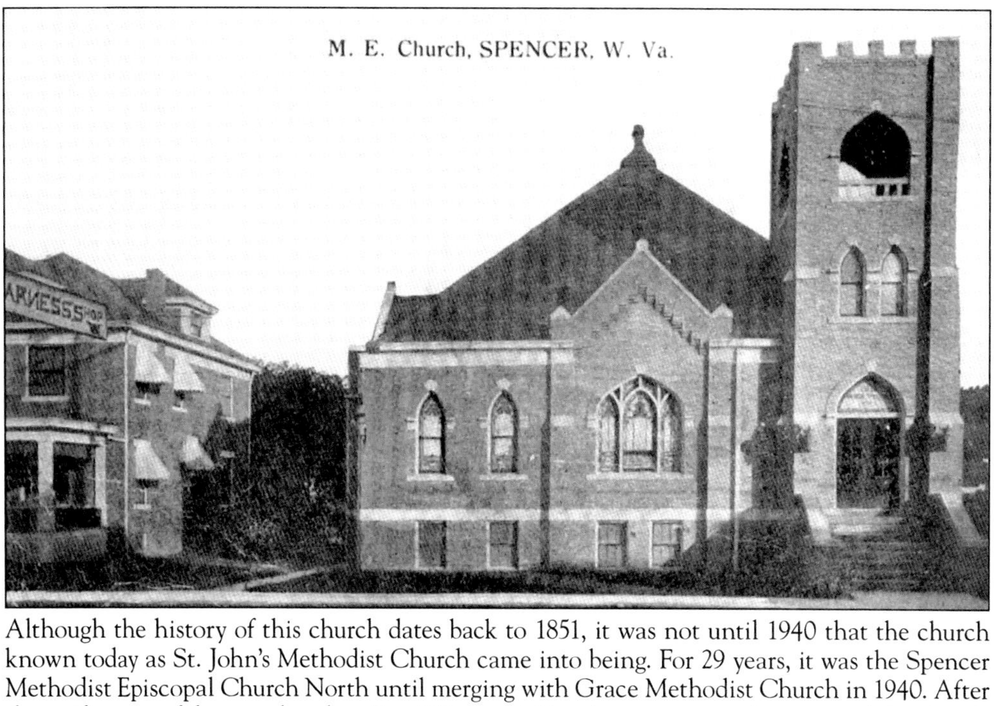

Although the history of this church dates back to 1851, it was not until 1940 that the church known today as St. John's Methodist Church came into being. For 29 years, it was the Spencer Methodist Episcopal Church North until merging with Grace Methodist Church in 1940. After the unification of the two churches, Rev. Winton R. Houck was appointed pastor, and the church was named St. John's Methodist Church. (Courtesy of Charlie White.)

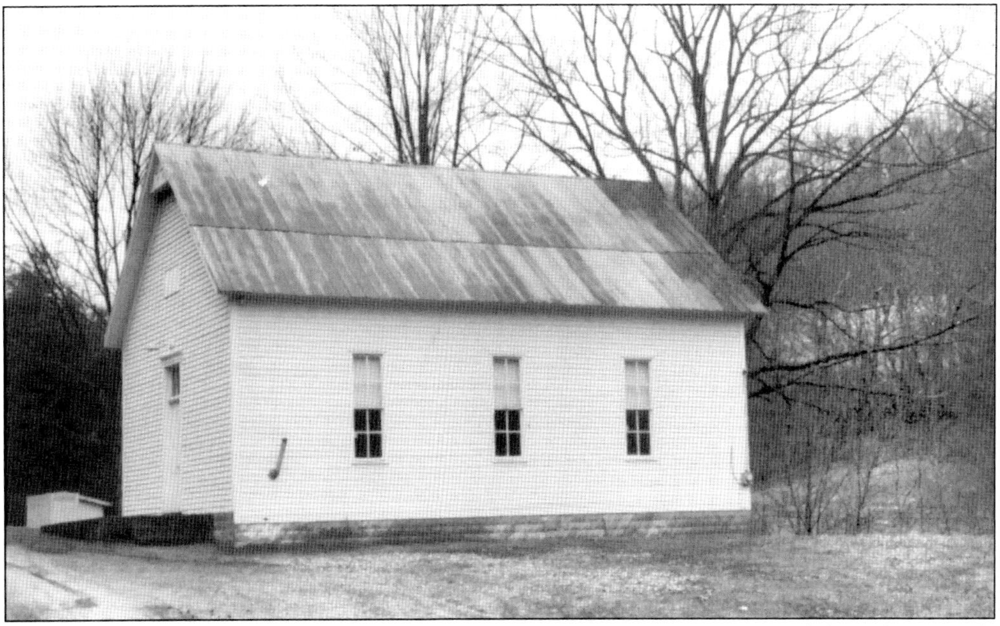

Clarence Methodist Episcopal Church is located on the upper waters of Middle Fork of Reedy Creek, and early meetings of this congregation were held in the old Union School near the mouth of Fetty Run. A church building was erected in 1896 on a site provided by the Harless family. The first pastor was Rev. Perry B. Fisher. Early membership included the Board, Fetty, Rhodes, and Sleeth families, among others. (Courtesy of Donna Walbrown.)

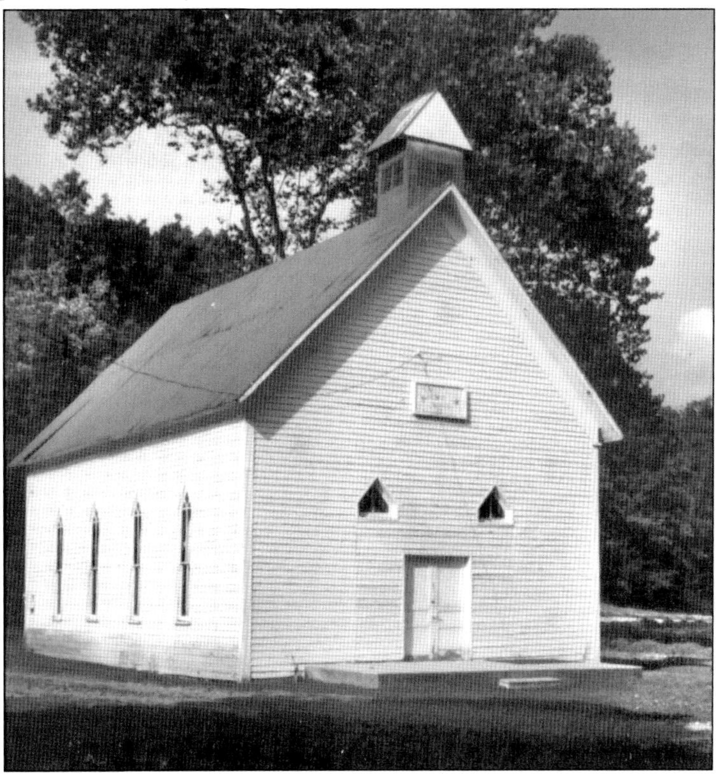

The Cherry Valley Methodist Church is located on Stover Fork of Reedy Creek. The earliest preserved records show a church in 1894 known as the Stover Fork Methodist Protestant Church. The land for the church was deeded in 1869 by Daniel and Margaret Roberts to the trustees of the Stover Fork Methodist Protestant Church. The first records under the name of Cherry Valley Church are dated 1896. (Courtesy of Donna Walbrown.)

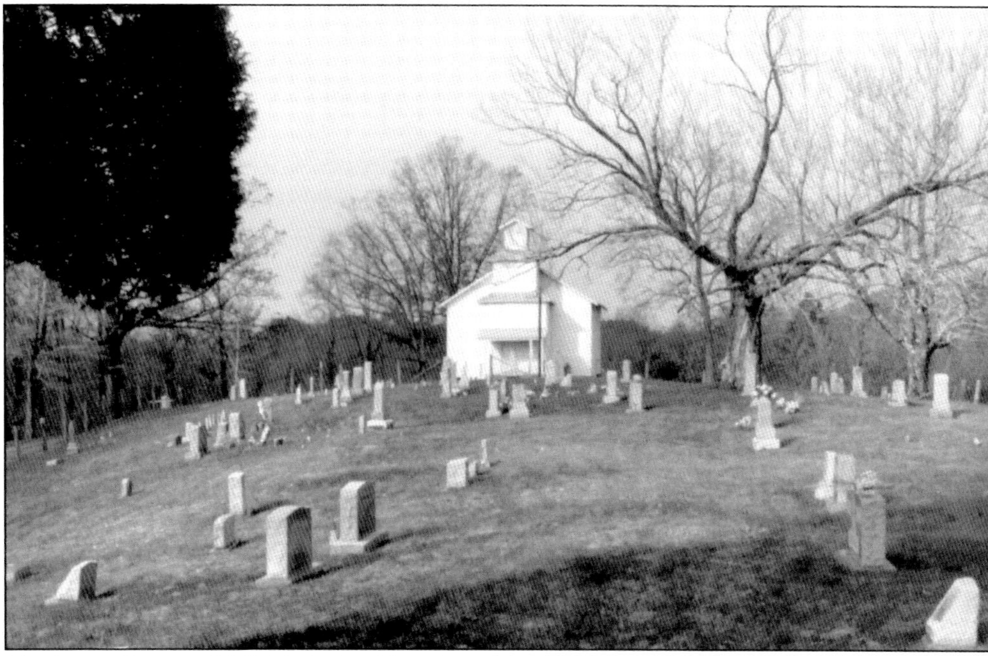

The Mount Herman (M.P.) Methodist Church was located on the waters of Mill Creek of the Pocatalico River in Harper District. The church was organized before 1900 and was the largest congregation of the Gandeeville circuit. For several years, it was one of the leading Methodist Protestant churches in the county. Services were discontinued in 1956. (Courtesy of Donna Walbrown.)

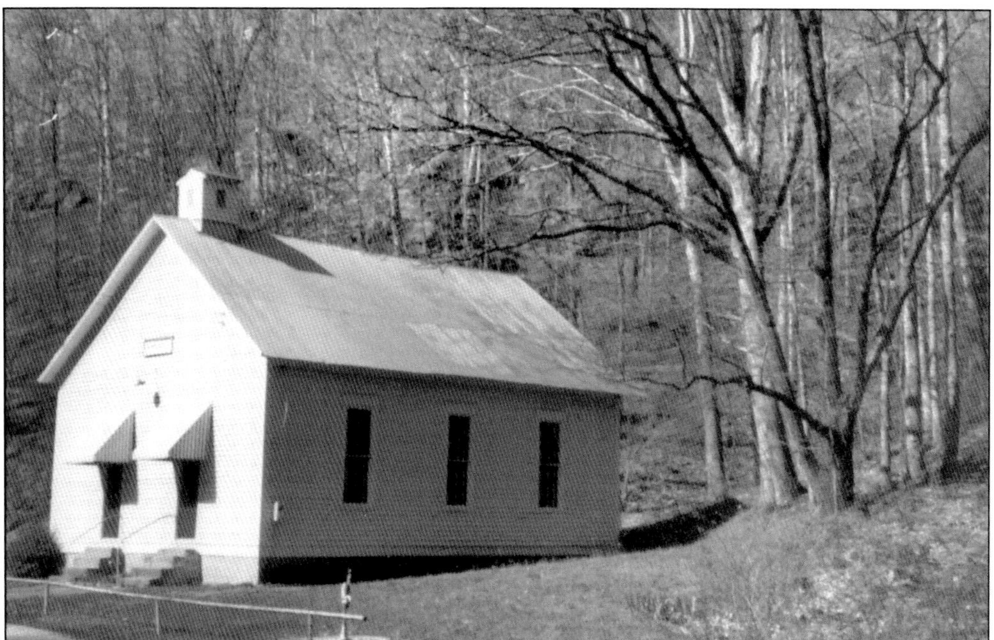

The Zion Methodist Church is located on State Route 36, about three miles southeast of Spencer. It began about 1866 in the home of Jeremiah Lewellyn. The first log church was built on his farm and was called the Spring Creek Chapel. A new church was built about 1885 on land deeded by J. G. and Ella Shilling and G. P. and M. K. Stone. (Courtesy of Donna Walbrown.)

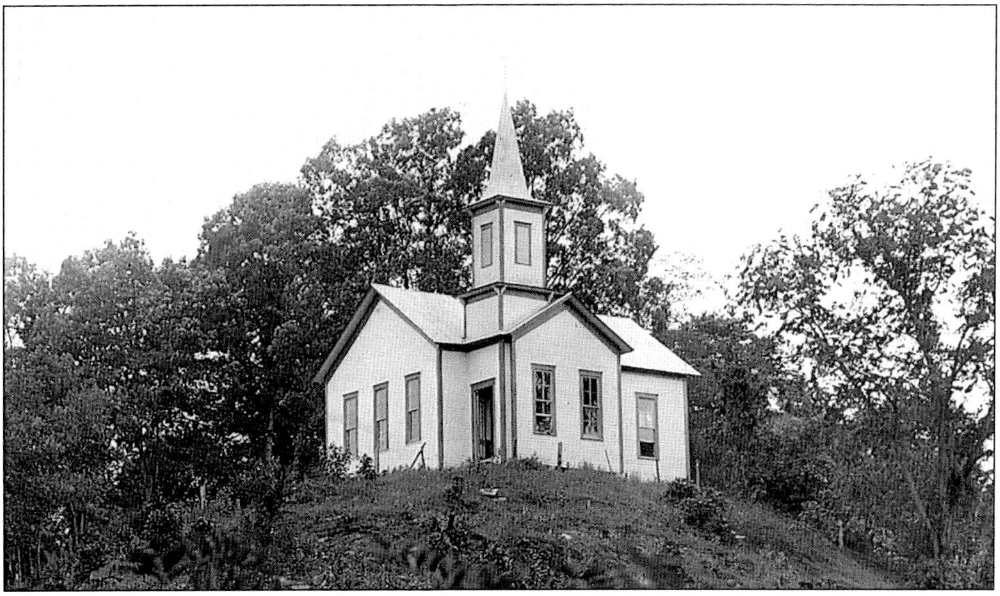

This Newton Methodist Episcopal Church is at least the second building housing the church. The oldest known Newton Methodist Church was located overlooking the village and is believed to have been built prior to 1880. That building would have been replaced by the building in this photograph. It was damaged by lightning and was torn down when the current church building was constructed in the 1950s on State Route 36. (Courtesy of Joyce Higginbotham.)

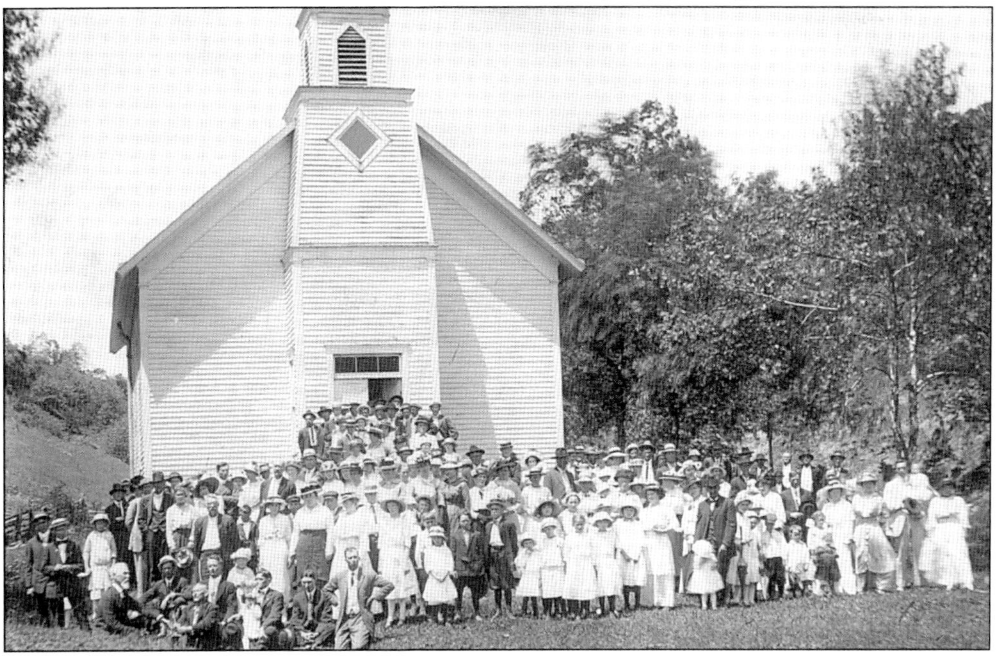

The Round Knob Union Church is located on Round Knob Creek of the Pocatalico River. This church was erected in 1911, and the deed specified that four denominations were to have use of the church. They were the Advent Christian Church, Methodist Protestant Church, Baptist Church, and Methodist Episcopalian Church. By 1956, a single pastor had been appointed to oversee the spiritual needs of the community. (Courtesy of Dr. Harry H. Camp Sr. family.)

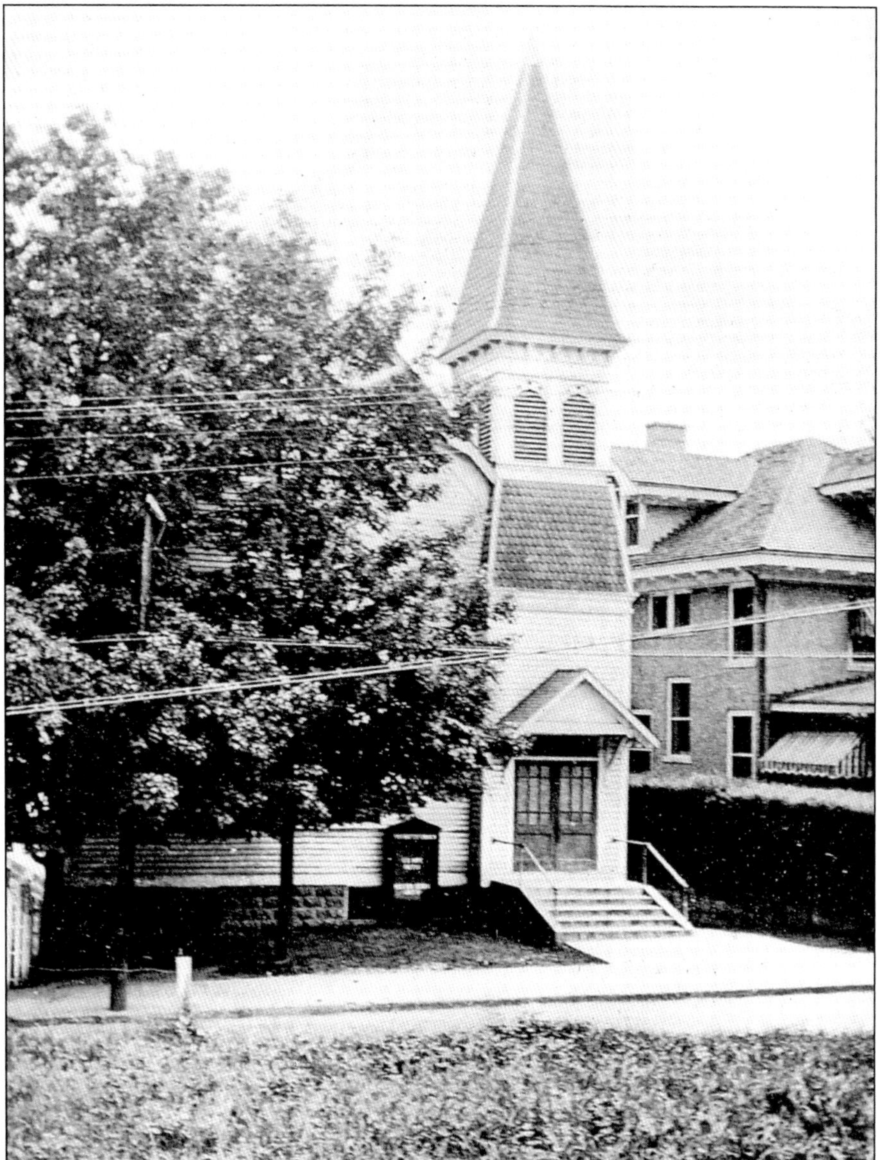

The First Baptist Church of Spencer traces its origins back to 1835 with Robert Tisdall as the founder. Members of the earliest recorded congregations included Elizabeth and Samuel Tanner, the first-known residents of Spencer. About 1860, the first established housing for the church known as the Spencer Baptist Church was constructed at the corner of Church and Main Streets. It was destroyed by fire in 1887. Services were held in other area churches until about 1891, when a lot was purchased from Martin W. and Rebecca Kidd, and the land deed located it "midway of the first square northwest of the courthouse and opposite Bishop Avenue leading to High Street." A new building was erected on this site, and the Spencer Baptist Church had a new home. The building was remodeled in 1924 and changes were made, including lengthening the original building and adding a basement. This building was torn down in 1961, and a new church building was erected on the site that is the present home of the First Baptist Church of Spencer. (Courtesy of Dr. Harry H. Camp Sr. family.)

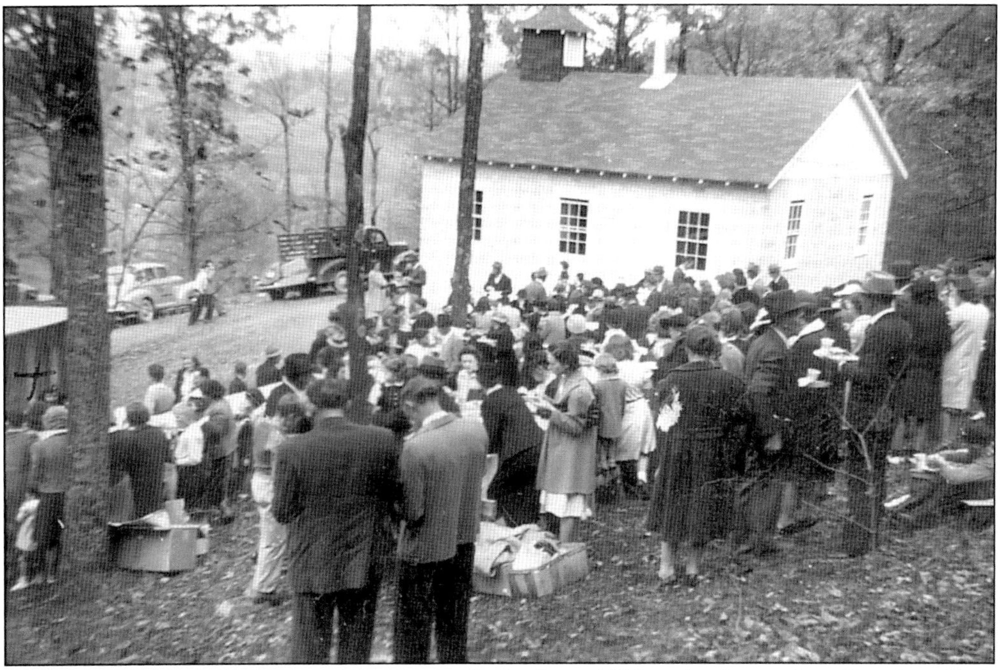
The Victory Advent Christian Church was built about 1929 and is located at Chambers Fork on the ridge between Rush and Clover Runs in Smithfield District on Banner Hill Road. The old Banner A.C. Church was built about 1905 on this site and was torn down and moved to its present location at Clover in 1928. (Courtesy of Donna Walbrown.)

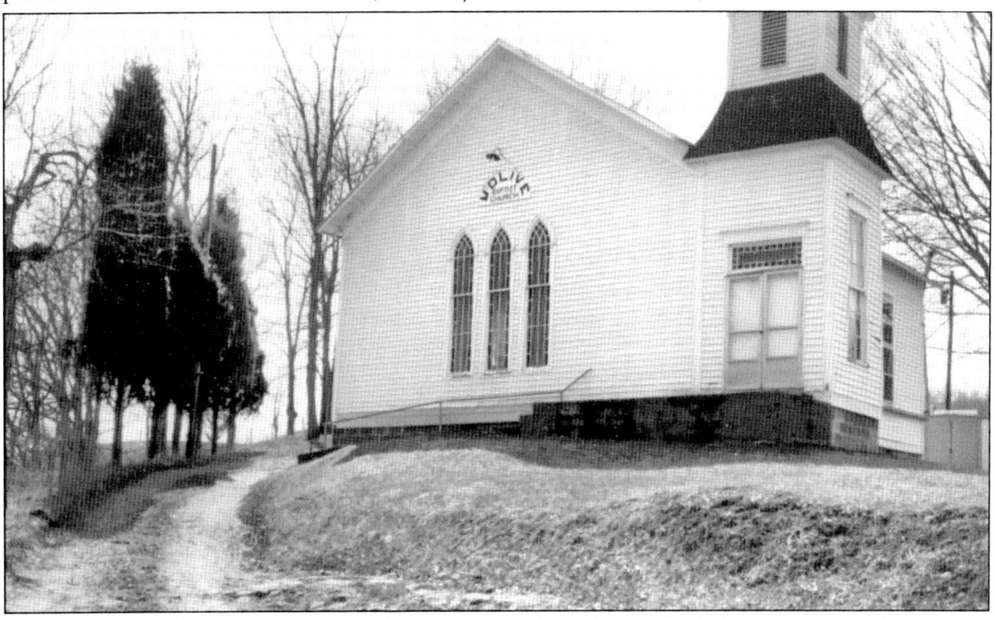

The Mount Olive Baptist Church is located on Tuckers Run of Left Reedy Creek and was built about 1888. The records show that this church had existed since 1856, and early meetings were held in a log house located at the intersection of Colt Ridge and U.S. Route 33. That building was destroyed, and the church relocated to the Thomasson School until the new building was completed. (Courtesy of Donna Walbrown.)

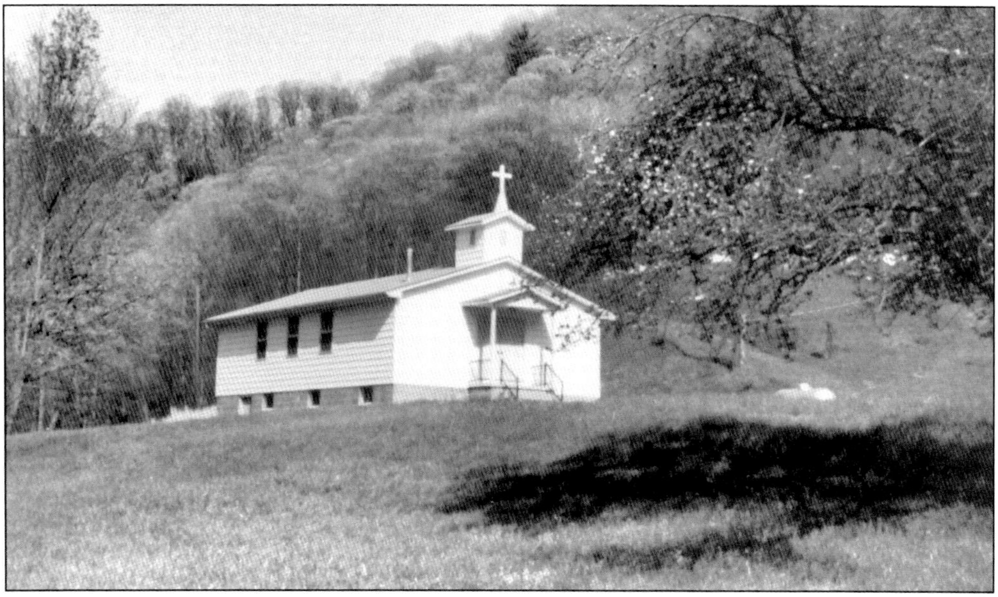

The Otto Advent Christian Church is located on Henrys Fork and dates from August 1919. The building was dedicated in 1925 as an Advent Christian church but welcomed all denominations. Over the years, the original building was updated and remodeled before burning in November 1981. A new building was constructed, furnished, and dedicated on May 30, 1982, and continues to serve the community and surrounding areas. (Courtesy of Donna Walbrown.)

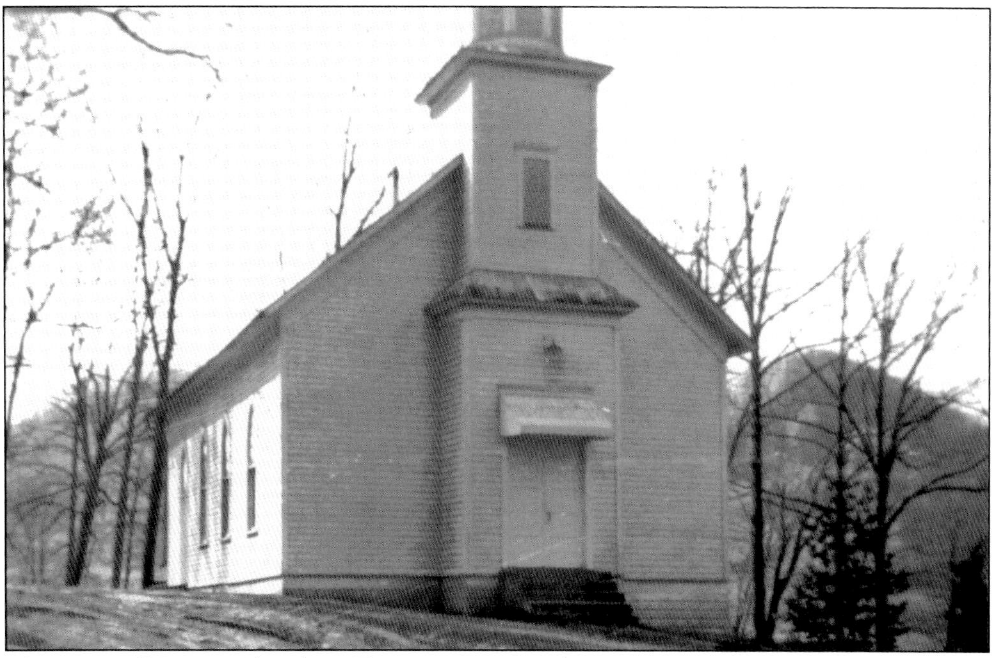

The Zion Hill Baptist Church in Elana was organized in 1848, and the congregation attended services in the Hollywood Baptist Church building near Uler until about 1914. Under the leadership of Rev. N. B. Hamrick, the first pastor of the new church, members joined with other residents of the Elana community to organize and build a church that they named Zion Hill Baptist Church. (Courtesy of Ruth Harold.)

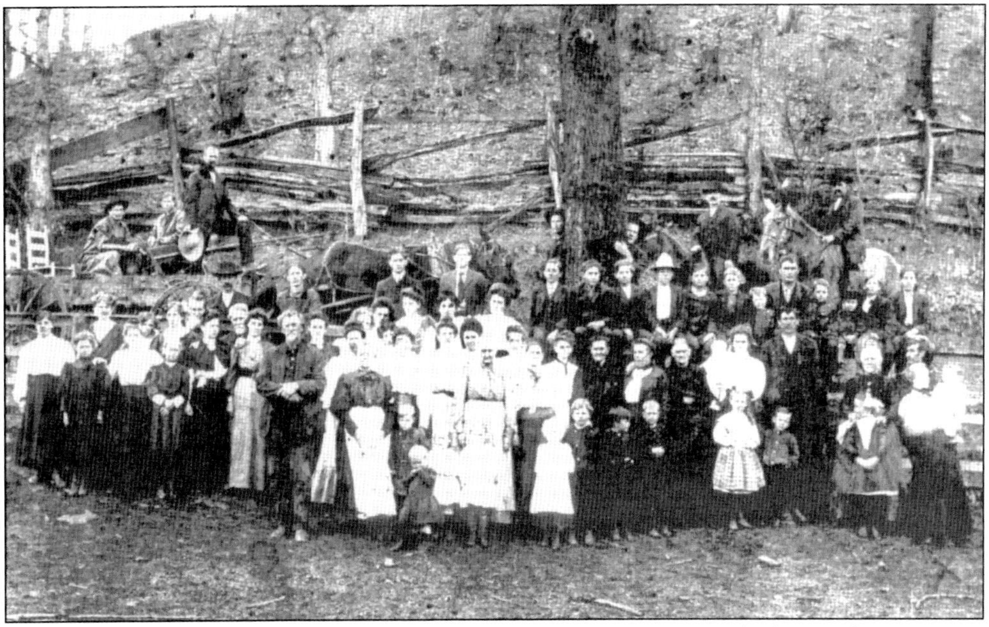

The Hollywood Baptist Church congregation first organized in 1848 at the home of James Keen. Services were held in the first Hollywood School building until a building could be erected near the Uler Post Office. The membership split in 1910 with one group organizing the Newton Baptist Church on April 12, 1910. Their new church building was completed on Hollywood Road in 1911. (Courtesy of Ruth Harold.)

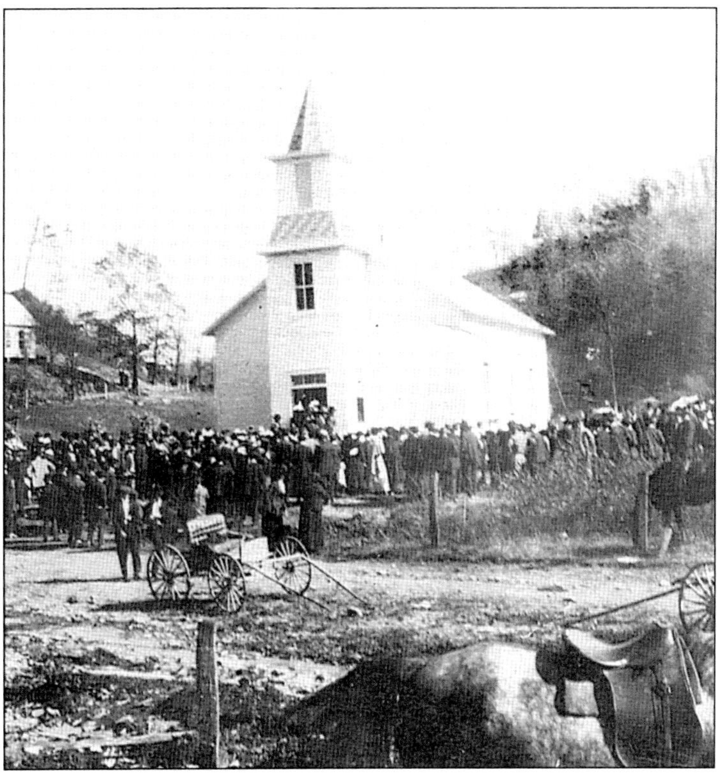

This is a photograph of the Slab Fork Church in Stringtown. (Courtesy of Jane [Taylor] George.)

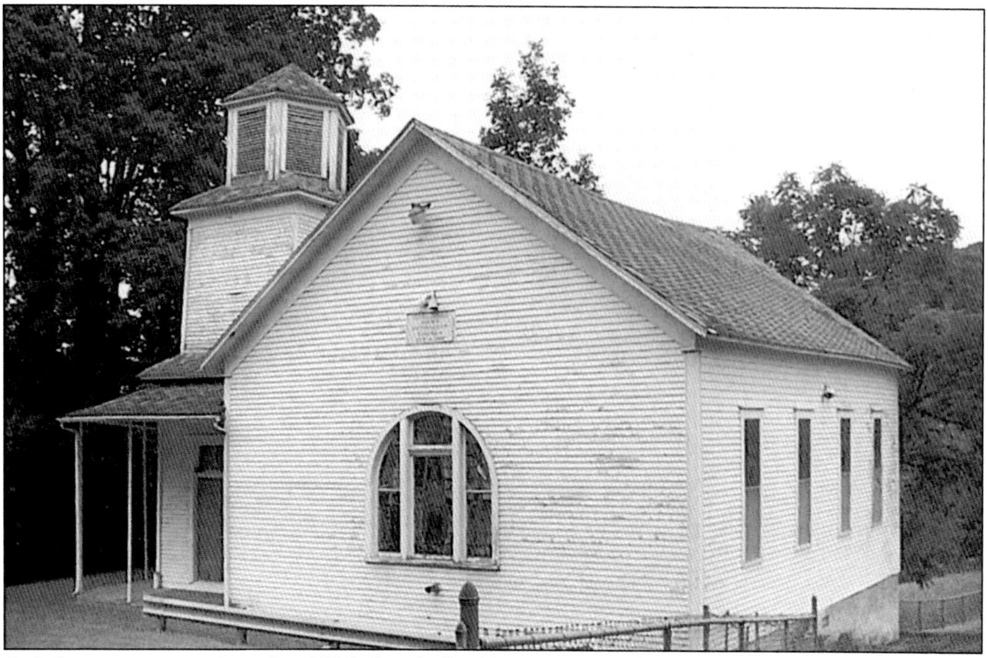

A dedication was conducted in 1905 after the building was erected on a lot conveyed to the trustees of the Amma Methodist Episcopal Church by John M. Geary and his wife, Phoebe. The land conveyed included a church lot and cemetery with tombstones dating back to 1886. The church survived for almost 100 years before closing for lack of membership. (Courtesy of Lisa Carper Stotts.)

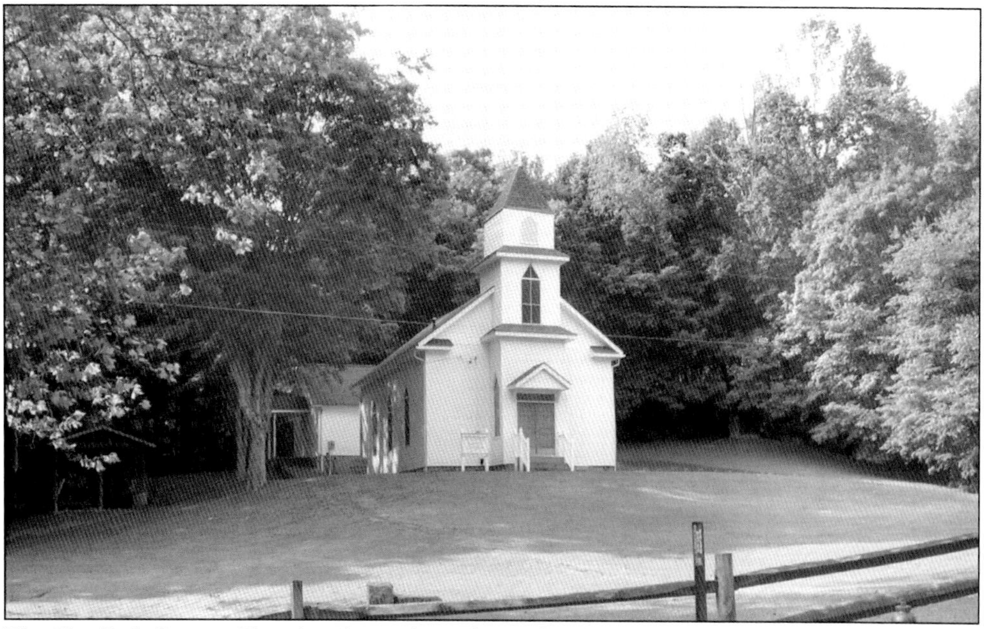

The Flat Fork Baptist Church is located on Flat Fork of the Pocatalico River and was the first church in Smithfield District. It was originally formed in 1842 with meetings held in the old log Flat Fork School. In 1875, a new frame church building served the church for many years until it was removed, and the present building was erected. It continues today and is one of the oldest churches in the county. (Courtesy of Jack Nida.)

Seven

COMMERCE AND INDUSTRY

In addition to the timber and oil and gas industries in Roane County, by the 1900s, there were other industries that were growing rapidly and contributing to the economy. Agriculture and livestock were increasing at a rapid pace in the rural areas, as manufacturing grew in the towns. Gristmills, sawmills, and tanneries were the early necessities of the new communities followed by the establishment of grocery and dry goods stores.

The two newspapers in Roane County, the *Times Record* and the *Roane County Reporter*, can trace their records back to the original publications in 1888 and 1877 respectively. These papers have pioneered many firsts in West Virginia and have accomplished many awards for their journalism. The first hospital in Spencer was built about 1901 by Dr. J. E. McQuain. The first resident physician of Spencer was Dr. Henry Nelson, who came to this area in 1855. He was also the first to engage in the mercantile business in the village of New California.

The Bank of Spencer was established in 1889, followed by the Roane County Bank in 1898. The Bank of Reedy (1902) was the third banking institution recorded in Roane County. Hamond H. Robey, the first to provide electric power in Spencer, established the first movie house in 1907, which he named the Nickelodeon. A new brick building was built in 1926 that houses the present Robey Theatre, one of the oldest continuously operating movie theaters in the country.

The first wholesale business in the county was a grocery business established about the year 1893 as the Wholesale Grocery Company. It was sold in 1903, and the Spencer Grocery Company was established in its place. Dr. Blackmore Thompson opened the first drugstore in 1868. In 1932, the Spencer Livestock Exchange began its operation, and the Spencer Department Store opened its doors in 1928. The Hardman Supply, second oldest business in Spencer, dates back to its inception in 1907. In June 1903, the De Gruyter Jewelry business was opened in Spencer. In the year 1914, Rex Arnott became the Chevrolet dealer and had been a Firestone Rubber Company dealer since 1908. Sam Simmons was a Plymouth and Dodge dealer established before 1920. Spencer Manufacturing Company, whose principal product was sweaters, began its operation in Spencer in 1948. Casto Rubber Company was producing rubber products as early as 1944 and would be sold to Monarch Rubber Company about 1948.

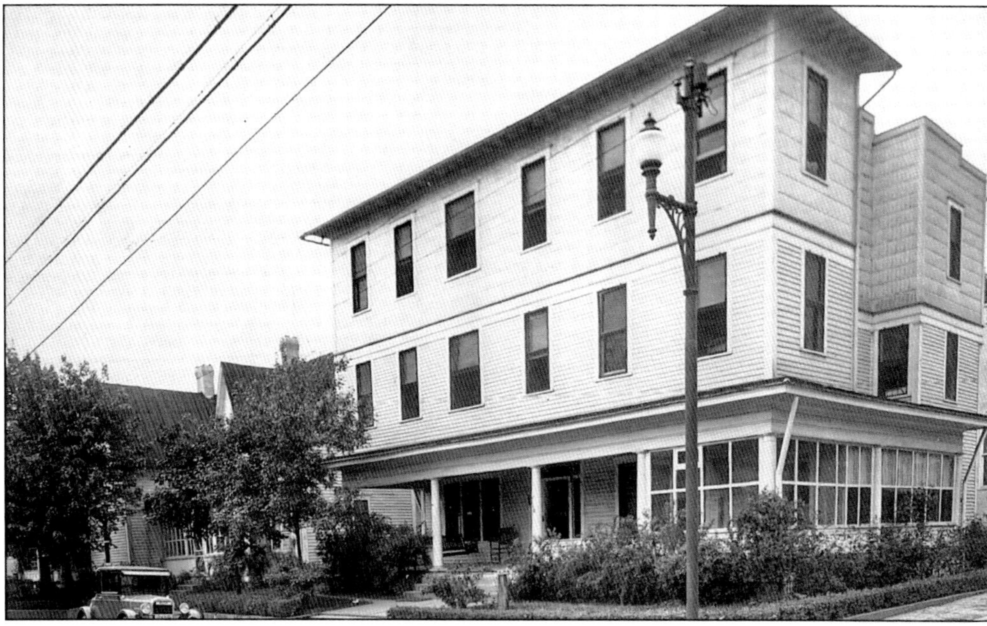

In 1921, Dr. A. T. Gordon and Dr. S. W. Bull purchased property known as the Lowe Hotel. The building was converted, and the City Hospital opened on June 20, 1921. In 1951, this facility was completely rebuilt, and the name was changed to Gordon Memorial Hospital. A nursing school was part of the institution from the beginning until 1950. (Courtesy of Dr. Harry H. Camp Sr. family.)

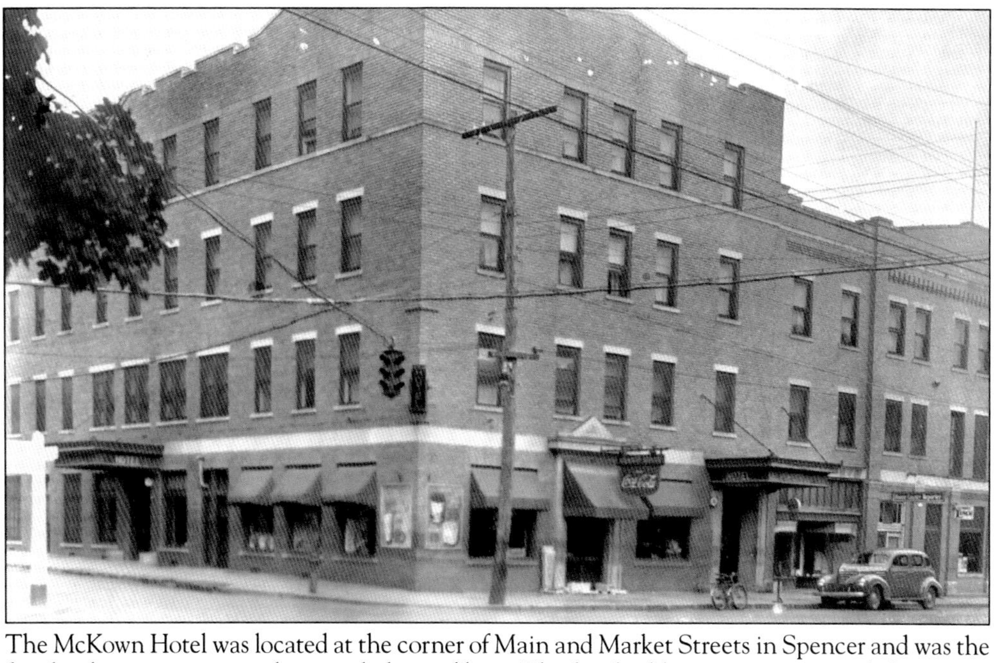

The McKown Hotel was located at the corner of Main and Market Streets in Spencer and was the first brick construction with water, light, and heat. The first building was constructed about 1903 and was known as the Grand Hotel, but it was destroyed by fire in 1914. It was sold to Ephraim W. McKown in 1915, enlarged to four stories, and called the McKown Hotel. It was later sold to the Lowe family. (Courtesy of Dr. Harry H. Camp Sr. family.)

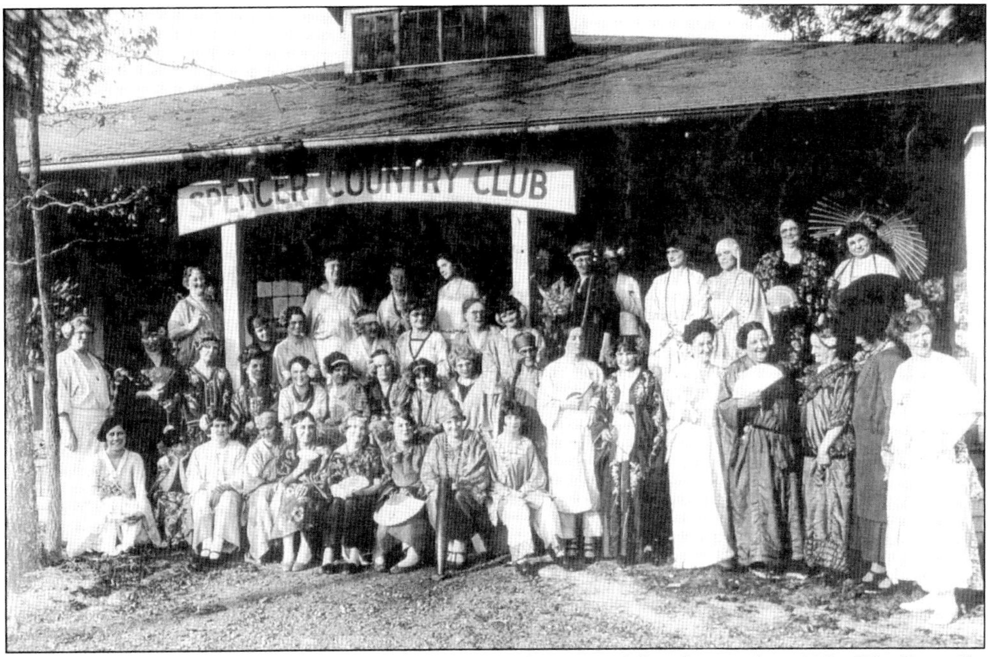

The Spencer Country Club was the site of many gatherings of the elite in the 1920s. The Priscilla Club, a ladies' group, was for many years the ultimate in Spencer society, especially for the matrons of the city. This photograph was a Japanese party given in the early 1920s by the club, and all members and their guests were attired in Asian costumes for the gala affair. (Courtesy of Bob and Patsy Welsh.)

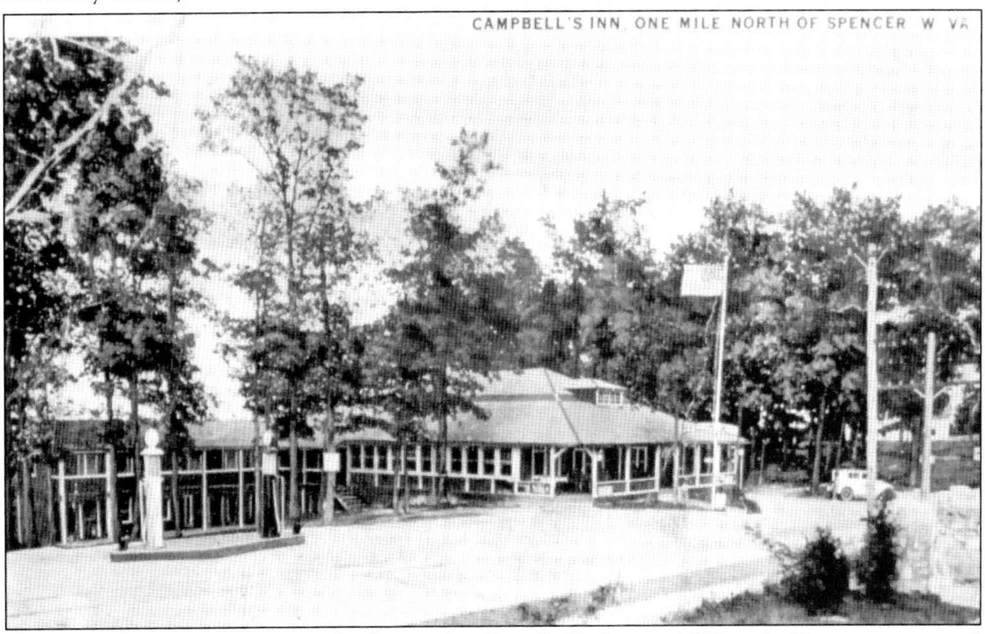

The Spencer Country Club evolved into the Campbell's Inn in 1927 with 17 tourist rooms, 2 dining rooms, and a dance floor. This brought a change in the clientele that frequented the new facility and provided a convenient location to conduct business for the local ladies of the night. (Courtesy of Bob and Patsy Welsh.)

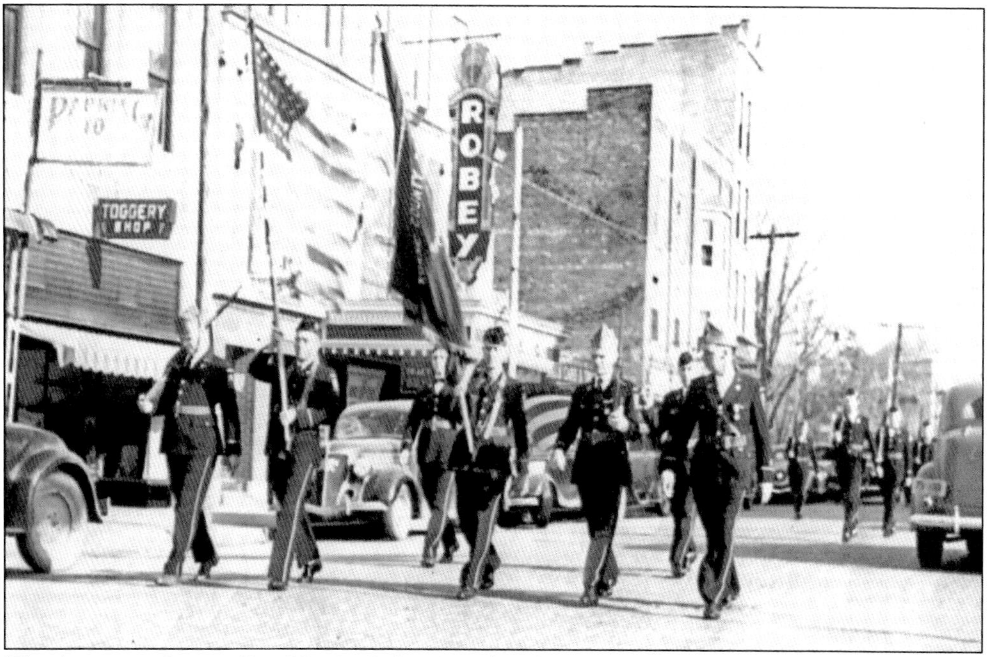

The American Legion Post No. 21 Color Guard and Legion members parade down Main Street in Spencer as part of the funeral procession honoring William Stine, the last Roane County Civil War veteran. He was born June 24, 1844, and died October 28, 1938, at 94 years of age. Capt. Harry Holswade leads the procession. (Courtesy of Carol Cronin.)

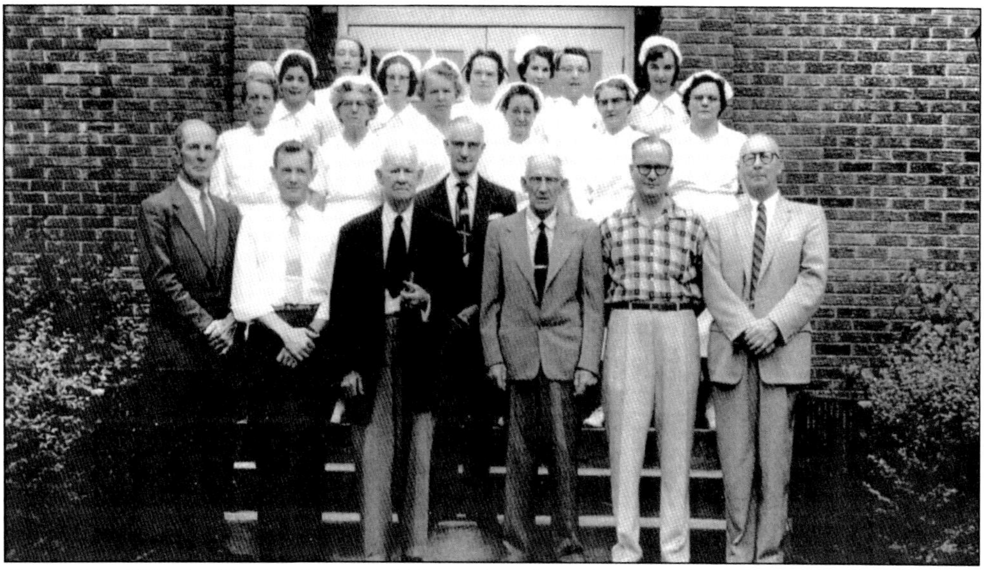

Pictured in 1956, the Gordon Memorial Hospital staff members from left to right are (first row) Dr. Rush C. Norman; Dr. Richard Brown; Dr. S. W. Bull; Rev. Carl A. Doddrill (hospital chaplain); Dr. A. T. Gordon (founder and superintendent); Dr. R. L. Calvert; and Dr. F. K. Stewart; (second row) Virginia Douglas, R.N.; Edna Stahlman, R.N.; Lucy Grant, G.N.; Stella Fleming, R.N.; Gladys Vineyard, R.N.; and Gayle Myers, P.N.; (third row) Yvonne Fields, S.N.; Hazeldean Gordon, R.N.; Madge Kendall, S.N.; Malissa Mace, R.N.; Dorothy McGrady, S.N.; Hester Brannon, R.N.; and Jean Lowther, S.N. (Courtesy of Carol Board.)

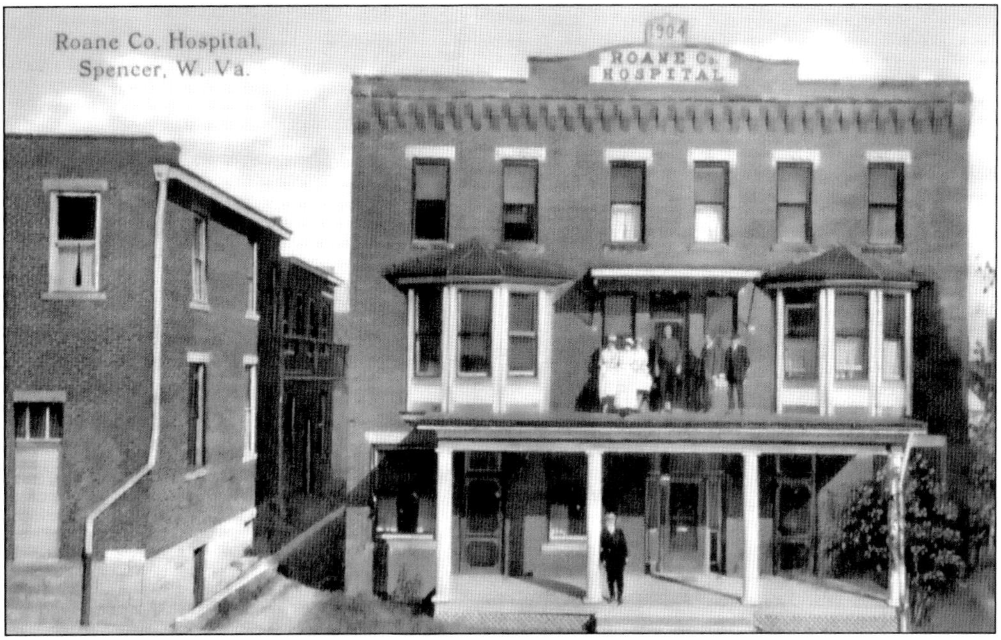

The Roane County Hospital was built before 1900 by Isaac I. Riley and was known as the Riley Hotel. In 1903, it was sold to Dr. Harlan H. Staats, who remodeled the building. The Roane County Hospital was later converted into the Lowe Hotel until 1929, when it was sold to Fred E. Vandale, and again the building was remodeled into a funeral home. (Courtesy of Carol Board.)

The Spencer Livestock Exchange was formed out of necessity as the number of farmers increased. In October 1913, one of the largest single shipments of cattle to date, 27 railroad carloads, left Spencer for Pittsburgh. The 4-H Clubs were increasing each year as education was required to improve the quality of the herds and maximize the profits for the farmers. (Courtesy of Fred Hardman.)

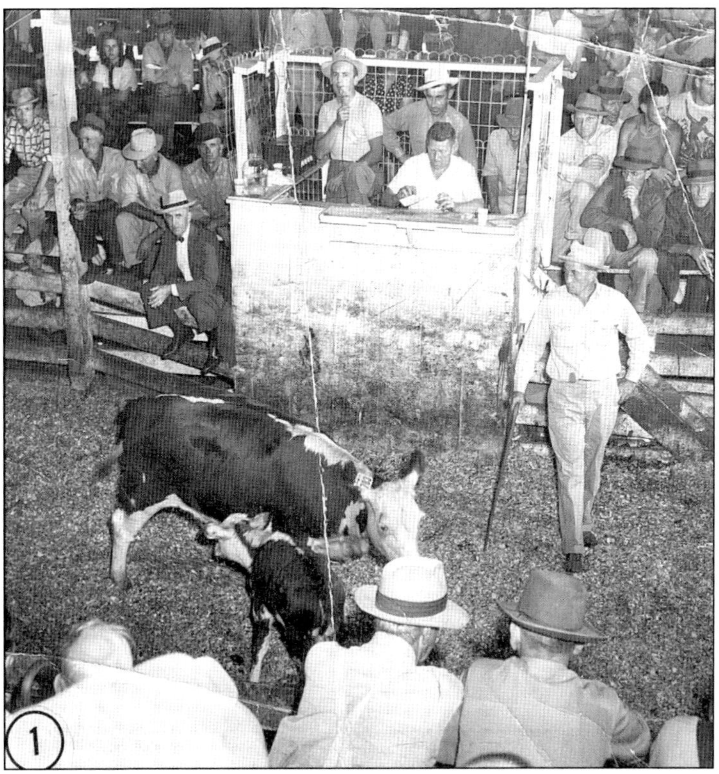

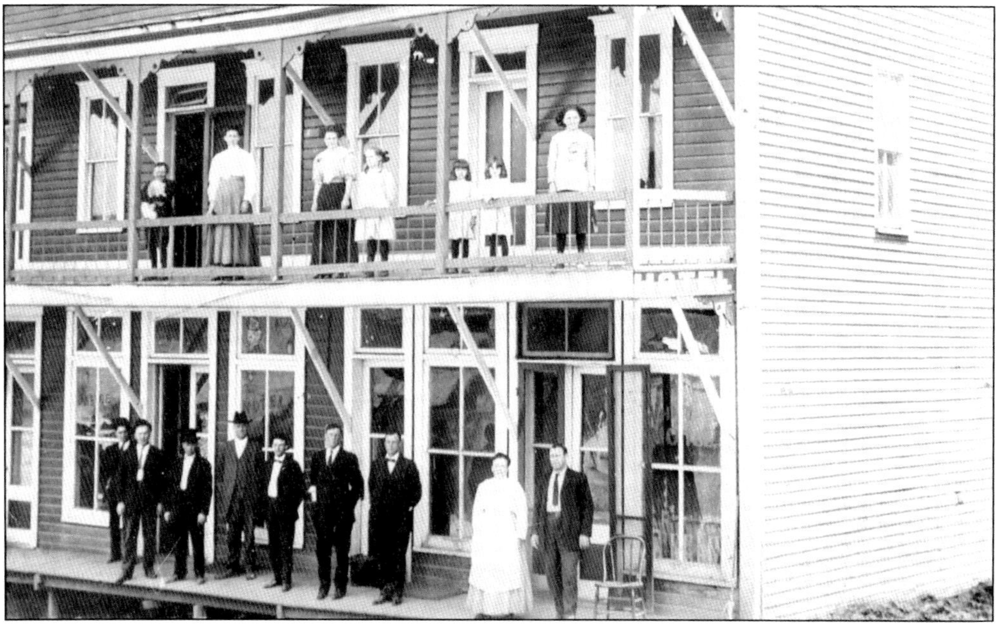

This hotel, owned and operated by John Whiting during the 1920s, was popular with railroad men, drummers, and other traveling men because of its proximity to the B&O depot. The Whiting Hotel was sold in 1934 to Dr. J. Marshall Depue, who remodeled the building and established the DePue Hospital, which opened for public service on November 16, 1934. (Ralph Nester Collection courtesy of Mark Sergent.)

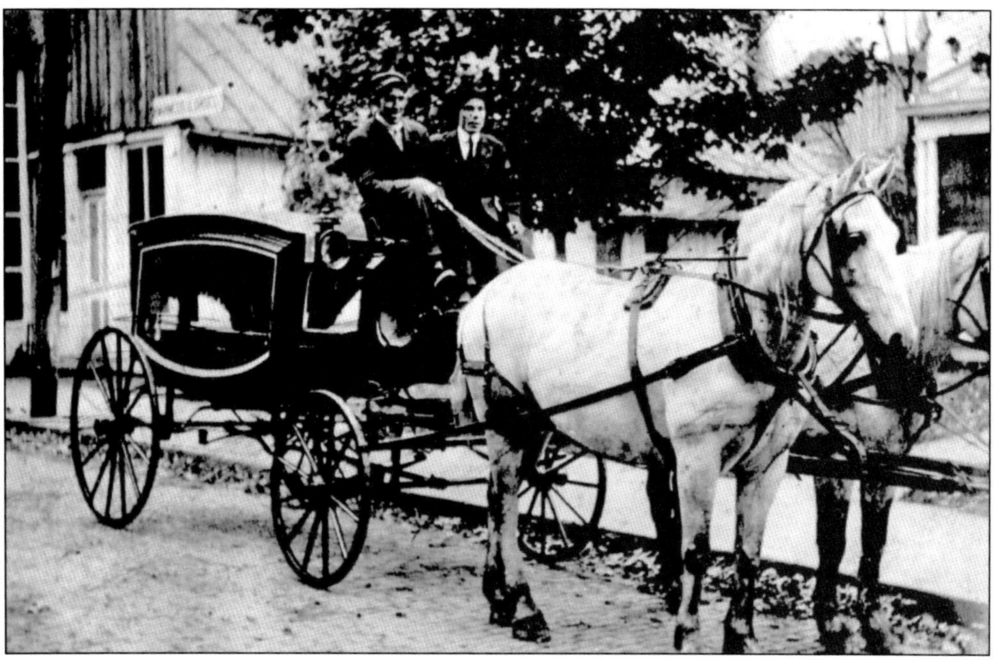

This photograph is typical of a funeral hearse in the early 1900s before the use of motorized vehicles became more common. It was owned by Vandale Funeral Home, and the drivers are identified as Jim Roberts (left) and Joseph Wolfe, both employees of Vandale Funeral Home in 1917. (Ralph Nester Collection courtesy of Mark Sergent.)

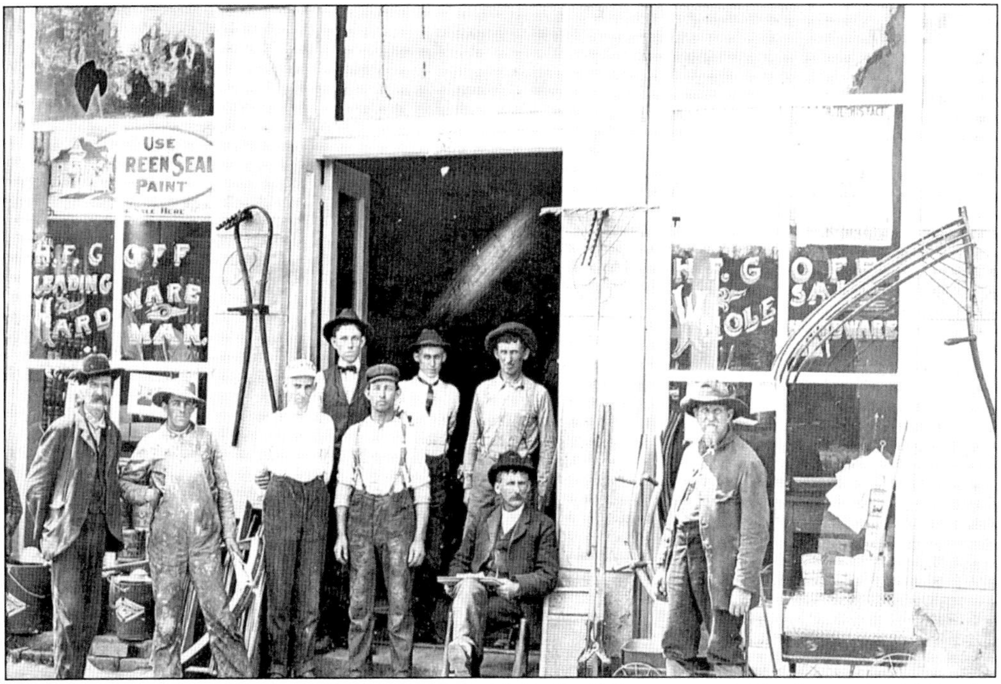

First listed among the merchants in 1898 as H. F. Goff Buggies and Hardware, by 1901, the name had been changed to H. F. Goff Hardware Company. (Ralph Nester Collection courtesy of Mark Sergent.)

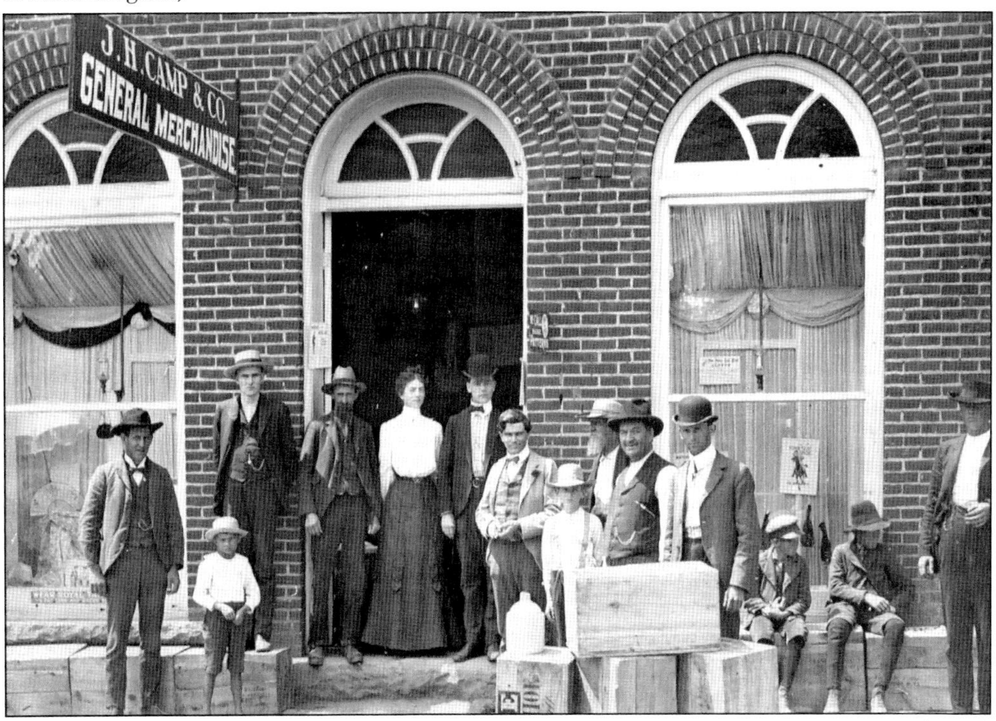

The J. H. Camp store started business in Spencer in 1896. It later became Camp's Dry Goods with Howard Camp as manager. (Ralph Nester Collection courtesy of Mark Sergent.)

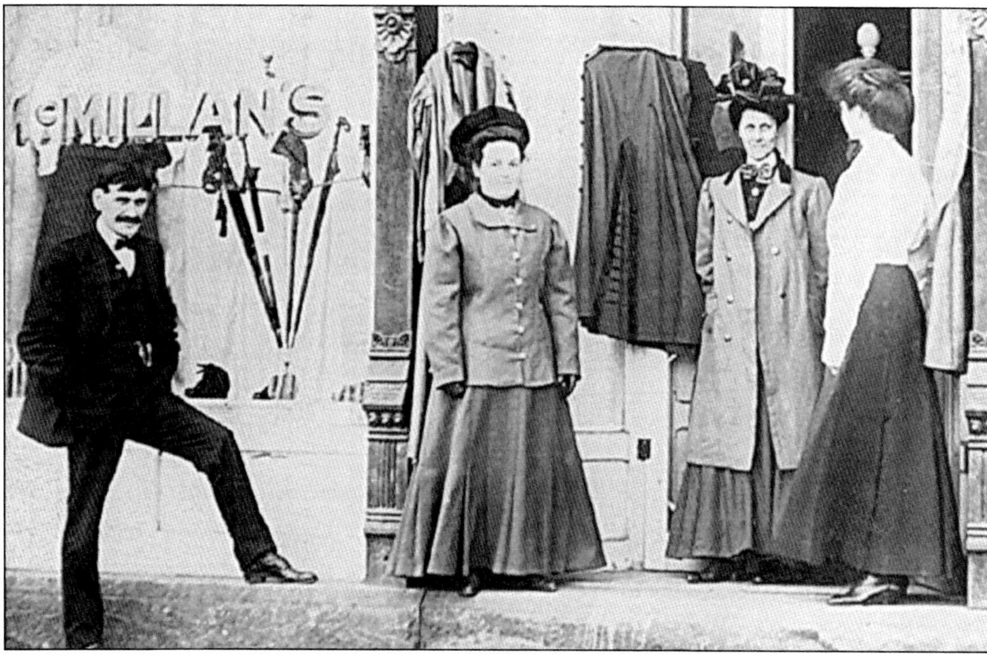

Orville McMillan operated the McMillan Ladies and Children's Wear store on this location until a fire in 1887 devastated the business section of Spencer and razed the original building. The above photograph is of the replacement building constructed after the blaze; however, it too was destroyed by fire on November 6, 1902. (Courtesy of Donna Walbrown.)

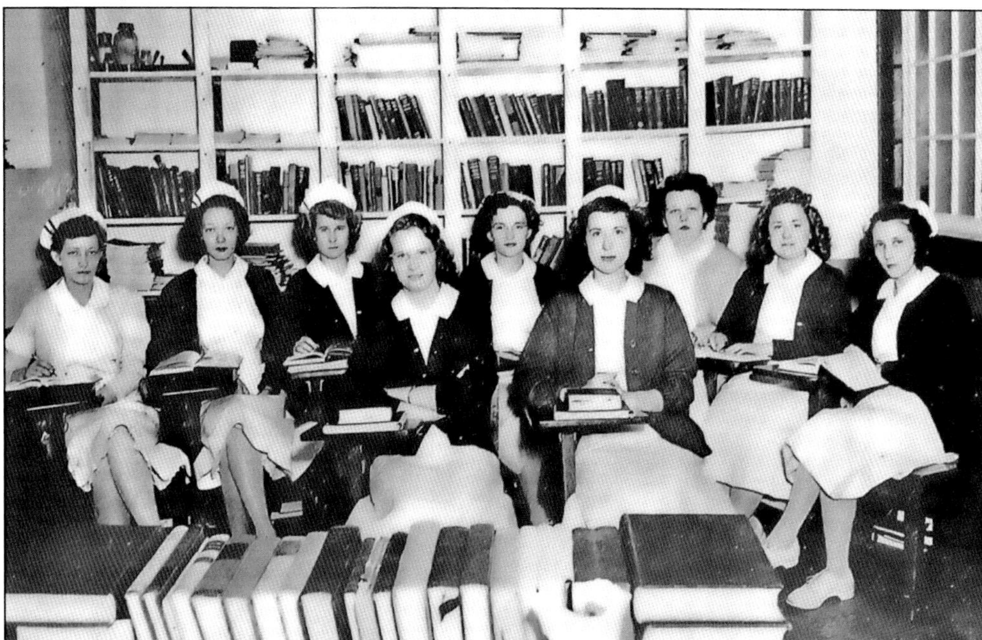

From the beginning of City Hospital, started by Dr. A. T. Gordon in 1921, until 1950, a nursing school was a part of the institution, with hundreds of girls from Roane and surrounding counties completing their training in this school and entering the nursing profession. (Courtesy of Carol Board.)

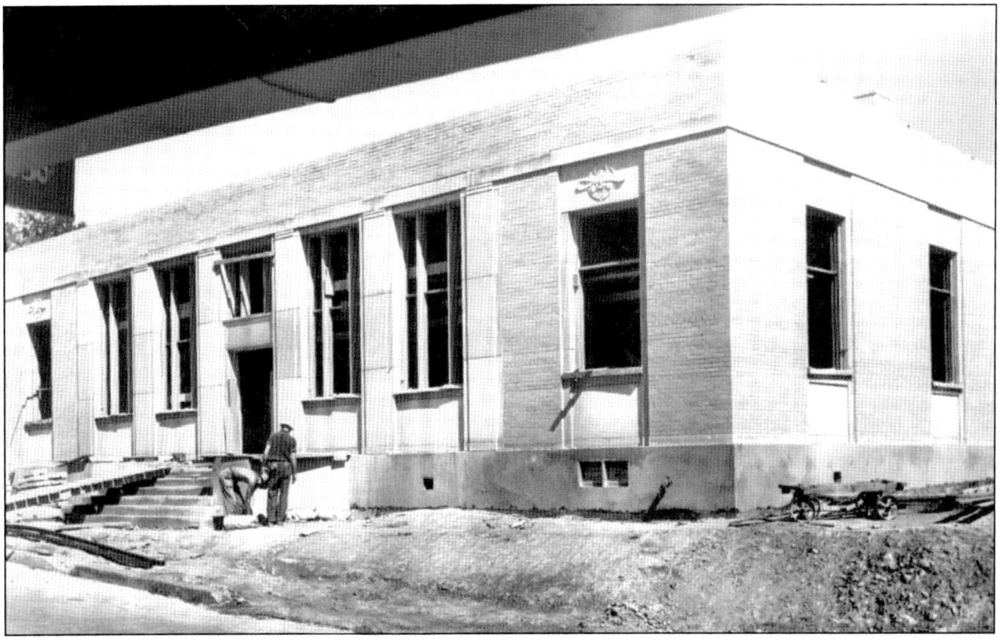

Prior to 1936, Spencer Post Office was housed in a building leased from H. D. and Cora Wells. In 1936, land was purchased for a new post office, and construction of the new building began in early 1937 and was basically completed by July 1937. The post office was moved into the new building the night of September 25, 1937, and was opened as usual on Sunday, September 26, 1937. (Courtesy of Carol Board.)

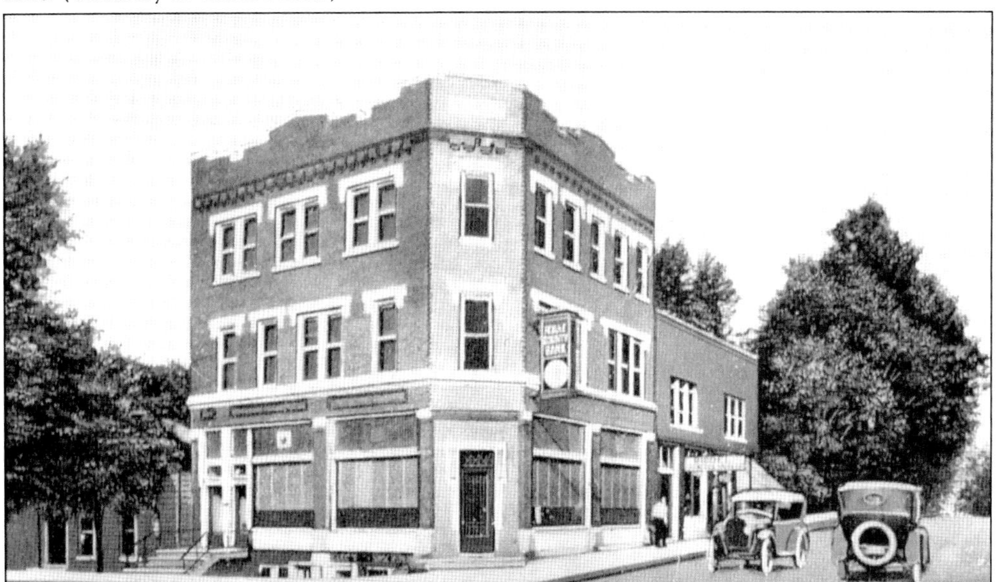

The Roane County Bank was the second bank established in the county. It first opened for business on August 8, 1898. In 1924, the Riddel Building on the northeast corner of Main and Church Streets was purchased and converted into banking quarters. It continued in this location until 1949, when its assets were sold to the First National Bank of Spencer, and the two banks merged. (Ralph Nester Collection courtesy of Mark Sergent.)

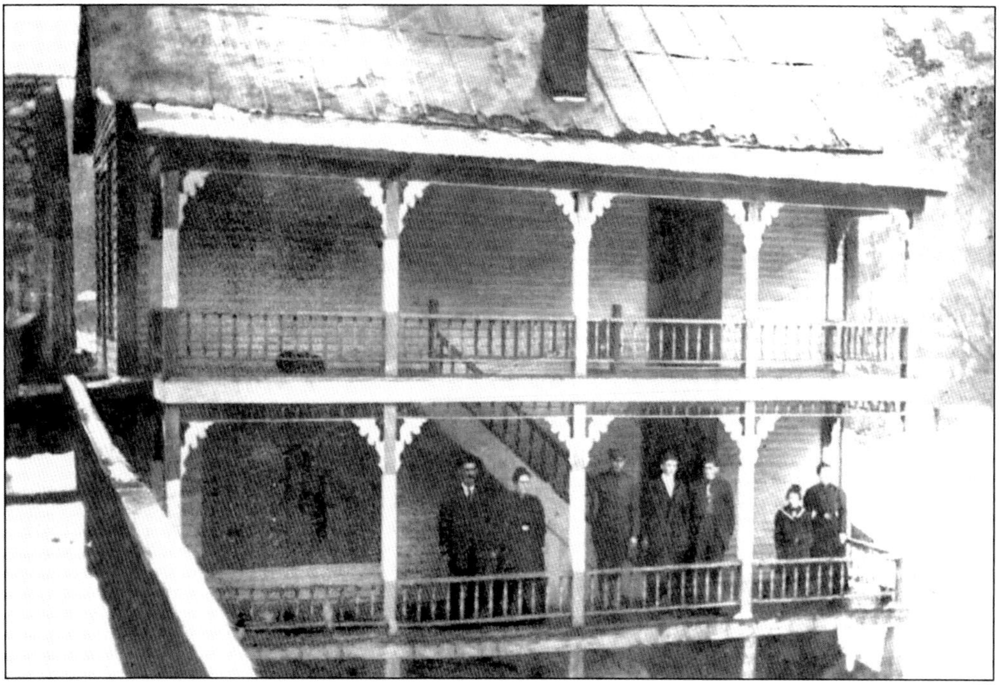

The Rogers Hotel was located in Newton and owned by Bennett Milton Rogers. It burned about the year 1903. (Courtesy of Marilyn Erion.)

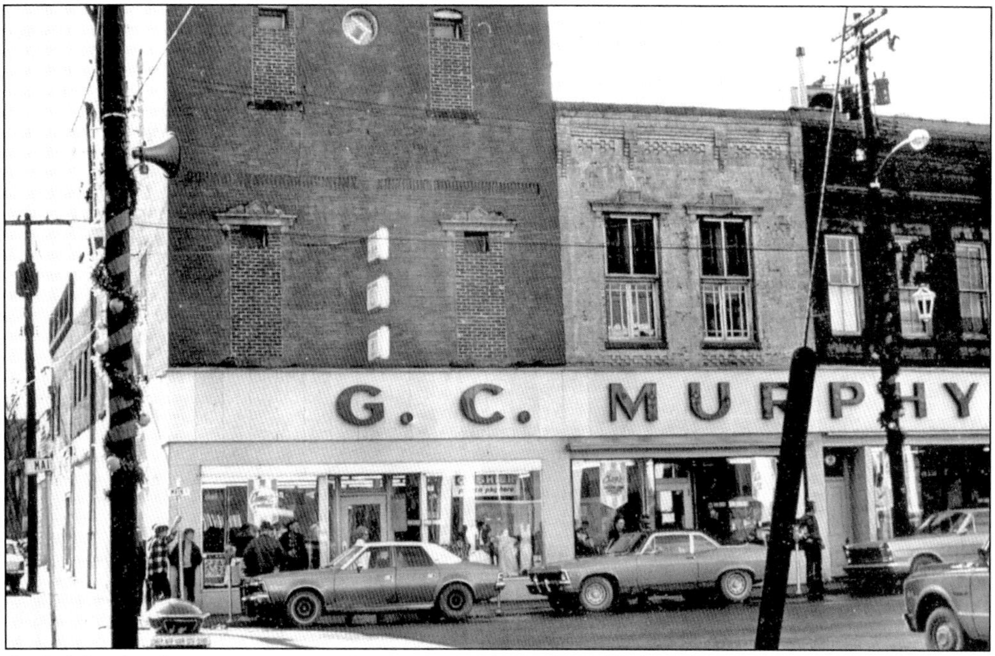

G. C. Murphy Company came to Spencer in 1936 and established their variety store business on Main Street. It opened November 14, 1936, with a sales force of eight clerks and Edward H. Hughes as the first manager. The store had a tremendous growth and by 1956 employed 26 regular clerks and an additional force of 18 clerks utilized during the holiday season. (Ralph Nester Collection courtesy of Mark Sergent.)

Eight

People of Interest

Any history of Roane County would not be complete without recording the part played by Jesse Hughes, noted guide, scout, hunter, and pioneer, whose exploits of the early days have become legends in this section of West Virginia. There are two principal reasons for giving recognition to this hardy pioneer. First this intrepid Indian fighter carried reports back to Harrison County that were responsible for the settling of Spencer and its adjacent territory. The second reason is that his daughter, Massie Hughes, married Uriah Gandee, for whom the village of Gandeeville is named.

Jesse Hughes was, no doubt, one of the most successful Indian fighters who ever lived. The famous 19th-century historian Reuben Gold Thwaites observed, "Hughes was a noted border scout, but a man of fierce, unbridled passions, and so confirmed an Indian hater that no tribesman, however peaceful his record, was safe in his presence." More importantly, Hughes was also a common man, dressing, equipping, and conducting himself in a manner appropriate to his time period, familiar and recognizable to the common people of the Virginia border lands. He died in western Virginia in the fall of 1829. The early settlers of Roane County owe a huge debt of gratitude to this man of the forest and the path that he created for each of them as they brought a new civilization to this part of the world.

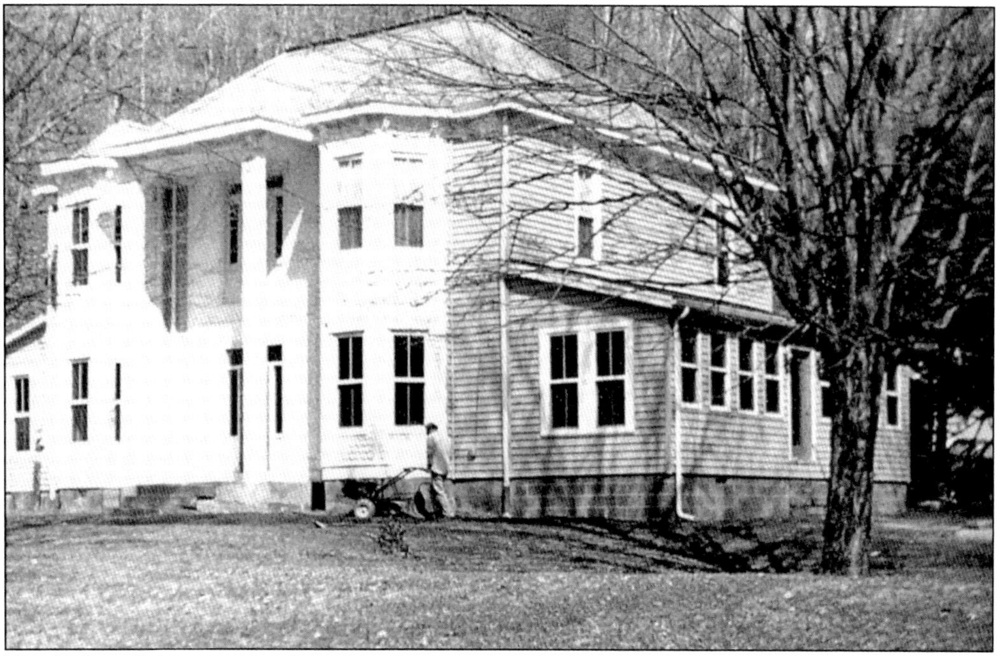

The Robert E. Lee Looney house on Sycamore Fork near Tariff was built by Sherrod Miller in 1908. Everett and Jeanette Moore resided in this house and sold it to Port Looney when they moved to Spencer. This is often called the Porter and Bess Looney house. It was restored in the 1980s. (Courtesy of Philip Crane.)

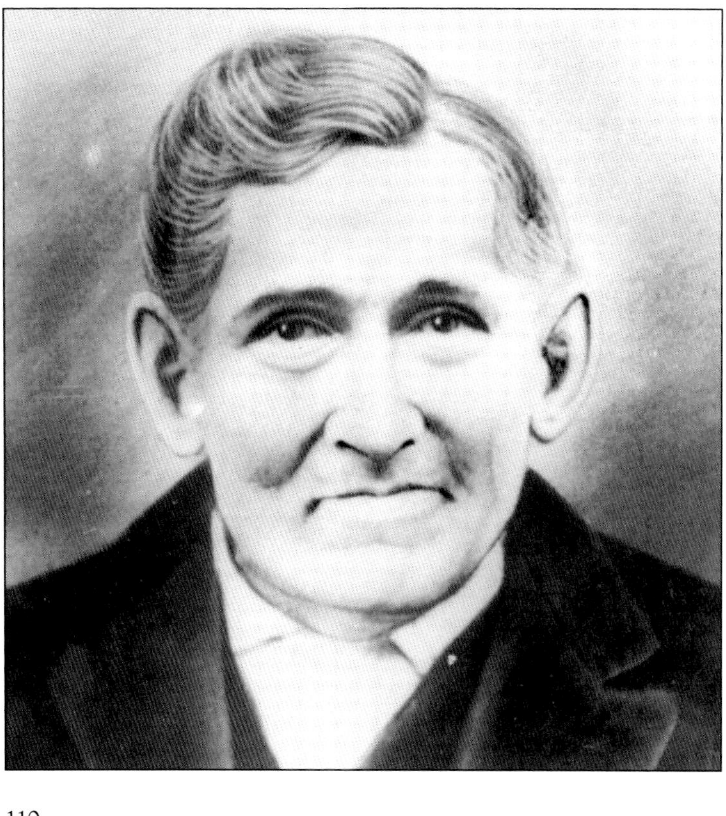

Peter Looney Sr. was born March 28, 1823, in Tazewell County, Virginia, a son of Robert and Catherine Stover Looney. Peter came to what is now Roane County in 1839 with his parents. He married Charity Vineyard in Kanawha County on February 22, 1844. Peter owned a large farm at the head of Canoe Run. (Courtesy of Philip Crane.)

Daniel Looney was born January 8, 1827, in Tazewell County, Virginia, a son of Robert and Catherine Stover Looney. He married Jeanette Ann Caldwell on April 1, 1849, in Kanawha County. Daniel owned a large farm and raised livestock on Sycamore Fork of Henrys Fork. He died December 30, 1883. (Courtesy of Philip Crane.)

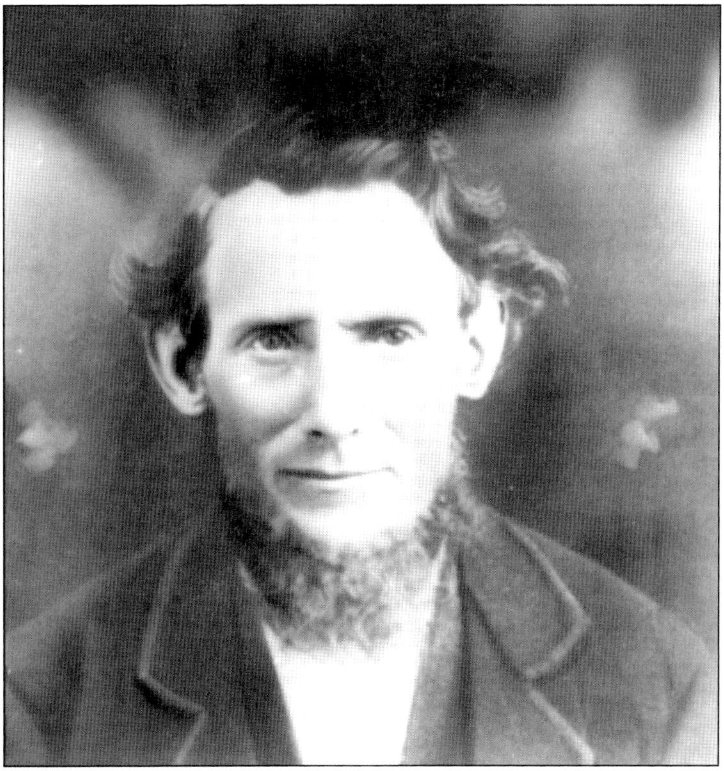

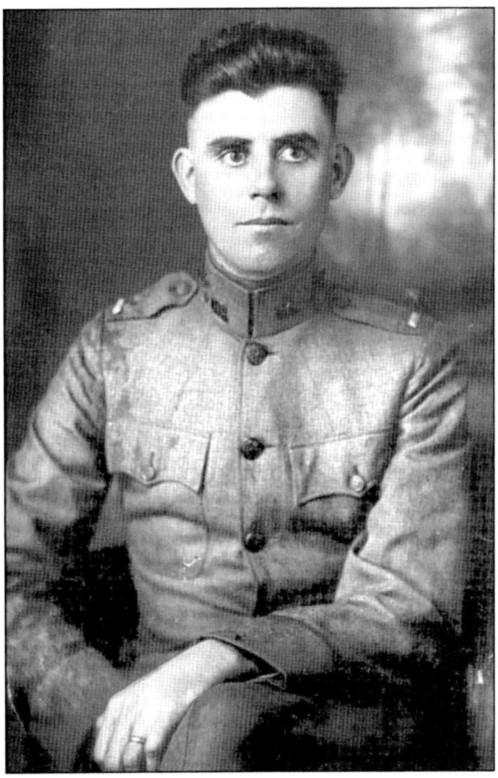

This is a picture of Fred E. Wright in his World War I uniform. In late 1920 or early 1921, he purchased the Phil D. Phillips Drug Store site in the Petty Building with entrances on both Main Street and Market Street and renamed it the Sinnett and Wright Drug Store. This business flourished for nine years until destroyed by fire on November 2, 1929, and was never rebuilt. (Courtesy of Dr. Harry H. Camp Sr. family.)

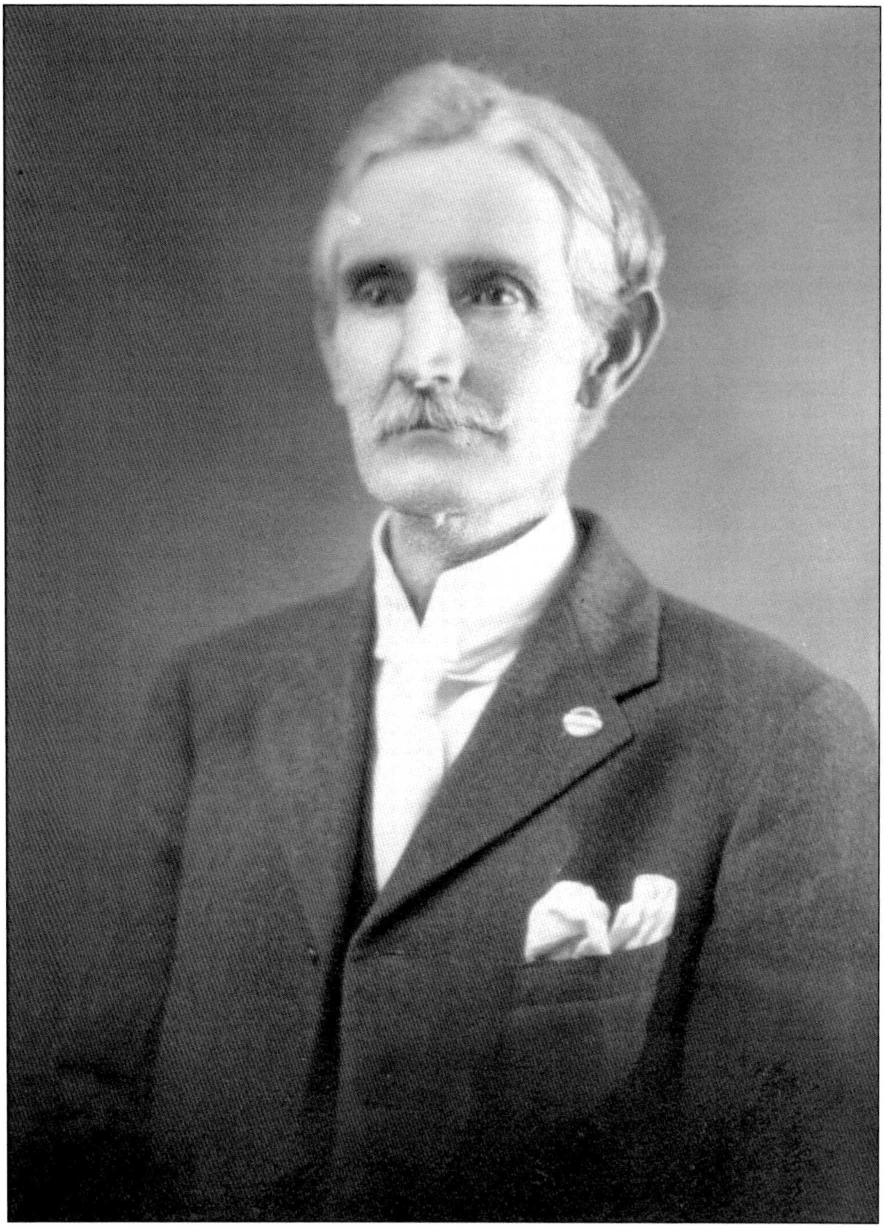

William Henry Bishop was born at Murrayville, Ohio, on December 14, 1860. He attended school in Ohio until the family moved to Reedy, West Virginia, where he attended subscription schools. He became a schoolteacher in Roane County, was principal of the town of Spencer schools from 1884 to 1885, studied law at Spencer under John G. Schilling and J. W. C. Armstrong, and was admitted to the bar in 1885. He attended Peabody Normal at Nashville, Tennessee, in 1886–1887 and was an instructor of civilization to the Jicarilla Apaches of New Mexico for over three years before returning home to practice law in Spencer in 1890. He married Gertrude Duling on July 7, 1892, was elected and served one term as prosecuting attorney for the county, and was a delegate in the state legislature for one term. He is the author of two books on state municipal law and *History of Roane County West Virginia, 1774–1927.* He also served as mayor of Spencer for at least two terms in 1894 and 1897. (Courtesy of Dr. Harry H. Camp Sr. family.)

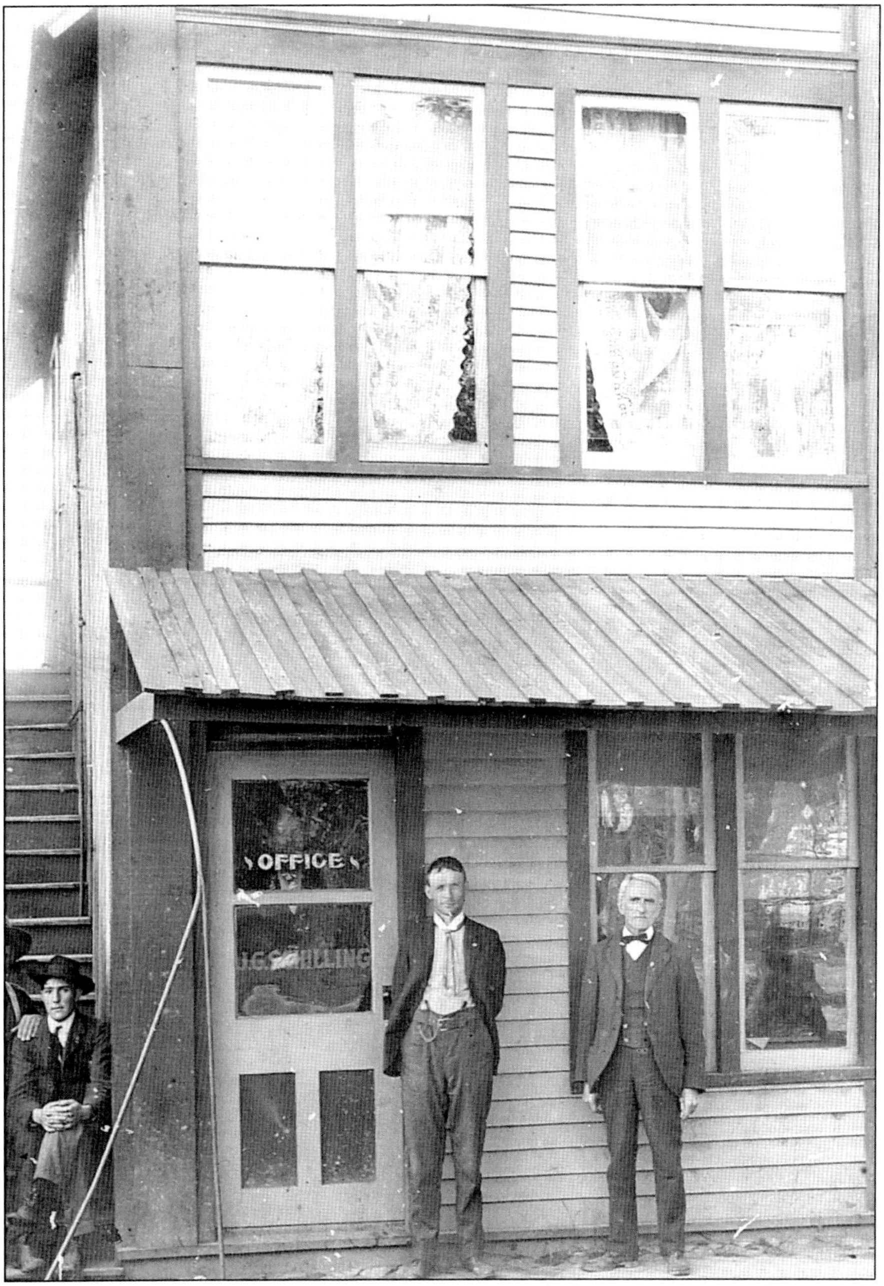

This was the law office of Judge J. M. Harper and J. G. Schilling in Spencer. John G. Schilling began his practice in Spencer before 1870 and was elected to a four-year term as county prosecuting attorney. It was in Schilling's offices that many students studied for careers as lawyers. He was elected as a delegate to the 26th State Legislature in 1903 and died at his home in Spencer in 1905 at age 69. Judge Jacob M. Harper started his law practice in Spencer in 1901 and was still practicing law in 1956. He served as county prosecuting attorney from 1924 to 1936 and was appointed judge of the Fifth West Virginia Judicial Circuit on July 8, 1956. This was the first time in the history of the county that a resident attorney from the county has held this high post. (Ralph Nester Collection courtesy of Mark Sergent.)

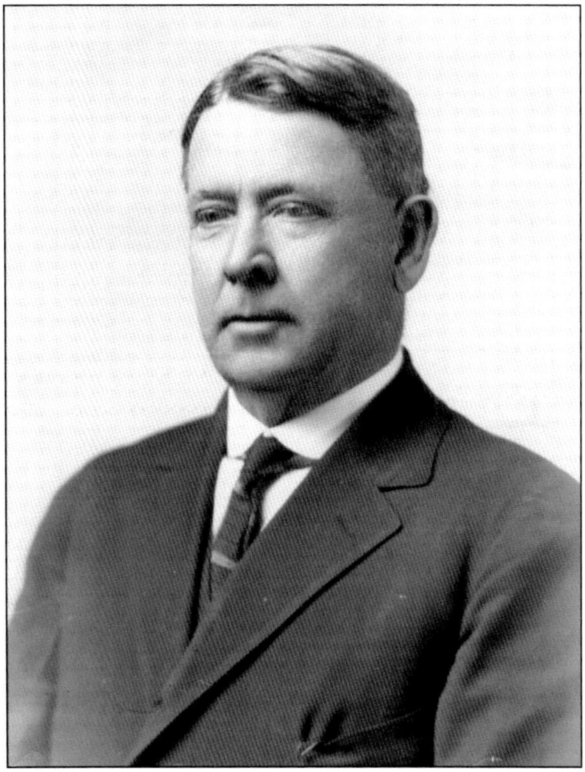

Amos E. Kenney was an attorney and mayor of Spencer in 1902–1903. During his term, the community of Alvord pulled away from Spencer over a much-disputed question of liquor sales. In 1903, Alvord was incorporated and held its first election. (Courtesy of Dr. Harry H. Camp Sr. family.)

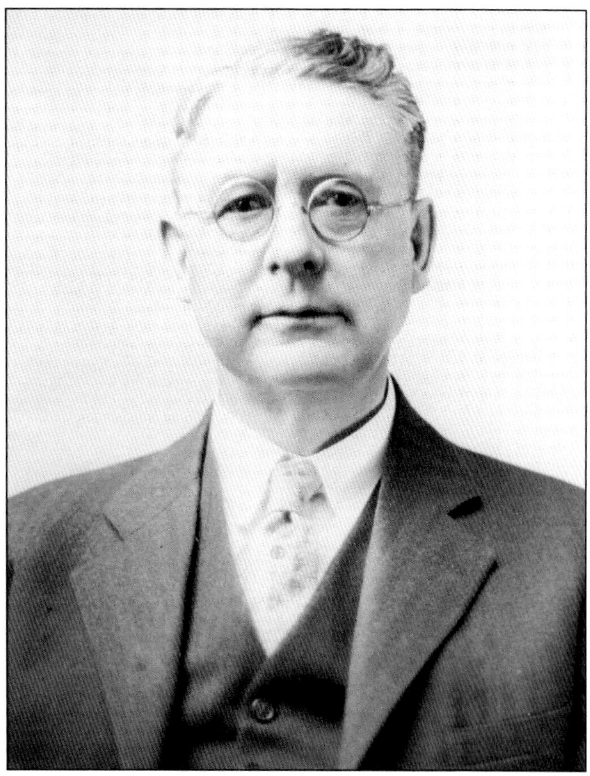

Born in Grantsville, West Virginia, in 1870, S. Paris Bell married Ona Stump from Gilmer County. Her ancestors were the first settlers of central West Virginia. He was an attorney and was the mayor of Spencer in 1921. He was a charter member and president of Spencer Rotary Club. (Courtesy of Dr. Harry H. Camp Sr. family.)

Dr. Holly L. Casto was a physician and surgeon in Spencer, a son of Charles C. and Margaret Casto. He was one of the officers of the Roane County Medical Society. (Courtesy of Dr. Harry H. Camp Sr. family.)

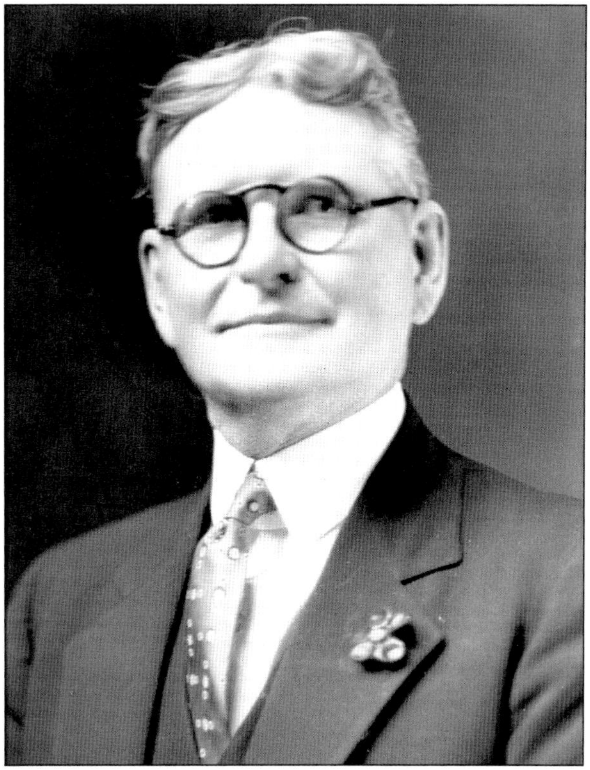

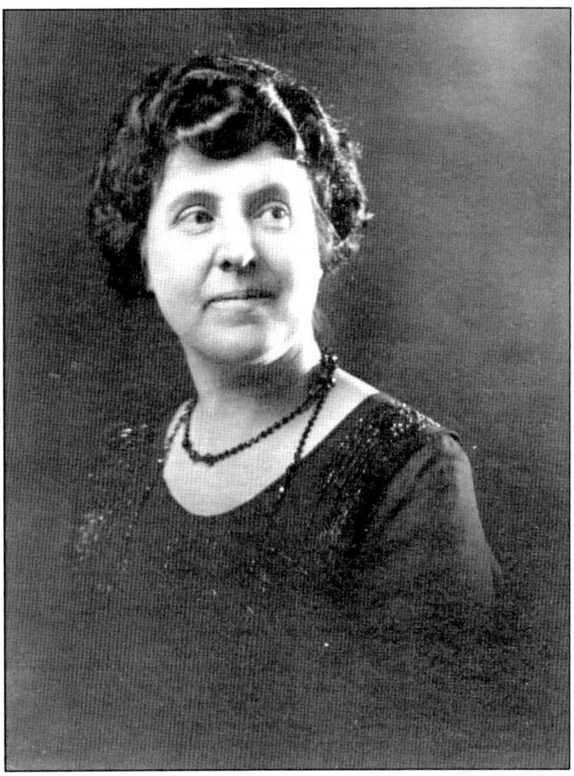

Mary (McMahon) Casto was the wife of Dr. Holly L. Casto. They were married in 1906, and May, her daughter by her first husband, married Frederick McIntosh Jr., a local businessman. (Courtesy of Dr. Harry H. Camp Sr. family.)

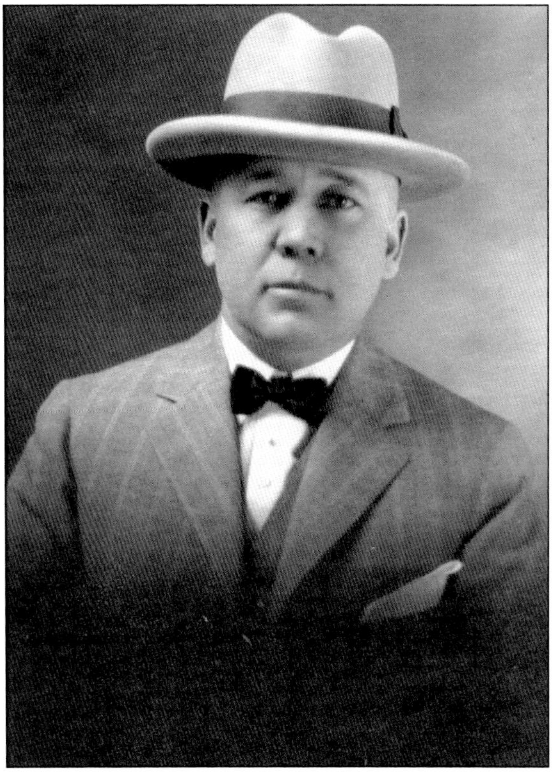

Mark Edward Hersman was a banker, oil and gas operator, schoolteacher, and mayor of Spencer in 1924–1925. He and John M. Looney formed the Roane County Progress Party because of a split with the Republican Party. He was a preacher of the Methodist Protestant faith and was a member of what is now the Memorial United Methodist Church. (Courtesy of Dr. Harry H. Camp Sr. family.)

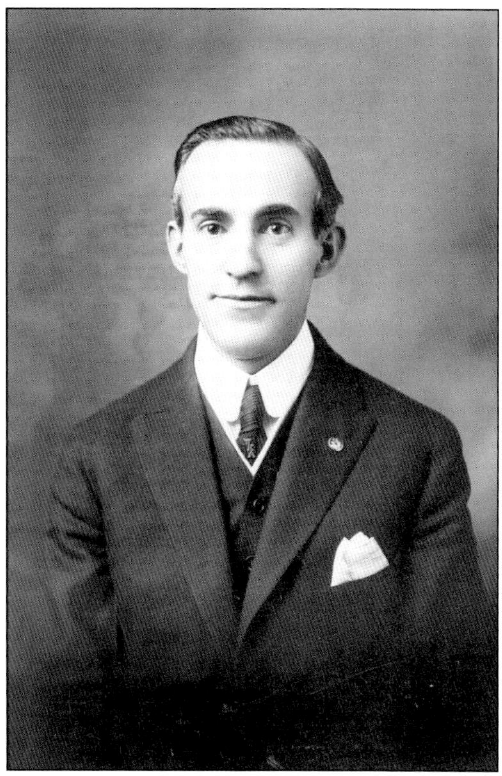

H. Laban White, a teacher and school administrator, was chosen to head the first Spencer High School in September 1911 in the old William Woodyard home. He served as superintendent of Spencer schools until the close of the 1917–1918 term, at which time he enlisted in the armed services and went to serve his country in World War I. (Courtesy of Dr. Harry H. Camp Sr. family.)

Belle Patterson Looney, wife of William M. Looney, was the first woman to be elected to the Roane County School Board and was a member of the Spencer City Council. (Courtesy of Dr. Harry H. Camp Sr. family.)

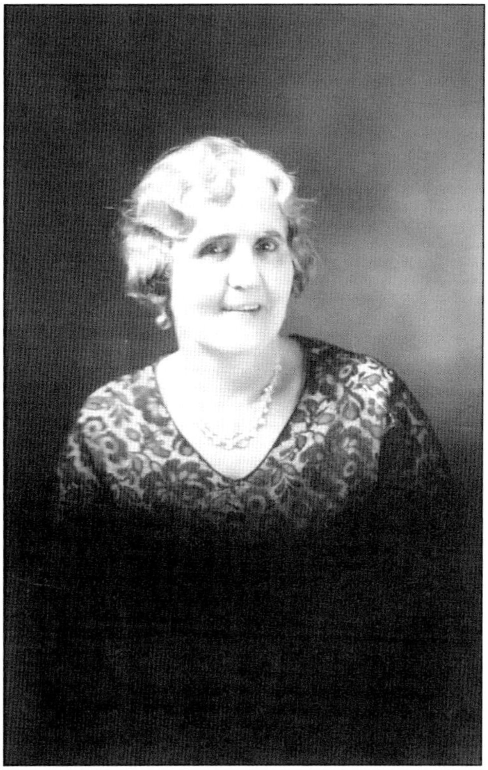

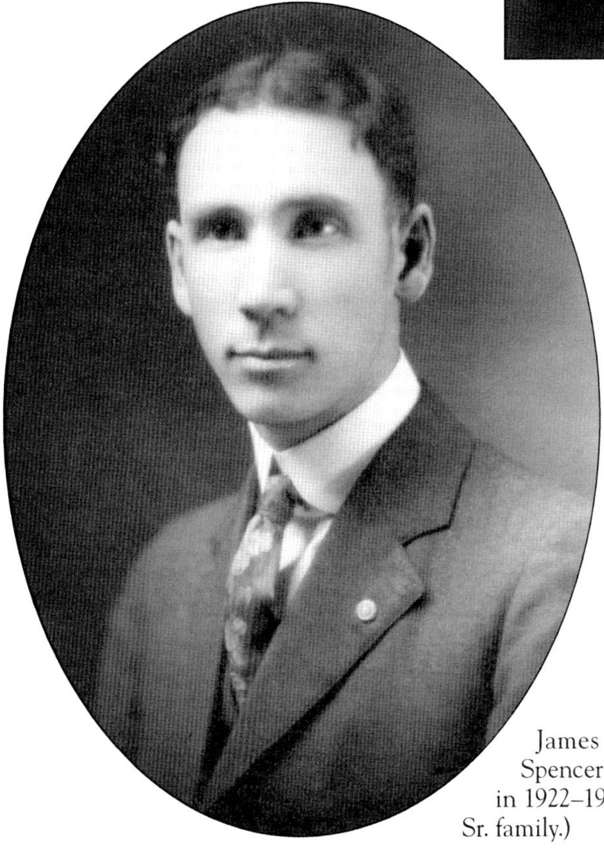

James Andrew Woofter was director of Spencer Summer School and Normal School in 1922–1928. (Courtesy of Dr. Harry H. Camp Sr. family.)

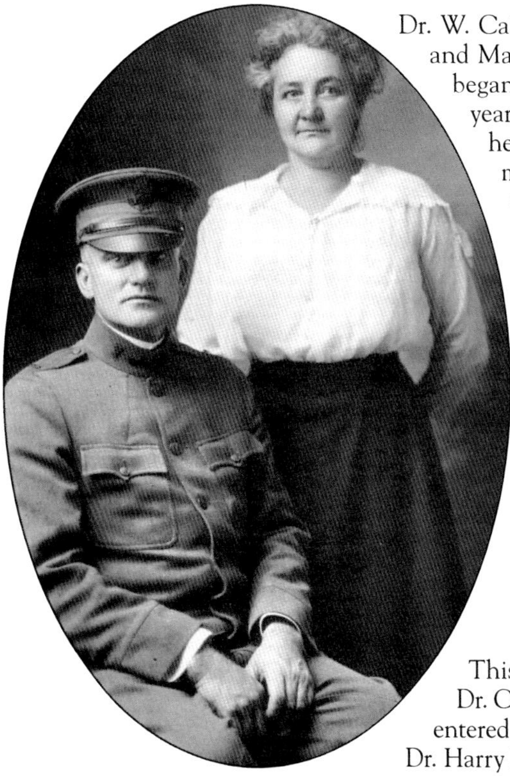

Dr. W. Calvin Camp was the second son of Henry C. and Margaret Ann (Hersman) Camp of Speed. He began his practice at Reedyville in 1907 and, two years later, moved his office to Gandeeville where he made his headquarters until 1919, when he moved to Spencer. (Courtesy of Dr. Harry H. Camp Sr. family.)

This photograph is of the Camp family in Spencer. Dr. Calvin Camp had nine brothers, and all but one entered the professional or business field. (Courtesy of Dr. Harry H. Camp Sr. family.)

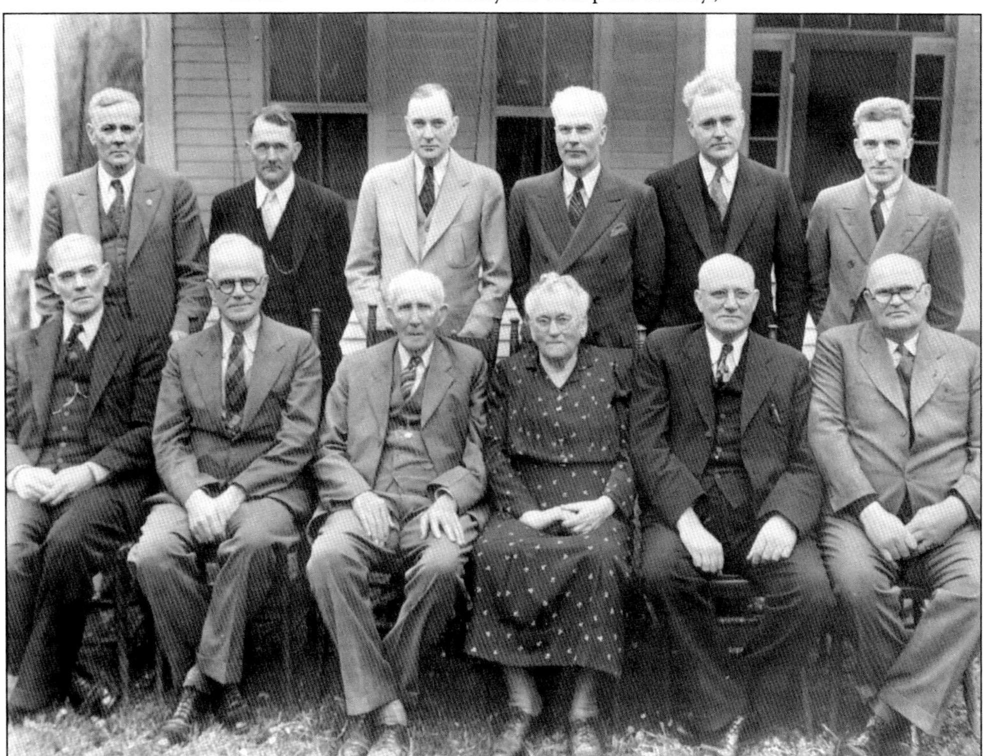

R. Worthy Shumaker was a graduate of West Virginia Wesleyan and in 1921 was chosen as principal and athletic director of Spencer High School. The 1921 football team with Schumaker as coach was undefeated. He was superintendent of schools in Roane County beginning in 1923. (Courtesy of Dr. Harry H. Camp Sr. family.)

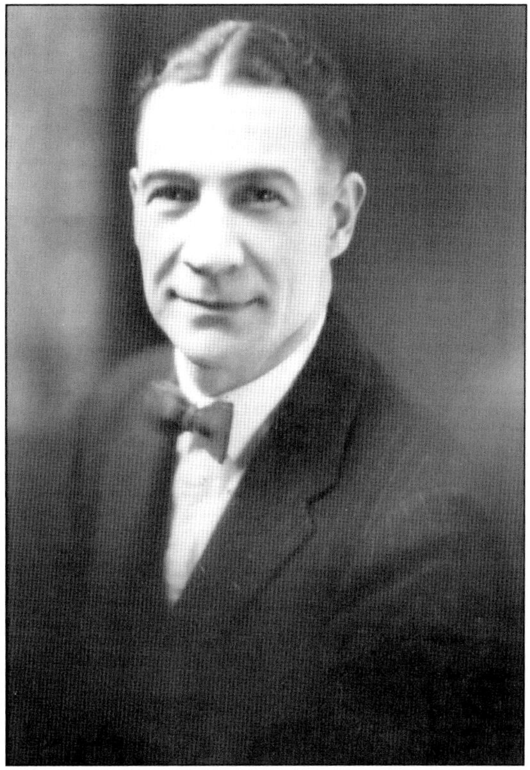

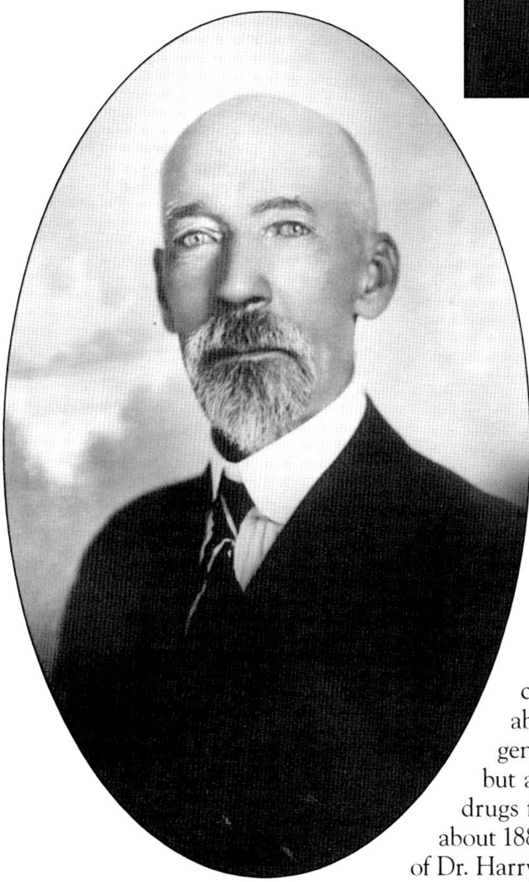

Dr. Daniel Webster Chapman was the first resident dentist in the town of Spencer. He continued to do praiseworthy dental work for about 50 years. He was in the drug business and general merchandising for a short period of time but always returned to his dentistry. Anesthetic drugs for "painless" dental work became popular about 1885. This picture was taken in 1912. (Courtesy of Dr. Harry H. Camp Sr. family.)

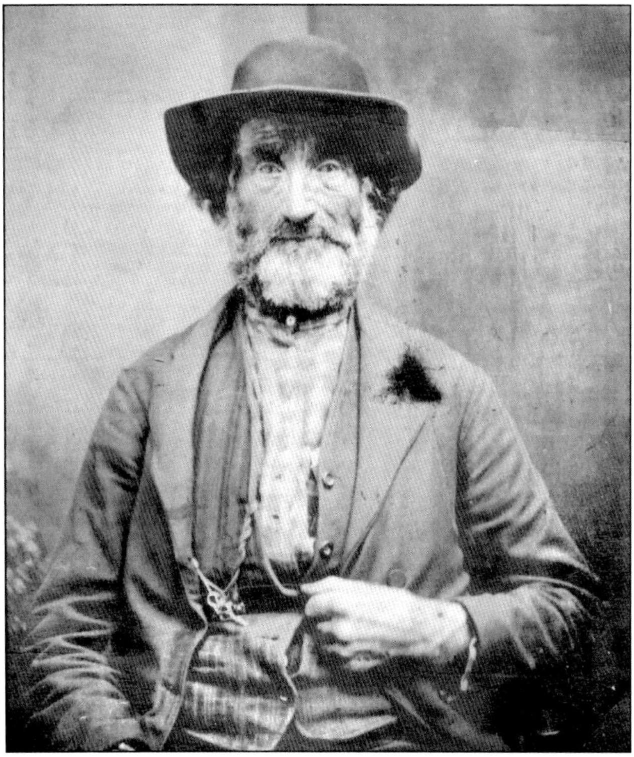

John Oscar Taylor was born 1814, the son of Elijah and Lydia (Bishop) Taylor. He married Anna Pennsylvania Hunt, daughter of William and Martha (Jackson) Hunt in June 1835. John and Anna and their family were some of the earliest settlers in what is now the Harper District of Roane County, arriving from Russell County, Virginia, about 1846. (Courtesy of Jane [Taylor] George.)

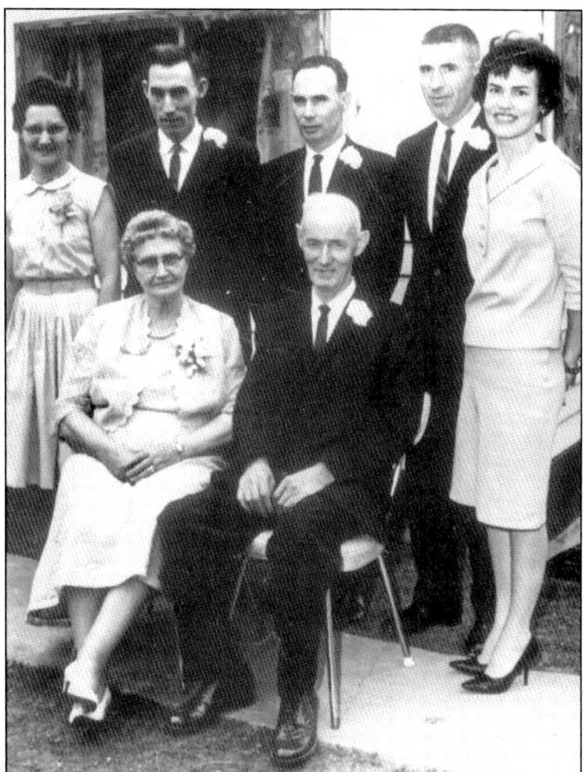

On April 5, 1964, Dan and Elsie Looney celebrated their 50th wedding anniversary at their home in Amma. Seated are Phoebe Almira (Carper) Looney, who was always known as Elsie, and Isaiah Daniel Looney, who was always known as Dan. Their five children are, from left to right, Madge (Looney) Crane, John William "Bill" Looney, Charles Edward Looney, Robert Bruce Looney, and Lenora Merle (Looney) Noble. (Courtesy of Philip Crane.)

Dr. A. T. Gordon came to Spencer from Jackson County early in his career and made this his home. In addition to establishing City Hospital in 1921 with Dr. S. W. Bull, he was also active in civic affairs. As a county commissioner, he and C. A. Lynch were involved in obtaining state funds for building a rock-base road on State Route 36 in 1932. (Courtesy of Carol Board.)

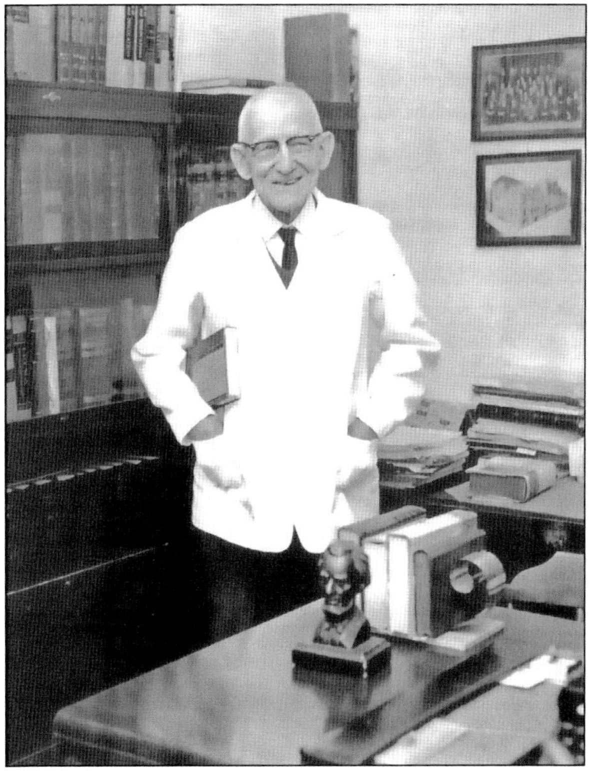

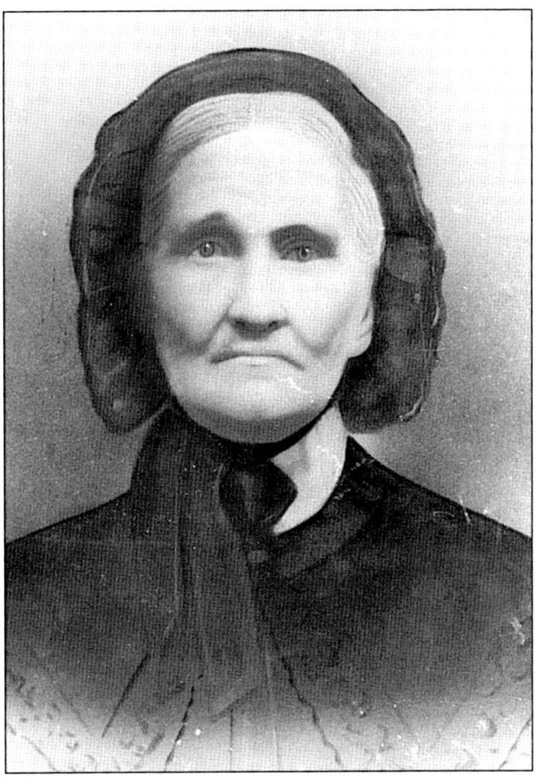

Elizabeth Almira (Ashley) Geary was the wife of a very prominent person in Roane County history. She was four years old when her family moved from North Carolina about 1823. During a time when Mathew Geary was buying staves for barrels to pack salt, he met Almira, who afterward became his wife. She died October 8, 1894. (Courtesy of Annabell [Geary] Copper.)

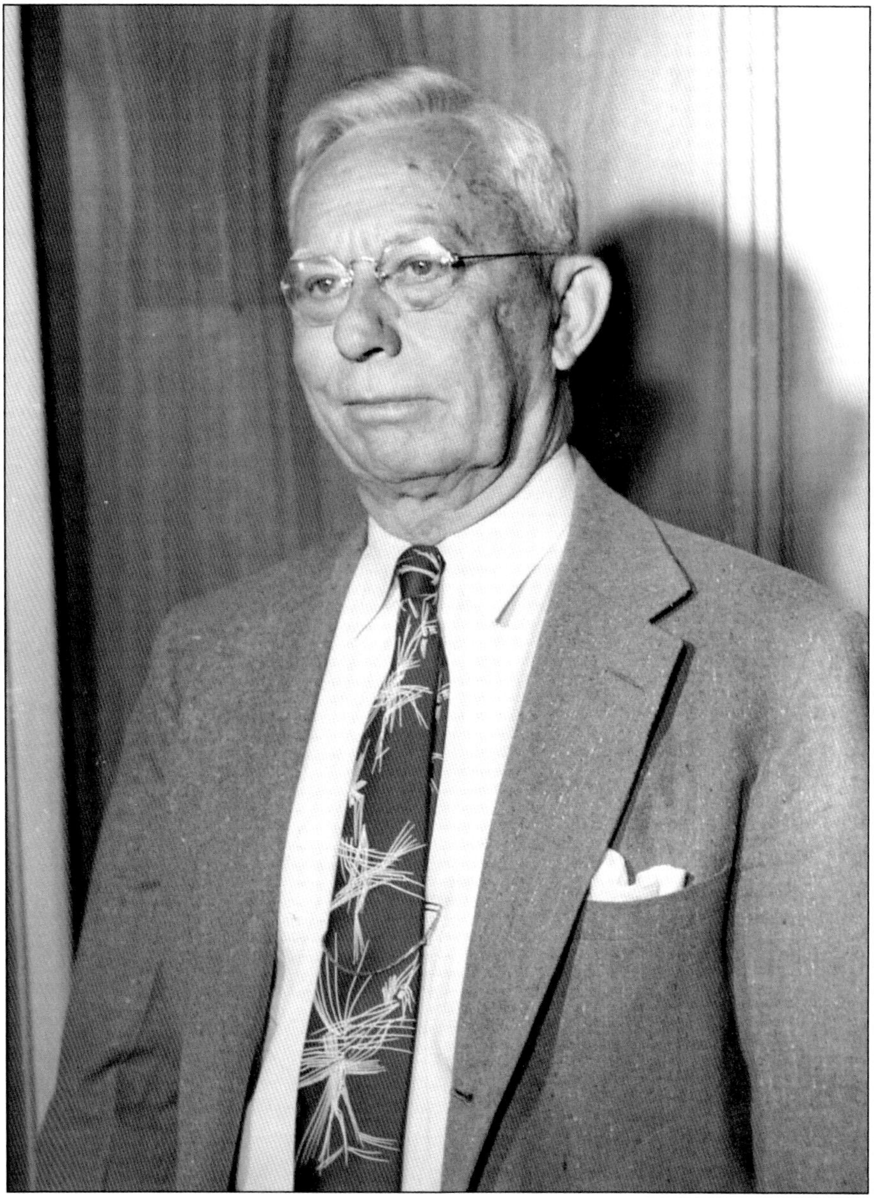

Wehrle Geary was one of Roane County's most illustrious sons and West Virginia's greatest "Merchant Prince." He had also been a delegate to the Wheeling Convention that formed West Virginia in 1863 and played a key role in the formation of Roane County. He attended the Roadside School, Sunday school, and church services at Rolling Hills, which was within sight of his father's home. He taught school in Clay County after receiving his certificate and in the summer of 1900 attended the Roane County Teachers Institute in Spencer. In 1904, he established the Diamond Shoe Company in Charleston. In 1925, he purchased additional property and in 1927 completed the new Diamond Department Store. In 1927, he built and completed the Daniel Boone Hotel, West Virginia's largest and finest hotel at the time. He was instrumental in bringing Morris Harvey College to Charleston from Barboursville and was a major contributor to its improvement and advancement. Wehrle Geary lived out his days in the Daniel Boone Hotel and was never married. (Courtesy of Annabell [Geary] Copper.)

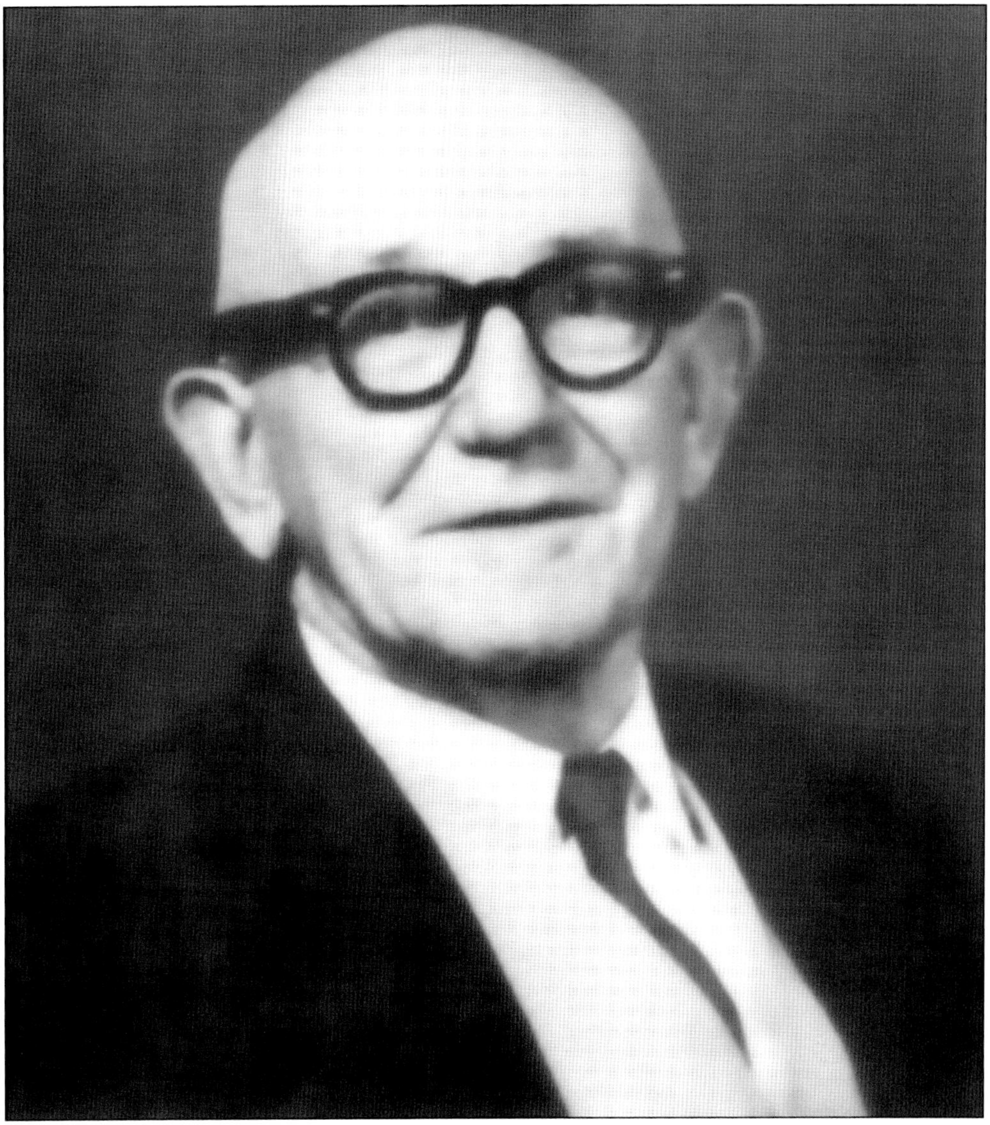

Hamond H. Robey was born in the Curtis District on February 28, 1881. He went to embalming school in Cincinnati and opened a funeral parlor in connection with a furniture business in Spencer with Rev. E. J. Harris. The funeral home was sold to Fred Vandale about 1910. In 1907, Hamond Robey went into the theater business and opened the Robey Theatre. He built a brick facility in 1926 that currently houses the Robey Theatre and installed equipment for the new talking pictures. Congressman Harry C. Woodyard gave the welcoming address for its opening. Hamond was a Mason, a charter member of the Rotary Club, a loyal Democrat, and a faithful member of what is now the Memorial United Methodist Church in Spencer. He continued to run the farm, raising cattle, sheep, and hogs. He died at 86 years of age on November 28, 1967. The Robey Theatre is one of the oldest continuously operating movie theaters in the country. Aaron Richardson, who continues to bring improvements for the enjoyment of the patrons in Spencer and surrounding areas, currently owns it. (Courtesy of Aaron Richardson.)

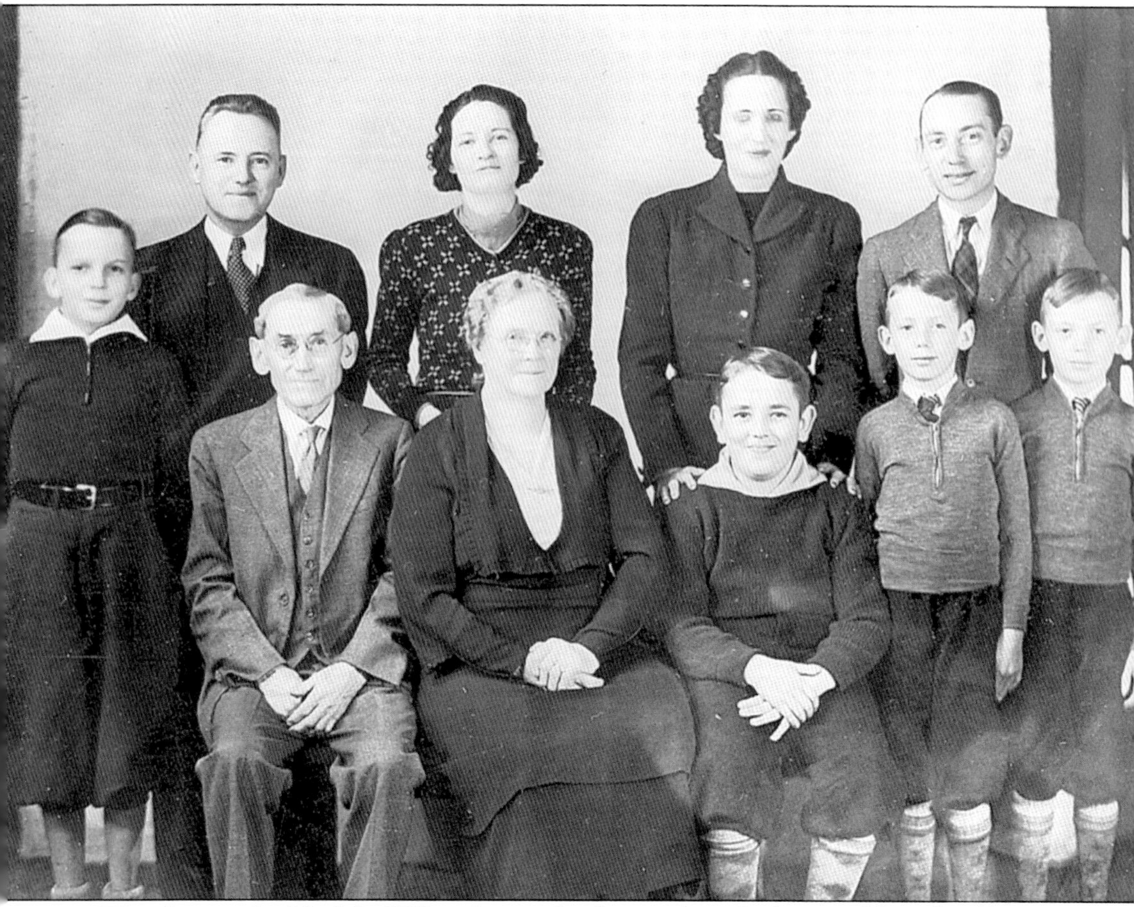

This photograph of the John William Looney family was taken after he moved from the old Loomey homestead at Looneyville to their new location in Spencer. He was a prominent schoolteacher in his early years and later became part of the managing personnel of the First National Bank in Spencer. John married Hattie Osborne on September 28, 1892, and they had two children, Harry Virgil and Ernest Ward Looney. Harry married Edna Bingman, and Ernest married Anna Mae King. Harry and Edna had one adopted son, William David Looney, and Ernest and Anna had three sons. Pictured from left to right are (first row) William David Looney, John William Looney, Hattie (Osborne) Looney, Ernest W. Looney, and twins James Francis and John Franklin Looney; (second row) Harry Virgil Looney, Edna (Bingman) Looney, Anna (King) Looney, and Ernest W. Looney.

This photograph of Henry C. Looney, his wife, Clara Maud (Hoff) Looney, and daughter, Ruby Gladys Looney, was taken in 1911. Henry and Clara also had three sons, Hubert, Darwin, and Gerald. Henry was a schoolteacher, merchant, and postmaster in Newton, where he lived all of his adult life. Ruby married Roy J. Nida and taught in the elementary schools of Roane Country for about 40 years, retiring at age 65. (Courtesy of Jack Nida.)

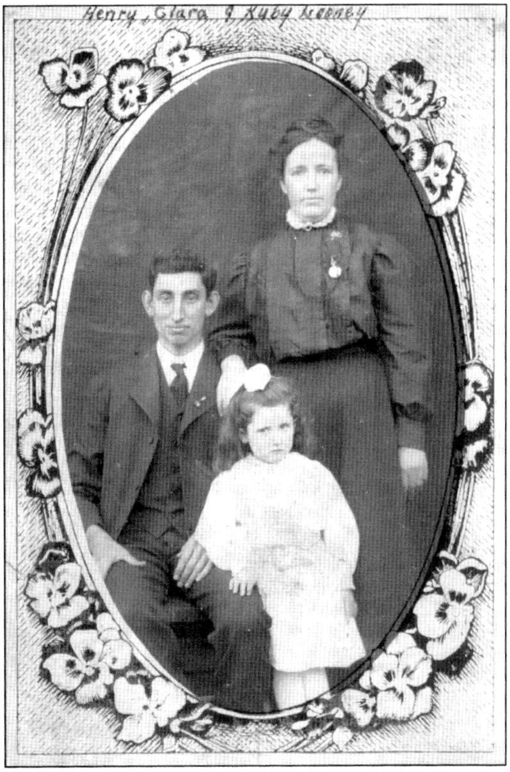

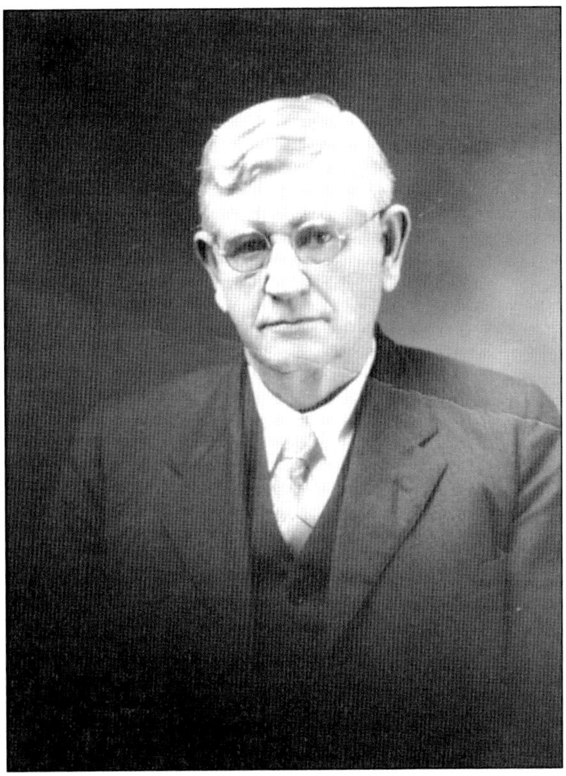

Harley D. Wells came to Spencer about 1884, and for more than 50 years, he figured prominently as a builder, businessman, civic leader, church leader, and public official in the early history of Roane County. He established the first undertaking business in the county and a furniture business. He opened the Wells Opera House about 1889, and it continued as an entertainment and cultural center until 1916. (Courtesy of Dr. Harry H. Camp Sr. family.)

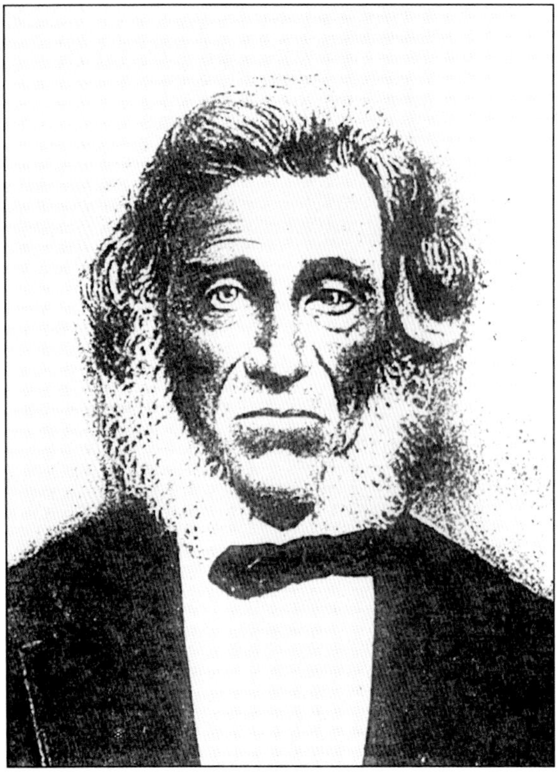

Nicholas Carper married Sarah Nida in 1837. Sarah was the daughter of Jacob and Sarah Harless Nida of Giles County, Virginia. Nicholas moved his family from the Shenandoah Valley in the spring of 1858. He purchased 310 acres of land on Shaver Fork. He died in 1886, and he and Sarah were among the first to be buried at the Amma Methodist Church Cemetery. Many of their descendants still reside in Roane County. (Courtesy of Jack Nida.)

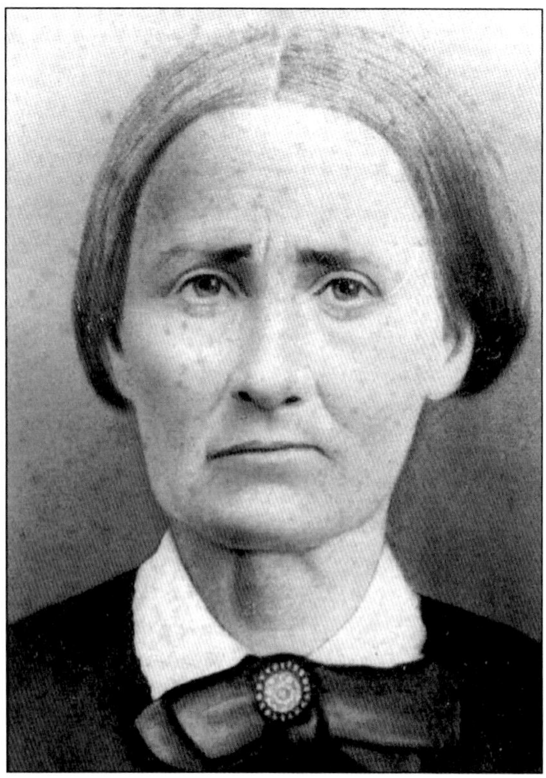

Sarah (Nida) Carper was born January 16, 1799, in Giles County, Virginia. When the family moved west, the wagons were pulled with oxen, and the trip took six days. Unlike most houses of that time that were made of logs, Nicholas and Sarah's house was of frame construction and one of the first in the area. Sarah died at the home of her youngest son, Harvey Carper, in Amma at the age of 87. (Courtesy of Jack Nida.)

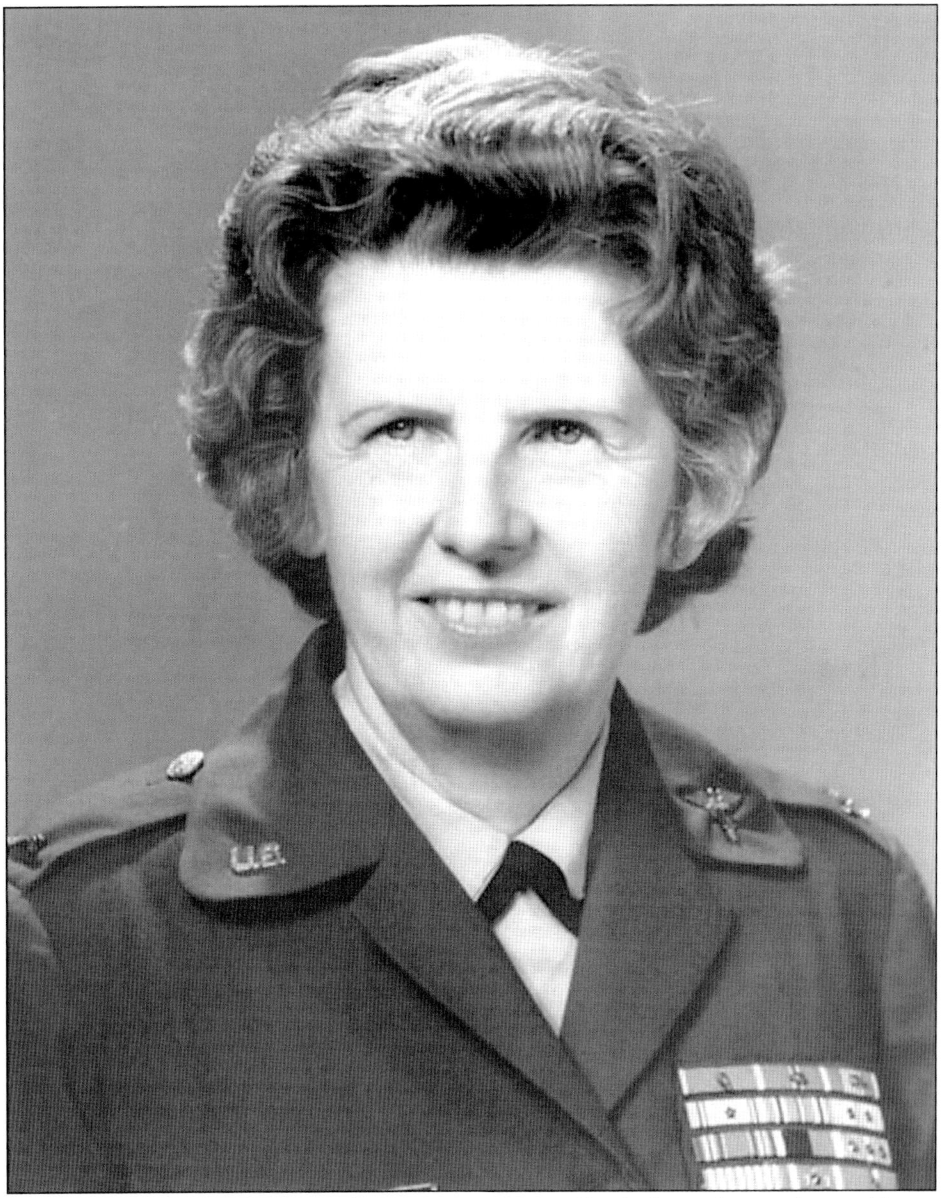

Col. Ruby G. Bradley was born on a farm on upper Spring Creek, five miles southeast of Spencer, and graduated from Spencer High School in 1926. She attended Glenville College and taught school four years in Roane County before entering the Philadelphia School of Nursing for training as a career nurse. Upon graduation in 1933, she went to work for Walter Reed Hospital in the surgical department, where she remained for six years, and enlisted in the Army Nurse Corps in 1934. She was serving as a nurse at Camp John Hay on Bagulo, Philippine Islands, and was taken prisoner on December 28, 1941. On February 3, 1945, U.S. troops stormed the gates of the Japanese camp and liberated Colonel Bradley and her fellow prisoners, ending her three years of captivity. She died May 28, 2002, in Hazard, Kentucky, at age 94 after a heart attack. Col. Ruby Bradley, one of the most decorated women in U.S. military history, was laid to rest in Arlington National Cemetery nearly 40 years after she retired from the army. She was honored with a military funeral in the historic cemetery overlooking the nation's capital. (Courtesy of Jack Nida.)